WHAT PEOPLE ARE SAYING...

"The writing challenges us to plunge into the Spiritual, not being influenced by the enemy... how to successfully survive the tragedies of our day, regardless of circumstance. It is certainly a wonderful book...to the extent that I have recommended this book to the Pastors in the Jurisdiction of which I preside."

> Jurisdictional Prelate Bishop F.E. Perry
> COGIC, Ohio Southern Jurisdiction

"I've had the privilege of reading a couple of manuscripts from Gregory. I enjoy his enthusiasm and positive outlook on life. I appreciated the way that he's able to bring out the inspirational aspects of the story."

> Cristy Lane
> International C&W/Gospel Artist

"Mr. Jones has gone beyond the afflictions and suffering found in the Book of Job in order to lift the readers to a depth of thought concerning Job's priestly functions, providing a protective covering for his children. A Must in every library and every home. Mr. Jones prepares us for the 21st Century. From a prolific pen comes purity."

> Dr. E.N. Blake
> Temple Bible College
> St. Paul Community Church, Dayton, Ohio

"In reading the Book of Job, Bro. Jones will challenge you and refocus your thinking. This book will cause you to face life with a renewed inspiration...This is a book for men and women who are eager to learn how to endure suffering, yet be a conqueror. It comes from the pen of someone who has learned the meaning of suffering without being defeated. I highly recommend the book for men and women everywhere and challenge you to hold on in spite of the Evil Forces of this world...."

> Mark L. Perry
> Administrative Assistant to Prelate Bishop
> Pastor, Williams Chapel Church of God in Christ
> President, MLP Ministries

"I commend you for the wonderful job you have done. Your work and research is reflected in the quality of the book. I believe that many people will be blessed by this book. May God bless you."

> Rev. Dr. Carl P. Adkins
> Dean of Day School
> Temple Bible College,
> Pastor, Golden Leaf Baptist Church, Cincinnati, Ohio

"This book is a beacon to anyone who, in life, has experienced sorrow, pain and suffering. The inspiring message which the author communicates reveals how an individual must walk upright in holiness, depending upon the powerful, sovereign GOD. We can all be encouraged and possess renewed hope through an understanding of the undeserved suffering of Job. I would strongly advise everyone to honor themselves with a copy of this new book by Gregory V. Jones, Jr."

Minister Robert Embree
True House of Faith Ministry, Cleveland, Ohio

"The chapter of Job in the Bible covers the unprecedented challenges of Job's life bestowed on him by Satan and allowed by Christ. The Book Of Job by Dr. Gregory V. Jones, Jr., inspires, directs, and refocus our attention and standing that God is still in control regardless of what happens in and out of our lives and any circumstances we find ourselves facings or involved. Dr. Jones is a prolific, gifted, and skillful writer who sanctioned God's spirit to guide his understanding, knowledge, and writing for presenting a unique and inspirational picture and view on the life of Job. His suffering physically, mentally, and spiritually gives us the desire to hold on and not give up! Yet, Job came through in flying colors, unscathed, and upright. From the reading of the Book of Job's Life, God's love, patience, and spirit will be increased and amplified in your life."

Dr. Wilbur L. Daniels, Sr.
Bishop
President and CEO of W. L. Daniels and Associates

"Gregory V. Jones, Jr. is a warrior for Christ. As you read through the pages of this book, it will become humbly clear what his vision for the children of God entails. You hold in your hands the gateway to living an upright life, as Job did, in spite of today's societal values. You are taught by Biblical references how to make decisions for your life based on principles taken from the Bible and not the principles of society. You are shown where to go and what to do when your faith is being tested. Job was severely tested and he stood on his faith. Gregory has been severely tested and will share that miraculous story with you in his debut book. There is no confusion in life choices when you base your decision on the word of God. Read Mr. Jones' words and be forever changed. His words plus the references from the Bible bring you to a higher level of understanding. The way he weaves Job's afflictions into today's turmoil is masterfully and reverently accomplished. You will not be disappointed."

Professor Diane Penn-Mickey

"This is definitely a story for the niche market the author has targeted. It has plenty of action, visuals, drama, conflicts and good characters."

Lynn Pembroke, Coverscript.com

"I appreciate the opportunity to review the screen play "JOB" by Dr. Gregory Jones. It looks like a very powerful piece of work. And we will encourage our members to go and see it and purchase the DVD. St. Stephen's is interested in discussing the possibility of doing a screening at our church. Blessings!"

> Bishop George D. McKinney
> Founder/Sr. Pastor
> General Board Member – C.O.G.I.C.
> St. Stephen's Cathedral Church of God in Christ Ministries
> San Diego, CA

"I am proud to pledge my support in promoting your screen play "JOB." I found it to be profound and captivating, especially in the manner in which you compared the life of "Job" to our present times. I would be elated to encourage our District and other churches in joining us in a viewing at our District Headquarters. We will also encourage our members to purchase the DVD and attend the movie. I am confident that this screen play and your endeavors will be blessed."

> Lanelle Perry, Ph.D.
> District Missionary
> Shaker Heights, Ohio

"Dr. Jones has a unique gift of grasping and communicating the glorious, and sometimes mysterious, truths of Scripture. After personally experiencing a devastating and prolonged illness, with intense pain and suffering, Dr. Jones writes from an insider's perspective captures the glory, majesty, and wisdom of our great God. In essence, the readers are challenged to make a paradigm shift in their thinking, not so much on pain and suffering, but on Who our God is. Our great God is sovereign and is in total control, not only over all creation, but also in the midst of our sufferings. He is a compassionate, holy, and loving Father, even if it appears to us He is distant or silent. As the author masterfully draws out principles and precepts from the book of Job, he shows the readers that God allows hardships and trials into our lives in order to grace us with a tremendous increase. This book is a must read! "

> Brett Williams, Editor
> Dallas Bible College (summa cum laude)
> Training in Theology and Biblical Languages

JOB

A Man for His Time, A Man for Our Time, A Man for All Time

"We cannot marginize, intellectualize, rationalize, or duly politicize another person's suffering. We lose out on the reality of that person's suffering"
-Gregory V. Jones, Jr., Author

JOB

A Man for His Time, A Man for Our Time, A Man for All Time

Gregory V. Jones, Jr., Ph.D.

CANDLELIGHT
PUBLISHING

CANDLELIGHT
P U B L I S H I N G

CANDLELIGHT PUBLISHING GROUP, LLC
Atlanta, Georgia

Job— A Man for His Time, A Man for Our Time, A Man for All Time

Visit our Website at www.jobthebook.net

http://www.candlelightpublishinggroup.com
for information on more resources.

Jones, Gregory V.
Job—A Man for His Time, A Man for Our Time, A Man for All Time/
Gregory V. Jones, Jr.

ISBN: 978-0-9709037-0-9

All Scripture quotations, unless indicated, are taken from the Bible, <u>King
James Version</u> Topical Reference Edition.

ATTENTION: WRITINGS & PUBLISHING ORGANIZATIONS, EDUCATIONAL
INSTITUTIONS, AND INDUSTRY PUBLICATIONS: Quantity discounts are
available on bulk purchases of this book for reselling, educational purposes,
subscription incentives, gifts, or fund raising. For information please
contact our Sales Department at info@candlelightpublishinggroup.com.

Edited by Brett Williams
Cover design by Tia Andrako, LA Graphics

Dedicated to the Memory Of

My mother, Artelia M. Jones. A genuine, strong, confident woman of integrity and character. Everything that I am, everything that I have become I owe to her. She introduced me to the Word of God and practiced it moment-by-moment throughout her life. For this I am eternally grateful. She raised the seven of us with strict discipline and love. She was a loving, caring mother on the battlefield of life. A woman with class, style, intelligence, and grace. A woman of strength and patience. She was a helping and healing hand for those in need. She set an example for us to follow. Her instruction and guidance remain with us today. One thing rings true that she encouraged us to constantly perform, "Always pray." O what a gorgeous woman of faith. I honor her with this book. Amen!

ACKNOWLEDGMENTS

I'd like to thank Prelate Bishop F. E. Perry for his support, encouragement and excellent advice for my book. He challenged me on every sentence, making for greater study, wisdom and understanding. Thanks, Pastor Mark Perry, Dr. E. N. Blake, Rev. Dr. Carl Adkins, Cristy Lane, Minister Embree, Minister Clinton Nixon, Dr. Curtis Lee, Bishop Wilbur Daniels, Ph.D., and Ramone Garret for your unending support and patience.

A special thanks to my editor, Brett Williams, a wise and thoughtful evaluator, blessed in knowledge and wisdom of the word. Thanks a million Brett! You are a winner!

Of course thanks to Deacon William Jackson, Elder Payton, and my sisters Zodra and Akinyi—constant partners with endearing patience and encouragement.

As always, my wife, Rosa, you deserve so much credit for your patience, support, encouragement and love. A soft touch or whisper of confidence and reassurance was a blessing.

God bless you all! Thank you very much!

FOREWORD

An untrusting world! A world prepared to confront, isolate, reject, question, and condemn God's authority. A people unconsciously ashamed of themselves, hesitant and reluctant to allow the light to shine on an otherwise dark agenda. Unknowingly, such people play into the hands of a satanic doctrine. Innocently, seducing spirits and doctrines of Satan have eased their way into the hearts and lives of men and women while God is subject to ridicule.

John Lennon penned the now famous lyrics: "Imagine there's no heaven. It's easy if you try." The author dares to take the other route: "There is a heaven God has prepared for persons who are ready to go back to him; a prepared place for a prepared people." There is also a hell. The Bible states that hell has enlarged itself for persons whom are not ready to meet God. The author encourages us to forget the "physicalness" of life and focus in on the "spiritualness" of life.

JOB – A Man for His Time, a Man for Our Time, a Man for All Time is a literary masterpiece that combines the methods of the King James Bible with the insights of a premiere author. You will learn much about the power and will of God. The power of God will amaze you. Within these pages, you will find wisdom, power, and a renewed sense of faith and hope in the Almighty.

Too many times a reader will be disappointed in a work of this nature because of the author's self-indulgence. In this work, we find an unselfish man who has used his talent to make good a promise that he made to God. In the author's own words: "Keep a vow with God after he lifted me up from the ashes."

As he stated, God's miracle of life and healing took hold in his life. Never before had he given himself to writing. He made a vow to God that, with His help, he would devote this work unto Him. The author's insights show us candid solutions to modern-day problems. Our focus has been on the suffering and patience of Job. The author takes us to new heights in the elevation of our Holy Father's power, knowledge, grace, wisdom and compassion. He places the focus on where it should be, on God, not man. This permits us to magnify God once we have denied "self," and submitted ourselves to Him.

There have been many writings on the book of Job. Some compositions have been mere translations. Additional writings have been a podium for questioning our Holy Father for His actions. Through all the writings, the message has been lost that, "we are His children and the sheep of His pastures." The author seeks no honor for this work. Quite the contrary, he seeks only that the Lord may be glorified by this work. He desires that the master of deception be rebuked and a worldwide change transpires in the heart of man.

Brothers should help brothers. We should lift up the holy name of God from the bounty that He has given to us.

Prepare now for battle! You are about to meet a man you thought you knew, and read a story you thought you understood. The author transports us to places that men have only dreamed. We will be present in the Grand Boardroom of the Almighty and the living room of Job. We will observe in silence the acts of the deceiver. Our chief adversary conducts his destruction with very few limitations. The power of God will be revealed. God's awesome power and authority cannot only will a planet into being, it can also refine itself to light on the shoulder of the Son of Man in the form of a dove. We will observe a triangle that few can comprehend. Servant, serpent, and savior all involved in what seems to be a life—and--death struggle. In reality, this struggle is the cornerstone that will train our children and us in today's world. The imagery used to display the pleasure and peril of being among the supernatural and the Almighty is more than the mind can conceive. You will find yourself gaining wisdom in every passage as God's perfect plan continuously flows from event to event. It is through this acquired wisdom that we can understand and take hope in the fact that God is always watching and protecting His children. There is redemption for even the poorest of spirits. Is God playing with his creations? No, not at all. He alone knows where every man, woman, and child fits into His ultimate plan for everlasting peace, salvation, and victory (Acts 17:22-31).

Job has qualified for spiritual boot camp. He is not the only trainee, nor is this a mock war. Job soon finds himself a "prisoner of war." To his captors' delight, sympathizers plague him within his own ranks! How true it is even in this day and time that no one stands with us except God. The release of Job is a surprise to everyone. His fair-weather friends and former persecutors return to him bearing gifts. This after God performs his own style of debriefing, which is so amazingly proper that it leaves no doubt in the reader's mind that God is pleased with his servant. We should not concern ourselves with the patience of Job, but rather the glorious patience of our merciful, graceful, and compassionate deity, God. Job could not have had patience without the blessed, exalted power of the Living God.

In modern times we face many difficult problems, struggles, pain, sickness, and suffering of all forms. Adversity strikes at the most inopportune time. During these times, like the patriarch Job, we have to depend completely on God. Satan's mission is to discourage us so we will faint and give up, quit, and lose hope. The Bible makes it plain, if you faint in the day of adversity your strength is small. The author reveals to us that in spite of the adversity, God remains in control of our lives.

This is a premiere work for Gregory V. Jones, Jr. This book will renew our blessed hope in the promise of the Almighty. It is prudent to be determined to wait on the Lord and be of good courage. God will strengthen your heart. Wait, I say on the Lord.

Welcome this book into your worthy collection. Share this moment with your family and friends.

Mark L. Perry, Pastor
Williams Chapel
Church of God in Christ

CONTENTS

PREFACE

T he Book of Job has created many confusing responses from all of us as to "why this just and upright man had to suffer." A man so filled with the love of God that God himself called him, "perfect and upright, and one that feared God, and eschewed evil" . . . a powerful statement from the Almighty regarding an earthly man. Is Job worthy of this description? Are we in a position to object to the ultimate judge's decision?

Often, our conditions and circumstances become complicated when sorrow or suffering attaches to the "good" or "just." Our over-sophistication can be an overpowering influence. The defining emotion becomes our fear of leaving our loved ones or being a burden to them. More important, we fear the final exit from this earthly domain. In particular, we fear death. We hesitate and refuse to elevate our limited and finite intellectual functions to that of a godlike spiritual thought process. We enjoy the "physicalness" of life rather than the godly practices of life. Satan has provided such a comfortable haven for us on earth through the pleasures of the flesh that we cannot receive the abundant life God has in store. We become complacent, while trampling in the debris left behind by a destructive, uncaring serpent that despises God and possesses a total disdain for man.

While facing a deadly infection in the hospital, I prayed to God to heal me. The doctors were confused about the source of my illness and the medicine necessary to cure me. I was facing death. I cried out to

1

God to heal me of the intense pain and suffering. I made a vow to write this book on Job and salute the Almighty as the absolute authority over all things in heaven and beneath heaven. My ultimate desire was to magnify, exalt and glorify the Most High. I am extremely enthusiastic and grateful that God healed me. Our God is a God of life, not death. This book is now complete and all credit is due to the Holy Father.

God blessed me with the power to see Him differently than I had in the past. When I became low, submitted to Him and confessed my sins, God kept His promise and lifted me up from the "ashes of despair." When we recognize and accept in our hearts that God is the supreme ruler, absolute authority, and power over all things in the universe, we reach a level of understanding to inherit the promise. God cannot and will not lie to us. Our best interest is always in the hands of God. In addition, when we elevate our understanding to the heavenly region we eliminate the limits of earthly knowledge. At this stage, we gather a clearer comprehension of God. Satan's mission is to limit our understanding to earthly knowledge and instruction. In the Book of Genesis Satan demonstrates his "power of deception" as he tricks Eve to sin against God in the Garden of Eden. The Bible reveals that the serpent in the Garden was "more subtil than any beast of the field" (Genesis 3:1). This creature possesses a level of cunning, deceitfulness, and treachery higher than any animal on earth. This is a riveting statement about the devil. He is artful in his ability to persuade. The serpent says, "Ye shall not surely die: For God doth know that in the day ye eat thereof, then your eyes shall be opened, and ye shall be as gods, knowing good and evil" (Genesis 3:4, 5). The serpent grips Eve's attention as her mind becomes blanketed in wonderment. She decides that the tree is "desired to make one wise" (Genesis 3:6). She was fooled and earthly knowledge and understanding were injected into the heart of man. Eve's desire to gain wisdom was derailed by the serpent's treacherous nature. She and Adam failed to attain all the "goodness" of God and settled for a lower form of human knowledge and instruction. God had commanded that the fruit not be eaten, but Satan won a temporary victory over us in our relationship with God. Obedience to God is our primary source of strength. God's strength gives us the power to resist the devil.

There are days when we fail to perform at our best. We do not get it right 100 percent of the time. We may get knocked down, and trampled on, but that does not kick us out of the race. Often when we encounter disappointment, sorrow, and suffering, we feel the urge to strike back at God. We seize on our physical resources rather than the spiritual treasures of the Most High. The great patriarch Job wished he had never been born, that darkness had come upon his birth. But, as Job meditates and examines his condition, his understanding returns and he eventually concludes, "Though he slay me, yet will I trust in him" (Job 13:15). This is the growth pattern that all of us go through in order to reach a higher understanding of the Lord God Almighty. The Old Testament Book of Daniel reveals the story of the great king Nebuchadnezzar, who ruled all of Babylon. King Nebuchadnezzar exalted himself before the Lord and the Lord struck him down to dwell among the beasts of the field (Daniel 4:30-33). Seven years later Nebuchadnezzar lifted up his eyes unto heaven and "mine understanding returned" (Daniel 4:34). It took Nebuchadnezzar seven years to re-gain a divine perspective. The most important point is that he became reacquainted with the Most High and acknowledged that God has "an everlasting dominion, and his kingdom is from generation to generation" (Daniel 4:34).

God is our master, our creator, and our lord and savior. His plan and purpose for us was ordained prior to the beginning of the world.

His understanding, knowledge, and wisdom are far greater than those of humans. He is the source of our strength. In the midst of the struggle we must elevate and lift up our countenance and face the challenge that God has placed us in. If selected, God has found us worthy of the challenge. Satan does not know what God knows. Satan failed all his classes when he had residence in heaven. That's why we need not condemn, doubt, or challenge the power of God. His love for us is beyond the imagination of the human intellect. We do not want our emotional and psychological significance misrepresented when it comes to "our feelings." We must suppress our emotions and psychological trauma. Why is it so difficult for us to grasp the wisdom of God? The truth and facts are simple: We prefer pleasure to affliction. Satan recognizes this weakness for pleasure in men and women and seeks to exploit it at every opportunity. When God selects us to suffer in His name, He is advising Satan that His saints are up for the workout. God does not debate with Satan over the issue. God is in control of all situations, but Satan will not yield until he has spewed every form of havoc on the landscape. Keep in mind that this is a being that has no desire for mercy or compassion. His entire makeup is confusion, deception, and destruction. We must go forward and upward with the mercy of God firmly planted in our minds and maintain our faith and confidence that God will deliver us in due time. We must say to ourselves, "I want God to give me that ring and crown of glory, I want it! God keep me strong and let your tender mercies prevail." Wherein lie the complexities of God's purposes for us? Our refusal to place God in the center of "all things" limits us in receiving the true harvest God has in store for us.

The New Testament encourages us to, "Bear ye one another's burdens, and so fulfil the law of Christ" (Galatians 6:2). No matter how complex the world may become, we must keep our sights on heaven. When we are consumed with fleshly matters we reject our inheritance. Our understanding becomes restricted and our level of comprehension becomes distorted. Our attachment to the spirit of God grants us wisdom based on righteousness. We become stronger as the Lord guides, instructs and teaches from a higher platform. We rejoice in knowing the truth, and our heightened understanding teaches us all the good things of God. The devil can't place any restrictions on God. God is everywhere and is the power that controls all things in heaven and earth. We are from below, God is from above; we are of this world; God is not (John 8:23).

In the Gospel of John 7:15, "And the Jews marvelled, saying, How knoweth this man letters, having never learned?" Jesus Christ responds, "My doctrine is not mine, but His that sent me" (v. 16). We must reject the limitations of earthly doctrine and instruction in our attempt to understand God. Our libraries lack sufficient volumes of literature to give us proper knowledge. When we manifest the God in us, we can understand His teachings and instruction and have perfect knowledge and understanding. Our perspective will take on a heavenly viewpoint rather than the limits of earthy knowledge.

Job admitted in the presence of the Lord that he was a vile and undeserving person. Job questioned and challenged many things that he did not understand while suffering under the supervision of God. Job realized that he had no foundation to stand before God and demand anything. Job said he was like "dung" before the Lord; like a worm in the soil. Job placed himself in a state of "nothingness" before the Almighty. How often do we extract our importance and become humble and meek before the Lord? How often do we take the focus off self and glorify the presence of the living God? Apostle Paul says, "For if a man think himself to be something, when he is nothing, he deceiveth himself" (Galatians 6:3).

In the end, Job was granted mercy and forgiveness from God. He received an increase that was larger than before. God always rewards his worthy and obedient servants.

While nailed to the cross the Son of God suffered more than any person that ever lived. He paid the ransom for our sins. He conquered death. Christ is our righteousness. Through Christ's righteousness we have power over the enemy. God showed us His love by sacrificing His only son that we might have salvation. He gave us this special gift. We did not earn it nor do we deserve His love and tender mercies. It is His gift of grace that sustains us. We owe God everything for granting us this marvelous opportunity to be seated in His presence. God has elevated us above the angels in heaven. God is great! God showed us His infinite "goodness" through Jesus Christ. What has Satan done for us?

Sorrow and suffering allows us to reign with God. We do not always witness the clear picture of God's purpose. In the end we recognize that God's eternal and blessed covering was with us the entire time. Even in the midst of our sorrow and suffering we eventually discover that God's all-powerful presence was working quietly and silently behind the scene. Let us not be discouraged by God's silence or quietness. Be patient and wait on the Lord. Be thankful for God's patience with us. We were designed for one simple purpose: to glorify God. When we manifest the power of the living God in us, we gain the advantage over our sorrows and suffering. The pain becomes secondary to the beauty of God. When we lift up, honor, praise, and exalt the Most High, we place ourselves in a position to receive the promise. He is the Lord of lords, King of kings and Champion of champions. He is the awesome master and creator of all things in heaven and beneath heaven.

How will we handle sorrow and suffering in the future? Affliction is only for a season, then God grants us joy in recovery. The Bible teaches us to pray in adversity and sing praises in our days of prosperity.

May this book on Job give you strength, faith, and confidence to believe that our Father in heaven is the only God we have to deliver us from evil. This is the God of Abraham, Isaac and Jacob. He is the God of our fathers. He is the beginning and the end. He is the craftsman who designed us in His image. He is the master of our faith.

I pray after reading this book you will refuse to inquire of God, "Why would you do this to me?" Instead, I pray that you will embrace adversity, convinced that the vainglory of Satan is insignificant when confronted by the overwhelming power of the living God. Heaven has a powerful angelic army prepared and ready to defend the throne of the Almighty. These warriors of God protect all believers from the hands of the enemy (Hebrews 1:14).

May the emotions of heaven blanket you while in the midst of the "smoldering ashes of despair." May God richly bless every reader with a "tremendous increase."

Gregory V. Jones, Jr.

INTRODUCTION

"Blessed is the man that endureth temptation: for when he is tried, he shall receive the crown of life, which the Lord hath promised to them that love him." – James 1:12

What is our curiosity regarding the plight of Job? Did he suffer enough? Did he suffer wrongly at the hands of God? These are perplexing questions for mere mortals to clarify. When confronted with questions of such paramount importance, we must elevate our thought processes to be more God-like in our conclusions rather than remain like man limited by his mortal capacity. The suffering of Job has challenged our intellectual processes for a long period of time without leading to a consensus or competent conclusion. Did Job's suffering glorify God or merely provide an indication of his level of stamina?

In contrast to previous commentators on Job, I pose the following question: "Why not me?" instead of "Why me?" Because only through the grace of God am I. What is the form of our curiosity? What shape will it take when we are confronted with the absolute and ultimate authority of God? God possesses the supreme power to totally annihilate a man, woman, nation, or planet. There is no match for God. God has an overwhelming supply of answers for all things.

In order to understand and maintain a clear focus of Job's ordeal, I went to the scriptures of King David. David was a man after God's own heart and he provides candid insight into the power and greatness of the Lord. I Chronicles 29:11, 12, 17 says,

> "Thine, O Lord, is the greatness, and the power, and the glory, and the victory, and the majesty: for all that is in the Heaven and in the earth is thine; Thine is the Kingdom, O Lord, and thou art exalted as head above all. Both riches and honour come of thee, and thou reignest over all; and in thine hand it is to make great, and to give strength unto all. I know also, my God, that thou triest the heart, and hast pleasure in uprightness. As for me, in the uprightness of mine heart I have willingly offered all these things: and now have I seen with joy thy people, which are present here, to offer willingly into thee."

King David provides us with a clear perspective of the majestic beauty of our Lord and savior. It is abundantly clear that God has the power, glory, and will to master and control all things. Through God, we have victory. This is His gift to us. It's essential that we cooperate with Him. God is masterful. God is All-knowing. There is no match for the Almighty. Man is inferior to God. Neither can Satan compete with God, his Maker. God's plan is so structured, complete and divine that it is beyond the comprehension and imagination of Satan. Satan cannot tempt God. God has complete control. In Job's case, God is in absolute, complete, and total control. God is also at the center of all situations and circumstances from the beginning to the end of Job's trials and tribulations. God is a master planner and supreme architect. Who can measure up to him?

Job, a man of timeless importance. A timeless wonder. A man of God with impeccable credentials, who faced a tidal wave of life's challenges and struggles (in modern terms: life's tragic vicissitudes). At the outset, Job possesses extreme wealth, influence, integrity, character, compassion, and the trappings of power. He becomes a man forced to look in the mirror at himself, to face himself as he really is, in his true nakedness, and in the true nothingness in the presence of God. Job does a complete introspection of self.

A number of established scholars have taken on the challenge of explaining and evaluating the Book of Job. Explicating the Book of Job appeared to be a difficult task for many religious scholars. Some scholars have devoted a large portion of their lives to the study of Job and his struggle. For all mortals, dissecting the mind of God is extremely difficult. Many scholars concluded that Job's pain and suffering was unnecessary; that God erred in making a righteous man suffer unnecessarily. Some scholars challenged God's system of judgment. When we read the story of Job, it's easy to question, "Why did God permit this righteous man to suffer?" Of course, no man would want to experience Job's plight. This was a struggle that many men could not and would not have undertaken or endured. When we pause and consider that Jesus Christ went to the Cross "willingly" to save the entire human race; where does it place our thinking?

Job possessed wealth beyond the scope of men of his generation. More important, he possessed integrity and character that stood up higher than his riches. His heart was filled with meekness and goodness. He was obedient to God and was in constant prayer for his family. God called him perfect and upright.

When God decided to let his servant suffer for a season, Job was convinced in his mind that he had been "upright" in every aspect of his life. He had surpassed every moral standard that God had set before him. In his thinking, he felt he could "measure up" face-to-face with God. Job felt he was flawless in every aspect of his humanity and, as a family man, had excelled in his duty, worship and sacrifice to the Lord. Is Job really as sharp as he perceives himself to be? Is Job as knowledgeable as he thinks? Can Job pass God's test of integrity, character, compassion, mercy, euthanasia, and patience? Can Job compete with God's holiness and glory? Is Job too "confrontational" to God about his works? Keep in mind, God endorsed Job as an "upright" man, a man that eschews evil. In the following verses from the Book of Job, we indulge deeper into the emotional torment that Job wrestles and tussles with while shackled by the hands of Satan. Job cries out in his mourning. He proclaims his righteous works for the poor and downtrodden. Job slowly plows through his anguish; constantly seeking the face of the Lord. Even in the midst of turmoil he cries out to the Lord. Job 30:25, 26 says,

> "Did not I weep for him that was in trouble? Was not my soul grieved for the poor? When I looked for good, then evil came unto me: and when I waited for light, there came darkness."

Job continues to expand upon his purity. He stands firm regarding his holiness. He questions those who wallow in sin and inquires before the footstool of God that he be judged in an equal balance. Job presents righteousness in its purist form. In Job 31: 3-6 we hear the voice of a mighty warrior for God. His voice is a cry for eternal mercy while shackled in the bowels of sorrow:

> "Is not destruction to the wicked? And a strange punishment to the workers of iniquity? Doth not he see my ways, and count all my steps. If I have walked with vani-

ty, or if my foot hath hated to deceit: Let me be weighed
in an even balance, that God may know mine integrity."

Job goes further to reveal his purification in Chapter 31:9,11:

"If mine heart have been deceived by woman, or if I
have laid it at my neighbor's door...; For this is an heinous crime; yea, it is an inequity to be punished by the
judges."

Job proclaims that he has not seduced another woman while
married. He has not committed adultery, fornication or any lustful,
illicit sexual act. Job has maintained the highest degree of decorum
within his marital vows. Job describes adultery as a "heinous crime."
He feared being punished severely for violating this commandment.
Job 31:12 clearly describes his feelings about adultery:

"for it is a fire that consumeth to destruction, and would
root out all mine increase."

ADULTERY

Job issues a direct condemnation of adultery. He rebukes the temptation to commit adultery. Job understood that lustful fantasies played
out in reality would demolish his soul. Desires kept unchecked can
cloud our judgment and lead us into an all-consuming fire of sin. Job
feared that God would strip him of his increase. Job feared losing all
of the prosperity with which God had blessed him. How many men
and women of wealth would embrace Job's stance on adultery? Let
us evaluate Job's standing on adultery and fornication as it relates to
modern-day society.

Today, all types and forms of sexual immorality surround us on every corner. Promiscuous behavior flows through literature, magazines and newspapers, movies, pornography and web site chat rooms just to name a few. It frequents the back rooms of offices, dining areas and the churches. People shout, "If it feels good, do it!" Where is our "self control"? Experts in the field of psychology rationalize adultery as having an "affair" or people are merely "doing their thing" or playing the "blame game" ("You made me do it"). Often, we view acts of adultery in film or gossip pages of magazines as a playful act and laughed off as "no big deal." This is how I do 'me'." The affair often has harmful consequences as the married couple search for love and affection in all the "wrong places." The Word of God commands us to acknowledge adultery for what it truly is—sin. God designed marriage to be holy; that a man and woman will find satisfaction through love within the marriage. King Solomon writes, "But whoso committed adultery with a woman lacketh understanding; he that doeth it destroyeth his own soul" (Proverbs 6:32). There is a lot of ungodliness in the world, but Solomon provides us with wisdom in order to govern ourselves more skillfully in life. We cannot disregard the importance of the family when we confront the issue of adultery. It destroys families. Families able to survive an adulterous episode have illustrated strong faith in the Lord of forgiveness, which is pivotal in matters of this magnitude. God has graciously provided an out through forgiveness. Jesus Christ showed us forgiveness when He forgave the prostitute caught in the act of adultery. And Apostle Paul warns us in Colossians 3:6, "the wrath of God cometh on the children of disobedience."

In earlier times, women and men were often stoned to death if caught in the act of adultery. Today adultery and fornication are tolerated with little alarm. It is often played out on theater screens as pay back, enjoyable pleasure, and revenge against an enemy. I don't feel you can locate a cheating spouse who finds comfort in marital infidelity. There are web sites across the Internet injecting pornography into the lustful fantasies of spouses. The Apostle Peter says, "Having eyes full of adultery and that cannot cease from sin" (II Peter 2:14).

Job makes it abundantly clear that the burning desire of adultery can consume a person. It can lead to destruction. In other words, adultery tears down the family. It's a tactic that Satan uses to destroy the heart of men and women. Adultery attacks so many corners of the family structure. The husband and wife are impacted; the children are hurt and torn between parents; in-laws become troubled and society as a whole is impacted by this hellish device. The very foundations of adultery are based on lying and deception. And the author of these devices is Satan. This orgy of disobedience places a stronghold on the man or woman and violates the commandment of God: Thou shalt not commit adultery.

In the New Testament, Jesus Christ says, "But I say unto you, that whosoever looked on a woman to lust after her committed adultery with her already in his heart" (Matthew 5:28). This is a powerful statement from the Son of God. Christ reveals to us that the mere thought of sexual immorality is a violation of God's commandment. Christ teaches us that self-gratification and fantasy driven urges are not for God's glory. Sex within the confines of the marriage, tapered with love was designed to glorify God.

When we reflect on the Old Testament story of Joseph, we are reminded of the seriousness servants of God take in the commandment to reframe from lustful pleasures of the heart. Joseph was tempted by Potiphar's wife and he asked the question, "How then can I do this great wickedness, and sin against God?" (Genesis 39:9).

Job demonstrates a morally sound life. He feared God and avoided evil on every corner and avenue. He was spiritually strong and found great pleasure and joy in serving God. His wife and children meant the world to him and he thanked the Lord for the many blessings bestowed upon his family. In order for us to inherit the Kingdom of Christ and of God, we must reframe from the awful displeasure that adultery can bring to the family.

Job recognized that pleasing God was essential to the foundation of his marriage. He understood that self-pleasure would not lead to spiritual gain but place him in a downward spiral leading to a dismal outcome. Satisfying pleasure, lust, desires, and urges of the heart cannot measure up to the divine claims established by the sacrifice and resurrection of Jesus Christ. We magnify and glorify God when we work within our marital structure to overcome temptations of the heart. Job shows us that we can achieve the goal if we set our hearts to it. God within and God overhead permits us to walk with a heavenly heart and preserves us from a successful attack from the enemy.

FAMILY LIFE

The Book of Job addresses more than the suffering of Job. It also addresses how he conducted his family life. Job was not only a great man, but also a great father and husband. He was well respected and admired in his community. Job 1:3 says,

> "so that this man was the greatest of all the men of the east."

Job 1:2 says,

"And there were born unto him seven sons and three daughters."

Including his wife and himself, this was quite a large household for Job to care for as the man of the house. Job was truly blessed. As an "upright and perfect" man, Job's children were respectful children that honored their parents and enjoyed the company of one another. When was the last time you enjoyed the company of your brother or sister? When was the last time you spoke to or visited with your brother or sister, mom or dad?

Regarding the atmosphere of Job's home life, the Bible states:

"and a very great household" (Job 1:3).

Take note of how Job's children enjoyed the company of each other:

"And his sons went and feasted in their homes, every one his day; and sent and called for their three sisters to eat and to drink with them" (Job 1:4).

True genuine happiness. What a great family! A family to be admired. What a blessed family. Let us examine how principled Job was regarding his children. I am adamant that The Book of Job transcends pain and suffering. Job performed a consistent act to protect his children under the grace of God. If we, as fathers, would take the time to perform the following on a daily basis, we would not have the societal problems with our children that we experience today. Children would respect and honor their mother and father. Children would not murder their classmates. Children would not kill their parents. Our children would not fall prey to occult and drugs. Job 1:5 says,

> "And it was so, when the days of their feasting were gone about, that Job sent and sanctified them, and rose up early in the morning, and offered burnt offerings according to the number of them all: for Job said, 'It may be that my sons have sinned, and cursed God in their hearts.' Thus did Job continually."

Honestly, fathers are we following the blessed example of Job? Are we truly handling our responsibilities? We also must walk "upright," always presenting the perfect example for our children to follow. Do we think of insulating our children first from God's wrath? Job illustrates to us that prayer (in earnest and continually) is the perfect insulation against sin. Prayer is the perfect weapon against Satan. The great philosopher Aristotle wrote:

> "We are what we repeatedly do. Excellence, then, is not an act, but a habit."

MARRIAGE IS SACRED

There is a certain beauty and excitement when a man and woman are joined together in holy matrimony. Family and friends gather together to celebrate the union of a couple under the blessedness of our Lord. It's a marvelous scene to witness.

God designed marriage to be holy. He created marriage for the man and woman to be happy, joyful, filled with growth and love. He created the marriage for the further expansion of love. Love is the foundation of marriage. "Commitment is the foundation" of marriage (Swindoll).

There are disturbing trends existing in our society today. The traditional family is under attack. People desire to design new forms of marriage and the dynamics of family. Some people want to test coupling together for a period to see how it works out. Same-sex marriages or unions have surfaced to impact the traditional marriage dramatically. The cry for support is well-documented. Some religious organizations support such unions. Some ministers have announced their support and have performed "same-sex" marriages in violation of church doctrine. Sympathetic ministers call the church doctrine too rigid for modern-day living. They state that the church should be eager to make an accommodation to homosexual individuals. State governments wrestle and tussle with laws to accommodate the supporters of same-sex unions. We do not condemn people for their choices but the ultimate question is, "Can two people be joined together and not be ordained by God?"

God laid the foundation of marriage in the Garden of Eden when he married Adam and Eve. Has the Word of God changed since the beginning of time? Can man adjust the mighty Word of God to accommodate his desires or ambitions? If same-sex marriage does not fall under the doctrine of God, whose doctrine does it fall under?

The Bible records that Job lived an upright life and had a "great family." Job lived according to the mandates of God, not man. He did not participate in evil. He avoided evil. The bible says there are "none like him in the earth." He was the ideal role model of what a husband should be within his marriage. We can learn and educate ourselves by Job's supremely endorsed example of wholesome living, living that brings about an "increase," not a "decrease." Job describes aberrant acts as "heinous crimes." The term "heinous" is defined in Webster's New Universal Unabridged Dictionary as: "hateful; odious; abominable; totally reprehensible." In blunt terms, any form of sexual activity outside of marriage was a sin before God and violated God's commandments. Job is so fearful of the act of adultery and fornication that he alludes to it in Job 31:11, "It is an inequity to be punished by the judges." We learn from Job that a marriage is a sacred institution, blessed by God and not to be disturbed by any negative force. In Matthew 19:4-6 Jesus says,

> "And he answered and said unto them, Have ye not read that he which made them at the beginning made them male and female, And said, For this cause shall a man leave father and mother, and shall cleave to his wife: and they twain shall be one flesh? Wherefore they are no more twain, but one flesh. What therefore God hath joined together, let not man put asunder."

When a man and woman become one flesh, no man or woman should attempt to separate this sacred union. God places marriage and family at the foundation of civilization. And no one has the power to break it but God. Job stood firm on the mandates of God.

God warns us of vices that can destroy the family in Leviticus 18:22-23, 25:

> "Thou shalt not lie with mankind, as with womankind: it is abomination. Neither shalt thou lie with any beast to defile thyself therewith: neither shall any woman stand before a beast to lie down thereto: it is confusion. Defile not ye yourselves in any of these things: for in all these the nations are defiled which I cast out before you."

God does not want us to contaminate ourselves by engaging in acts that attack the foundation of marriage. God is a patient, merciful, and compassion God. He detests violations of His commandments. God commands us to be pure of heart, holy and just. He objects to participation in corruptible behavior. God is clear in His commandment, that it is an "abomination," to lie with beast of any type, that it creates "confusion," and do not "defile" oneself in these things as it defiles the nation. The entire society is impacted by this behavior. God wants us to live a good life. He has placed us in a position to rise above the angels. Do we want to dine in the presence of God? God designed us in His image. We are a reflection of God. He did not create us in the image of lower animals. We cannot allow ourselves to be deceived that our physical "urges" and "pleasures" in this life are more important than God's principles. We are commanded to be holy and walk in the path of righteousness. God's Spirit is in us. We have a sacred temple within us that is holy. God provides us with enough gifts to enjoy ourselves in this life. He is preparing a better place for us in heaven. God wants us joyful and happy. He does not want us attached to earthly urges and pleasures that are corruptible and serve only the father of evil and wickedness. King Solomon writes in Proverbs 3:5-7:

> "Trust in the LORD with all thine heart; and lean not unto thine own understanding. In all thy ways acknowledge him, and he shall direct thy paths. Be not wise in thine own eyes: fear the LORD, and depart from evil."

God wants us to trust him. What we perceive to understand with the human eye, we must deny and trust in God's holy knowledge, understanding, and wisdom. We must deny ourselves and believe that God has our best interest. God will provide us the right answers and point us in the proper direction. However, we must fear God, reject evil on all levels and never allow our eyes to believe and accept earthly images of "pleasurable urges." When we reject these urges, we resist Satan's attempts to control our mind. We are commanded to manifest the holiness of God.

Apostle Paul writes, "Now the body is not for fornication, but for the Lord; and the Lord for the body" (I Corinthians 6:13). Paul elaborates, "What? Know ye not that your body is the temple of the Holy Ghost which is in you, which ye have of God, and ye are not your own? For ye are bought with a price: therefore glorify God in your body, and in your spirit, which are God's" (I Corinthians 6:19, 20).

In the Book of Titus 1:2:

> "In hope of eternal life, which God, that cannot lie, promised before the world began."

The goodness of God is eternal. Jesus Christ describes a creature totally opposite of God in John 8:44:

> "Ye are of your father the devil, and the lusts of your father ye will do: he was a murderer from the beginning, and abode not in the truth, because there is not truth in him. When he speaketh a lie, he speaketh of his own: for he is a liar, and the father of it."

GOOD VS. EVIL

It is clearly stated by the Book of John that Satan is the master of deceit, a liar in all forms. He is always tempting us to act contrary to God's commandments and covenants, desiring that we reject good and replace it with evil. Matthew 4:21 says,

> "And Jesus answering said unto him, it is said, Thou shalt not tempt the Lord thy God."

Our primary mission in life is clearly illustrated in James 4:7,

"Submit yourselves therefore to God. Resist the devil, and he will flee from you."

All of Satan's devices are based on a platform of evil. There is no good thing in him. He wants to make us stumble. He attempted to make Christ slip up in the wilderness after a 40 day fast. He failed because Christ understood where all "goodness" resided. Christ performed a mighty good work with the shedding of His blood on the Cross. Christ's work on the Cross revealed God's total "goodness." The Son of God slayed the Destroyer. We can only reach the higher good in life through Jesus Christ. Apostle Paul understood the divinity of Christ. He knew the Messiah had arrived and ascended into heaven with full power and authority. That's why Paul always concluded his writings and speeches in the following manner:

"The grace of our Lord Jesus Christ be with you" (Romans 16:20).

God prefers us to be more spiritual in our behavior and attitude. God desires that we perfect the habit of worshipping Him with body, mind, and soul. Corruptible habits cannot proclaim residency in the Kingdom of God. He does not want us to fall victims of the flesh. The flesh will return to its original place the dust of the earth. Man can destroy or inflict pain or suffering to the flesh, but God is Master over the spirit and flesh. Let us be strengthened by God's doctrine, not weakened by it. Let us elevate our present level of thinking to a godlier manner of reasoning---supreme wisdom. God commands us to be like Him. God commands us to be in harmony with one another. What is our problem today? Why do we accept 'wrongness' instead of righteousness? God has forgiven us for our transgressions. We must serve God. God has given us the greatest opportunity to be saved and receive salvation.

We must believe in God with all our heart, mind, soul, and body. God is a light source when we face darkness. Do not second-guess God. Accept God for what He is, the absolute authority over all things in heaven and beneath heaven. No one is as sacred and holy as God.

Why do we fear suffering over pleasure? Why do we prefer pleasure and relaxation rather than pain and affliction? Do we have the spiritual fortitude to endure suffering and await the outcome? We do not know the limit of our suffering. We want God to give us the conclusion without the introduction. We want the crown without the Cross, Easter without Good Friday, heaven without death, victory without pain.

We will learn from the story of Job that Satan will exhaust every opportunity to destroy man. This is an untrusting creature with a strong power of persuasion, unmatched under mortal standards. Remember, this serpent held a high position of authority in Heaven. He decided that his position in heaven was not high enough, so he set out to become like The Most High. Pride engulfed his heart. His lust for power and authority engineered his thinking. He became consumed in creating mutiny in heaven. The devil commandeered a third of the heavenly angels and started war in heaven

God decided that he and Lucifer could not co-exist on the same turf. Someone had to depart from heaven and surely wasn't going to be The Most High. Lucifer set the stage for his permanent disbarment from heaven. His urges and pleasures overtook sound judgment. We cannot take from God that which belongs to Him. In the end, God's judgment on Satan was eternal damnation in Hell.

Folks, as Job found out, Satan and Hell are real. Satan never discusses or describes his place of residence. Yet, he does everything to recruit us to join him in his "cesspool of iniquity." Our Lord and savior have given us a clear description of what Satan and Hell is like. God will not fool or confuse us.

Satan will attack Job on every physical level to destroy his character, integrity, and uprightness. Job will illustrate the faith and trust in God that is necessary to combat the forces of evil. Job shows us how to wear the "full armor" of God.

The scriptures reveal that Job had a "great family" and in order to have a superb family in the presence of God we must maintain the priestly examples of Job. Satan's mission is to destroy the family. Satan is jealous of a happy family. He will do any unjust act to destroy the family of man. Satan was restricted from attacking Job's family because God maintained a hedge around him. In other words, Job's home was off-limits to Satan. Job constantly prayed for his family to protect and insulate them from sin. He thought of his family first instead of himself.

We will learn through the saintly behavior of Job that God is the centerpiece, the cornerstone of "all things." A renewed spirit will strengthen us when we fall to our knees like Job and admit to the Holy Father that we "are vile." Our mind and spirit will become stronger with godly knowledge, understanding, and wisdom. We will comprehend that adultery; fornication, same-sex unions and homosexuality are sinful urges and pleasures designed by the architect of wickedness and deceit.

Satan is racing against time. He has failed and lost all authority and position he once had with God. Will you not follow the God that has total authority over all things? The Book of Job will show us what transpires when God steps on the premises to deliver his righteous sermon to Job. What happens to Satan when God arrives? Glory to God! God has the Almighty muscle, strength, and power to do as He pleases. We cannot permit Satan's pride and arrogance to fool us. Satan "fears God." When we consider sinful pleasure, let us consider the words of God; "Hast thou an arm like God? Or caust thou thunder with a voice like Him? Look on every one that is proud, and bring him low; and tread down the wicked in their place. Hide them in the dust together; and bind their faces in secret" (Job 40:9, 13). Glory to Almighty God!

This is the God of Supreme glory, majestic beauty, power and might. God saw the proud posturing of Lucifer and brought him low to dwell in Hell. We cannot manifest pride in the presence of God. The Supreme honor and holiness of God is beyond any high earthly standard.

After reading this book you can rest assured that God sent us the true priest and chief cornerstone for all of mankind to follow.

"For such a high priest became us, who is holy, harmless, unde-filed, separate from sinners, and made higher than the heavens; who needeth not daily, as those high priests, to offer up sacrifice, first for his own sins, and then for the people's; for this he did once, when he offered up himself"(Hebrews 7:26, 27).

> Our Lord and savior fulfilled the law and is consecrated forever more (Heb. 7:28). We can rest in the faith that Christ Jesus is our mediator "who is set on the right hand of the throne of the Majesty in the heavens" (Hebrews 8:1).

When we are stripped of everything in this life we can only look to Christ Jesus for an answer. It is Christ who took us from the bondage of sin. He paid the ransom with His blood. The death, burial and resurrection of Jesus Christ are the key to our salvation. There is no other religious master but Jesus Christ. That's why we need not waiver when struggle, pain, or suffering knocks at the door.

God will accomplish what He sets out to do. He will not fail us. We must continue to praise God throughout our ordeal and offer up our struggle, pain, and suffering as a living sacrifice. Get excited that our suffering is only for a season and the love of God will prevail. Each man or woman will be rewarded according to the will and grace of God. His eternal mercy and compassion will overwhelm us. Job shows us that if we trust in the Lord, we will dine in His holy temple with Him.

Let us trust in God. The Lord has a seat of righteousness and crown of glory reserved in heaven for those that maintain uprightness, avoid evil, and fear Him. Remember, all things fall under one deity, the God of Abraham, Isaac, and Jacob. The great and wonderful "I AM"!

Glory to Almighty God!

CHAPTER 1

COUNCIL MEETING
BEFORE THE SUPREME CHAIRMAN

"The Lord is my rock, and my fortress, and my deliverer, my God, my strength, in whom I will trust, my buckler, and the horn of my salvation, and my high tower." – Psalm 18:2

We hear and read about the personalities of many of our great entrepreneurs, chairmen of large corporations, and companies valued in the billions. We read and hear how these great men built their companies with their knowledge, persistence effort, personal desire to achieve, willingness to take on the challenge, insightfulness, anticipation of the needs of society, and how to profit from them. We read and hear about the cockiness, aloofness, directness, arrogance, self-centeredness, and abrasive styles many chairmen of large corporations possess. And we read about the downfalls of many chief executives as they parade in front of cameras in handcuffs. A roaring echo is overheard, "Greed is good."

Where is God? No chairman sits on the board of any corporation in the world without God's approval. It's not the votes of the Board of Directors that elevates one to Chairmanship; it is based completely on the will and power of God. God is the Lord of lords, King of kings, Champion of champions, and Chairman of chairmen. When God steps into the Board of Directors room there is no mistaken who is in charge. Such a meeting occured in Job 1:6:

> "Now there was a day when the sons of God came to present themselves before the Lord, and Satan came also among them."

Picture the atmosphere in heaven when Satan parades down the corridors to the Holy Boardroom. Satan is an imposing figure of beauty; pacing with an air of arrogance and swollen pride, lustful eyes of deceit, a tongue like a dragon, and a profile of shadows, suggesting darkness. With two-thirds of the angels remaining in heaven, one can imagine his cynical disposition while strutting through the hallway of Heaven.

Here is Lucifer, an angel of light, a creature, and a spiritual being. He belongs to the order of angels called Cherubim. He is an angel of power, a prince. He demonstrated and maintained the composure of nobility, as described in Ezekiel 28:12:

> "Thus said the Lord God; thou sealest up the sum, full of wisdom, and perfect in beauty."

Satan was the highest of all the angelic beings. In the mighty position Lucifer, he carried a lot of influence in heaven. He was able to coerce one-third of the angels to follow him and deny the Almighty Creator. God describes the position Lucifer held in heaven in Ezekiel 28:14, 15:

"Thou art the anointed cherub that covereth; and I have set thee so: thou wast upon the holy mountain of God; thou hast walked up and down in the midst of the stones of fire. Thou wast perfect in thy ways from the day that thou wast created, till iniquity was found in thee."

God became angry with Lucifer when iniquity was found in him. God's wrath came down hard on him. It is important to fear God; never denying His rightful power and elegance. Ezekiel 28:16-19 says,

"By the multitude of thy merchandise they have filled the midst of thee with violence, and thou hast sinned: therefore I will cast thee as profane out of the mountain of God: and will destroy thee, O covering cherub, from the midst of the stones of fire. Thine heart was lifted up because of thy beauty, thou hast corrupted thy wisdom by reason of thy brightness: I will cast thee to the ground, I will lay thee before kings, that they may behold thee. Thou hast defiled thy sanctuaries by the multitude of thine iniquities, by the iniquity of thy traffick; therefore will I bring forth a fire from the midst of thee, it shall devour thee, and I will bring thee to ashes upon the earth in the sight of all them that behold thee. All they that know thee among the people shall be astonished at thee: thou shalt be a terror, and never shalt thou be any more."

The original position that Satan enjoyed was stripped from him. His authority ripped from his hands. Satan's jealous rage consumed him and God cast him down to the bottomless pit. It was similar to a five-star general stripped of his rank and authority.

Imagine heaven for a moment. Heaven's beauty is beyond human comprehension. The home of God has a clean, clear atmosphere of complete purity -- totally holy, a temple, a sanctuary of divine inspiration, with streets lined with gold, and many mansions built of the purest spiritual qualities and materials, mansions built in the air, supported by the clouds. John 14:2 says,

> "In my Father's house are many rooms; if it were not so,
> I would have told you."

Seraphim with six wings levitate around the throne of God. Cherubim surround the throne, flying to and fro, serving God as needed, in addition to the Sergeant at Arms, the archangel Michael. Cherubim are similar to the National Guard, to be called on at any time, as God commands, maintaining proper order, according to God's commands. Remember, "There was war in heaven: Michael and his angels fought against the dragon and the dragon fought and his angels. And prevailed not: neither was their place found any more in heaven" (Revelations 12:7,8). Michael, his angels and the blood of the Lamb defeated the Devil (Revelation 12:11). The Devil was permanently deported from the confines of heaven. Michael is the most powerful enforcer in God's heavenly kingdom. He is the true protector and defender of God's turf, blessed with the power to defend, and to defeat any opponent, under the blessed blood of Jesus Christ. Proper order will be maintained during God's holy board meeting.

THE COUNCIL MEETING

Seated on the right hand side of the throne of God, in His magnificence, is Jesus Christ. Jesus Christ is the Second-in-Command in

Heaven; obedient to his Father. Heaven is described as "the home of righteousness" (II Peter 3:13). The Lord says: "heaven is my throne" (Isaiah 66:1).

The most imposing, powerful, and exalted being in heaven is God. The angles worship Him continuously, shouting "Holy, Holy, Holy!" The power of His mere presence is overwhelming to all those assembled. God is feared, even in Heaven. He is worshipped, and heavenly songs of praise ring like perfectly strung instruments. He is crowned with honor, wisdom, understanding and grace. His face provides all the light in heaven, brighter than a thousand suns. He wears the breastplate of salvation. He is cloaked with the whitest of white robes; a robe made only for this God. He is a voice of power that sounds like "many waters." His presence is intimidating, his entire body being wrapped in "agape love."

This is a Holy Board meeting. The Chief Executive Officer has arrived and His sons are assembled. Christ and the Holy Spirit are present. God, Christ and the Holy Spirit are in one accord on all matters. In addition, the various Directors "present" and "submit" themselves before the Holy and Exalted Father. This was a meeting of The Board wherein each member had to submit in a humble fashion, advising the Father of his business. This is a board meeting in which the Supreme Chairman is in absolute control and command. God's mere presence is "COMMANDING," creating "fear" in the minds of all the Board members. This Supreme Chairman does not need, nor does He seek, the APPROVAL of any board member to have His way. God, as Supreme Chairman, makes His own decisions, without any suggestion or hint from anyone. He is the Absolute Authority in the Boardroom.

The Supreme Chairman opens the meeting by inquiring of Satan, with a commanding voice, in a tone that would warrant immediate response and total submission:

> "And the Lord said unto Satan, whence comest thou?"
> (Job 1:7)

Satan responds in Verse 7:

> "Then Satan answered the Lord, and said. From going to and fro in the earth, and from walking up and down in it."

The Supreme Chairman recognizes the prideful arrogance of this former member of his inner circle. God continues an exchange with Satan regarding one of His favorite sons on earth. Job 1:8 says,

> "And the Lord said unto Satan, Hast thou considered my servant Job. That there is none like him in the earth, a perfect and an upright man, one that feareth God, and escheweth evil?"

Remember, the Supreme Chairman comprehends the internal character of Satan. Satan realizes he cannot tempt God because he "fears and trembles" before the Supreme Chairman.

Satan provides a full report on his observations of God's perfect servant:

> "Then Satan answered the Lord, and said doth Job fear God for naught?" Hast not thou made an hedge about him, and about his house, and about all that he hath on every side? Thou hast blessed the work of his hands, and his substance is increased in the land" (Job 1:9, 10).

Satan's report provides us with a clear insight into how he sits quietly by, observing every movement by Job, listening in on every conversation, attempting to find some crack in his armor; calculating how he can persuade Job to sin against God. Satan's entire focus is creating opportunities to inject confusion, deceit and destruction on the landscape. He is quick to express his observations about Job. Seemingly, Satan knows everything about Job, overlooking one key component – Job's commitment to God. Can Job maintain until God calls him home?

Satan has been watching, observing, critiquing and recording Job in his attempt to persuade him to dishonor God, to curse God to his face and to depart immediately from him. Satan realizes that Job is armored with the shield of God, that he cannot penetrate this "perfect and upright man." Job is a righteous man who fears his Lord and savior. But, Satan had been checking out Job to uncover a way to penetrate this godly man's armor. In pursuing this objective, Satan has a higher aim. Satan offers a proposal to the Supreme Chairman in Job 1:11,

"But put forth thine hand now, and touch all that he hath, and he will curse thee to thy face."

Satan gains pleasure when we sin against God. He desires that every possession that Job has be stripped from him without warning. He wants Job to be left with nothing. Some may question, "How can a man live with nothing?" God provides us with all our needs. Even Job's basic necessities for living are suggested to the Supreme Chairman for removal. Some of you may be thinking now (and you need to consider this when you think about sin again): "What type of creature would take away everything from a man and expect him to survive?" Secondly, "what type of creature would be so insensitive as to suggest that everything a person has be removed from him?"

35

Obviously, such a person or character would be lacking empathy and would have very little sympathy for the oppressed. Such a character would lack dignity, honor, or kindness. That person would have to be a devil, a dragon or an angel of evilness and wickedness beyond human comprehension, a being so evil that only GOD can control. Not only does Satan want everything snatched away from Job, he also wants Job to "curse God to his face." Satan wants Job to commit the ultimate sin.

IN HIS PRESENCE

All of us sin and fall short of God's glory, but why suggest the worst possible outcome: "curse God to his face?" First, no person including Satan has the power, nerve or will to stand in the presence of the Almighty God and curse Him to his face. No amount of wickedness in a person could force him to stand before the Master in all his holiness and "curse him." Second, no man can stand before God and do anything but bow to the Father and humble himself. Consider for a moment that you are before the majestic beauty and glorified presence of God. It would be "overwhelming." How could one make an "utterance" before God? God's power and glory would be too "shocking" to even comprehend. To witness the Father one-on-one would be the most humbling experience we would ever experience. The mere power and will of God's presence would force one to kneel down before God's footstool in humility, meekness, love, and fear. No man can stand in the presence of God and say or do anything.

It is wise to abide by the rules of God and fear Him. We must not overlook or forget that only one being created the heavens and earth. There was only One Craftsman to the Universe. There is only one Ruler over mankind --- the Lord God Almighty. In addition, I hope we learn at this stage that the pleasures of the flesh, the physical-ness of our thought processes must be eliminated, and a more spiritual process must be inserted in its place. Further, we must pause for a moment and consider if sin is worth it. Satan is in the business of destruction, taking away those things we consider precious. His mission is to make our lives miserable. Satan wants to take away our "increase" and decrease it to "nothing." Is it necessary to curse God to his face when all earthly items are taken from us, when all of our creature comforts are taken away? What do we have left? Can we carry on? Can we keep the faith? Can we still trust God? Satan believes if his request is granted that Job will curse God and die.

The Supreme Chairman responds to Satan's request without trepidation.

> "And the Lord said unto Satan, Behold, all that he hath is in thy power; only upon himself put not forth thine hand. So Satan went forth from the presence of the Lord" (Job 1:12).

God grants Satan permission to consume all that Job possesses. However, God places a restriction upon Satan to follow to the letter: "only upon himself put not forth thine hand." Satan cannot take Job's life in his pursuit to tear down this righteous man of God. Satan departs from the Supreme Council meeting swiftly to carry out his aerial assault on Job's "increase."

Prepare for a rocky ride as we depart from God's Boardroom into Job's living room. Stay tuned for frequent reports of devastating circumstances pushed into the face of God's servant Job. Job has no idea what is about to happen to him. Job knows nothing of God's decision at his Board meeting to use him to glorify God, to show Satan that God's "upright and perfect man"--who fears God and

37

eschews evil--will maintain until God decides, "That is enough." Prepare to learn that God's good and faithful servant will not fall prey to the temptations of the "angel of light," but will continue to receive God as his ONLY Master, trusting in God at all times, and glorifying His name. Finally, God's servant Job will not "curse God to his face," as Satan had so confidently stated to God in the Boardroom of heaven.

SATAN'S ASSAULT, THEN AND NOW

Get ready for an assault upon a human being by a being of absolute evil and wickedness. Only seconds pass before total destruction is complete. We are about to witness suffering of the highest degree, suffering beyond man's imagination, suffering that God authorized on an "upright and perfect man." Remember, every one of us is only a "nanosecond" from being in Job's condition. Keep this latter point in mind when we observe and meditate on Job's suffering. We have valuable lessons to learn in life. We need God. Imagine, just for a second, the scenario that would result if God allowed this creature to run rampant on earth, doing as he wished, without control. Imagine it! We must trust in God in order to receive glory. Remember; never be ashamed to know Christ. Examine yourself -- are you prepared to go into battle for Christ? As stated in the Boy Scout Manual, "BE PREPARED" for this eventuality. Place your arms around a brother who is suffering. As we prepare for the assault of Satan, it is always more prudent to go into battle with Christ than without Him. Let us get ready and brace ourselves. God has a surprise for Satan, Job, and us. God knows the real outcome is in His favor. Through God, we have VICTORY. The assault is about to happen. Trust in God. AMEN.

The scene at Job's compound is "business as usual," another blessed day in the name of the Lord. Job, his children and servants are carrying on their daily activities in a seemingly pleasant, peaceful atmosphere. All of a sudden, the aerial attack from Satan strikes. It's an attack far worse than the attack of our Air Force's B-52 bombers. Satan's bombardment is a specific, direct attack on the heart of a godly man. Job is a man who had avoided evil all his life. We observe his world being flipped upside down by a creature of mass destruction. Here is a holy man put to the test of his faith and trust in the Lord. His wealth and riches are insignificant. Job was not trapped by materialism. This is the time frame where men and women of great courage find out what they are made of. This is the true test of one's inner spiritual commitment to God.

The following scripture describes Job's children's merriment together:

> "And there was a day when his sons and his daughters were eating and drinking wine in their eldest brother's house" (Job 1:13).

The children were having fun, enjoying the company of each other. The following scripture describes the level of destruction which ensued and how swiftly it happened. Can Job maintain? Can Job reject the temptation of Satan and not curse God to his face?

"And there came a messenger unto Job, and said, the oxen were plowing, and the asses feeding beside them: And the Sabeans fell upon them, and took them away yea ,they have slain the servants with the edge of the sword; and I only am escaped above to tell thee. While he was yet speaking, there came also an other and said, Thy sons and thy daughters were eating and drinking wine in their eldest brother's house. And behold, there came a great wind from the wilderness, and smote the far corners of the house and it fell upon the young men, and they are dead; and I only am escaped alone to tell thee"(Job 1:14, 15, 18-20)

THE IMMEDIATE REACTION

This precise news was delivered to Job by his surviving servants-- news to shake the spirit of any man. This was news that Satan believed would force a man to rise up and curse his God to his face. Is Job such a man? Can Job lose everything around him and still "praise" the name of the Almighty? Can Job carry the cross until God comes? Conversely, will Job condemn the most Holy Father? Let us witness Job's actions after hearing the negative news.

> "Then Job arose, and rent his mantle, and shaved his head, and fell down upon the ground, and worshipped. And said, Naked came I out of my mothers' womb, and naked shall I return thither: the Lord gave, and the Lord hath taken away; blessed be the name of the Lord. In all this Job sinned not, nor charged God foolishly" (Job 1:20-22).

Job illustrates that even in the midst of horrifying pain and suffering we must glorify God. There is a Higher Power at work in our daily lives. We do not govern our own affairs. Job shows us that we cannot become servants of our own passions. He shows us how to place a shackle on our desires to be hostile towards God. He shows us how to grab hold of our emotions and humble ourselves to the throne of grace. This is a mighty work performed by Job. Job reveals that when adversity arrives we must submit to the power and authority of God.

How often do we charge God foolishly when danger, destruction, or death comes into our path? How often do we tell God that He has wronged us? How often do we ask, 'why me, Father?" rather than, "why not me, Father?" When we charge God foolishly, we are charging God wrongly. Thus, we must seek forgiveness immediately and trust in God.

Upon hearing all the news, Job gets his mantle, shaves his head and humbles himself before the Father. He submits himself to the Father and blesses the name of the Father in heaven in a total, submissive manner. Job glorified and magnified the Lord; the God who sits at the head of the council table in heaven, where He rules as the Supreme Chairman over "all things" in heaven and beneath heaven.

PETER: ON PROLONGED SUFFERING

The Epistle of I Peter 5:10 provides us with wisdom from the Most High. Satan is a strong adversary and the disciple Peter reveals the necessities required for prolonged combat:

> "And the God of all grace, who called you to his eternal glory in Christ after you have suffered a little while, will himself restore you and make you strong, firm and steadfast."

Glory be to God who sits high above the stars, exalted in His holy temple and glorified. May we be strengthened by the reading of his holy word for the good, sanctification and edification of our souls. We pray: O heavenly Father, have mercy on us. We did not comprehend at first, Father, but the purpose of thy mission is clear for us to see. Although we do not welcome this suffering and affliction, Father, if it is your will, proceed, Father, with thy will and power. I command all things into thy hands. O heavenly Father, I await thee, Father. In the name of Jesus Christ our savior, who suffered for us all. AMEN.

THE COUNCIL RECONVENES

Again, God calls a council meeting with his sons in heaven. Job 2:1 says,

> "Again there was a day when the sons of God came to present themselves before the Lord, and Satan came also among them to present himself before the Lord."

The Supreme Chairman questioned Satan directly as to his whereabouts, knowing that Satan had failed in his hostile and brutal assault against his servant Job. As always, Satan responds to God in an evasive manner. Job 2:2 says,

> "And the Lord said unto Satan, From whence comest thou? And Satan answered the Lord, and said, from going to and fro in the earth, and from walking up and down in it."

Instead of Satan acknowledging his complete and absolute failure in getting Job to "curse God to his face," Satan uses his traditional, evasive technique. Satan refuses to give God credit. Observe closely how God controls his Boardroom by refusing to even acknowledge "double-sided" responses from Satan and proceeds to His true mission, His faithful servant Job. We listen in as God delivers his command:

> "And the Lord said unto Satan, Hast thou considered my servant Job, that there is none like him in the earth,

a perfect and an upright man, one that feareth God, and escheweth evil? And still he holdeth fast his integrity, although thou movedst me against him, to destroy him without cause. And Satan answered the Lord, and said, Skin for skin, yes, all that a man hath will he give for his life" (Job2:3, 4).

SATAN'S MISSION

In verse 3, God acknowledges that Job maintains his perfection and unrighteousness before the Lord: "still he holdeth fast his integrity." God is adamant regarding our "integrity." He wants us to maintain, to be steadfast under all conditions, never losing sight of the ultimate goal which is to "carry that cross until the Lord comes." Have mercy on us, Father. Deliver us from evil. Glory to your name, O heavenly Father. Peace. AMEN.

God also uses the term "destroy" in verse 3, stating clearly, "to destroy him without cause." God vividly advises us that Satan's campaign and sole mission is to bring destruction. Satan does not arrive on the premises for a peaceful chat or meal at the table of brotherhood. His ultimate and absolute purpose is to embarrass man before God, and to instill doubt in the mind of man regarding God's overwhelming love, grace, and forgiveness for us. Further, Satan illustrates his jealousy of Jesus Christ, the only Son of God, and tries to tear down any symbol of recognition of God's Son. Almost as an afterthought, Satan further desires to destroy man physically, in hope of provoking God's wrath.

Jesus Christ said,

> "Come unto me, all ye that labour and are heavy laden, and I will give you rest" (Matthew 11:28).

Praise God, who sits most high and exalted above all for sending His Son Jesus Christ for our benefit. Praise God for looking down from His mighty throne of power to have mercy on us, to examine our weaknesses and, from His holy observation point, conclude that his Son, Jesus Christ, was the only person equipped to come into this world in human form, face every temptations, and remain sinless. Praise God further, that the Son of Man would receive victory over the grave in order that man may experience salvation before the Lord. Father, we love you and accept your Son as our true and only savior. Father, we trust in you and pray for your continued mercy, grace, and protection from evil things and forgiveness. Father, as we travel along life's highway, we ask for these things in the name of Jesus Christ, our Advocate, Deliverer and Redeemer. AMEN.

According to God's written word, Job was a perfect and upright man, one who fears God, and eschews evil. And still he holds fast his integrity, as a blessed servant of God. It is safe to conclude that Job enjoyed the blessing of excellent health, too.

SATAN'S SECOND ATTEMPT

Satan failed miserably. But, this failure did not dissuade him from a second attempt to rip Job to remnants of his former self. After Satan's failure to persuade Job to curse God to his face by destroying his increase, Satan suggests to God that "Skin for skin, yes, all that a man hath will he give for his life" (Job 2:4). Satan is making a suggestion, not giving an order to God. Satan humbly submits his suggestion to God in hopes that God will grant him a second opportunity to destroy this "good and faithful servant." Satan feels his second attempt, if granted, will provide him with an adequate forum to destroy Job and his godly nature. Satan hates it when we honor God and follow his commandments and covenants. He is extremely jealous, highly committed to destroying man and strongly engaged in the elimination of any positive images of our Lord's Son, Jesus Christ. In Job 2:5, Satan refuses to accept defeat:

> "But put forth thine hand now and touch his bone and
> his flesh, and he will curse thee to thy face."

Satan is a competitive creature. He does not give up easily. He strongly feels that if he destroys the health of a man, that man will give up hope and curse God for his illness. Satan is convinced that man fears death and will not embrace it like life. Satan believes that man will point an accusing finger at God and curse Him to his face. That man will charge God foolishly. The Apostle Paul reminded us in New Testament scripture, "absent from the body, and to be present with the Lord" (II Corinthians 5:8).

God renders his final decision to Satan at the Supreme Chairman's Council meeting. Let us be reminded that Satan failed miserably in his first attempt with Job, and now requests a second audience in order to prepare properly a new strategy to destroy Job, to place Job in such a weakened position that he will "curse God to his face." The Supreme Chairman makes up his mind and states the following:

> "And the Lord said unto Satan, Behold, he is in thine
> hand; but save his life" (Job 2:6).

Job is not aware of this decision. Once carried out, Job feels he is facing impending death as a direct result of Satan's bitterness. God grants Satan a portion of his request and places his own decree within the directive, "save his life." God clearly illustrates that he is in total control of all situations and circumstances. It is required of Satan to follow God's directive to the letter, without any deviation whatsoever. Job's subsequent (and prolonged) illness is described in Verse 7 of Chapter 2:

> "So went Satan forth from the presence of the Lord, and smote Job with sore boils from the sole of his foot unto his crown."

PRESENT-DAY QUESTIONS

God's heavenly meeting is adjourned for a while. We journey back to the earth to view the supreme suffering of a "perfect and upright man, that eschewth evil and feareth God."

In the present day, would you inquire, "Lord, why did you perform such an act on this innocent man?" Or, would you inquire, "Job, you must have done something sinful to God for this thing to be placed on you?" Or, do we praise and exalt the name of the Lord and humbly confess to Him that we will carry the cross until He calls us home, denying ourselves in the process, convinced in our hearts that God knows what is best for us and God will not fail us? In sum, God will reveal himself at the appropriate time. Only God knows that time. I would encourage, do not charge God foolishly for the things we do not understand. Trust in God and keep the faith. The writer in the Old Testament strengthens us as we walk the journey with Job:

> "The Secret things belong unto the Lord our God: but those things which are revealed belong unto us and to our children forever, that we may do all the words of this law" (Deuteron omy 29:29).

When we are weakened by misery, it is because God has failed to reveal the true purpose of His mission. First, consider, how the Son of Man behaved on the Cross. He took on the sins of man which granted us the opportunity to reign with Him and come into the congregation of His Father. Our suffering is minute in comparison to what Jesus Christ endured on the Cross. God will surprise us. If we wait patiently on the Lord, we are assured of receiving the Promise.

The day will soon come when each one of us must come face-to-face with the Supreme Chairman of the Board. God does not need consent or a majority vote in order to conduct His global business. His blessings are not restricted by a set budget. There is not an independent board to review His decisions. The "economy of God" has unlimited riches, wealth and treasures. His storehouse is filled to over-flow. His business plan was written prior to the origin of the world and has stood the test of time. He has not had to make any adjustments. His plan is perfect. He does not need to make alliances with forces of evil in order to manifest His power and authority. God is completely "debt-free." But, we are eternally indebted to God for sending His Son to pay all of our bills. We were bankrupt until Christ paid the ransom demand. It's time for us to cast our vote and make that final commitment: heaven or hell. There is only one proxy that stands between man and God. Cast your vote now!

Meeting adjourned.

CHAPTER 2

IN THE BELLY OF THE BEAST

'Job's physical ambush by Satan'

"Be sober, be vigilant; because your adversary the devil, as a roaring lion, walketh about, seeking whom he may devour." – 1 Peter 5:8

As far as earthly possessions are concerned, Job has lost everything. He's bankrupt. The devil has ripped away every form of material gain. This evil adversary does not possess empathy or sympathy for Job's demise. This was a fun-loving game for the devil. Satan's demons leapt with laughter at God's perfect servant.

The only thing left for Job is his health, and he was thankful for that. Nevertheless, Satan decides to present for the Lord's consideration; a massive attack upon Job's health. He touches Job's body and poisonous boils surface from the top of his head to the soles of his feet. The boils are so horrible that Job performs the following act:

> "And he took him a potsherd to scrape himself withal; and he sat down among the ashes (Job 2:8).

49

There was no known cure for such an illness in Job's time. Job cried out for mercy and compassion, seeking the Lord's immediate intervention. He wanted to be restored to his former greatest and not face this disgusting trial and tribulation.

God has many methods to bring about healing. Jesus Christ illustrated many different techniques to healing. In Job's case, he did not fully understand why his life had turned upside down. But, as time moved along he decided to trust God. We must seek God and not rely on our own understanding. God possesses the power and authority to heal. Man can treat an illness, only God can heal.

THE ELDER'S REACTION

Job is so disfigured and repulsive that the elders that visit fail to recognize him. Shadows of death flash through the mind of Job. Is Satan accurate when he states, "All that a man hath will he give for his life" (Job 2:4).

Job is suffering massive pain and anguish. And when the elders recognize that the disfigured person is Job, they perform a traditional ritual:

> "And when they lifted up their eyes afar off, and knew him not, they lifted up their voice, and wept; and they rent every one his mantle, and sprinkled dust upon their heads towards heaven" (Job 2:12).

The elders wept at the sight of Job. They felt the intensity of his pain and suffering and performed a ritual by sprinkling dust upon their head towards heaven. The evil and wicked disease that Satan placed upon God's good and faithful servant reveals a lot about Satan, a creature with the power and terror to create ugliness and damnation in a cruel and unusual form--a creature of complete evil and wickedness.

However, Apostle Paul writes in the New Testament scripture:

"Be not overcome of evil, but overcome evil with good" (Romans 12:21).

Paul encourages us to overcome evil with good. As difficult as Paul's words are to absorb when we are in the midst of the struggle; it reveals an honest portrayal of how to conduct ourselves when pain and sufferings knocks at the door. Do we open the door and embrace pain and its traveling companion, suffering? Or do we peek through the key hold and curse both parties to depart immediately from the premises?

God believes in putting us to the test. We may have to take the test over and over in order to pass; but ultimately through faith and trust in the Lord, we will endure and get the passing grade. God is about "goodness." When we are confronted with evil, Paul writes

"That ye may with one mind and one mouth glorify God, even the Father of our Lord Jesus Christ" (Romans 15:6).

There are tremendous teachings in the Old and New Testament scriptures on how to govern our lives when pain and suffering attacks our body. Remember, we are only a nanosecond from being in Job's position. Job's present state shows us that no man can boast about his wealth or health when the Lord Almighty is the Master of our faith. Apostle Paul advises us about highly elevated thinking of self:

"For I say, through the grace given upon me, to every man that is among you not to think of himself more highly than he ought to think; but to think soberly, according as God Hath dealt to every man the measure of faith" (Romans 12:3)

Instead of us giving up on God, we are encouraged throughout scripture to maintain our faith, love and trust in God. God desires that we endure through suffering. Our heavenly Father would never encourage us to consider euthanasia, mercy killing, suicide, or assisted-suicide as a conclusion to our pain and suffering. Pope Benedict XVI said euthanasia is a "false solution" to suffering.

We must resist and not submit to the desires of Satan. The devil's mission is for us to "curse God to his face." It should never be our mission to assault the Creator of all things in heaven and earth, but exalt and magnify the "Father of glory." How could we muster up the power to curse God to his face? We should keep our focus and commitment on God, even if we must carry the cross to death. In life or death, we are with God. We are not alone. When we cross the river Jordan, Christ will be there. Apostle Paul says,

"For none of us liveth to himself, and no man dieth to him self. For whether we live, we live unto the Lord; and whether we die, we die unto the Lord: whether we live therefore, or die, we are the Lords. For to this end Christ both died, and rose, and revived, that he might be Lord both of the dead and living" (Rom 14:7-9).

God gives us the full picture, based on faith, love and trust in Him. God is waiting on us in life, as well as in death. Satan never gives us the full picture. He takes a portion of what God states, and distorts it to fool us and make us servants of sin. Jesus Christ conquered death; Jesus Christ received the Victory. Jesus Christ went into hell and Satan could not hold him. Jesus Christ took back what belonged to His Father. No longer does death have a sting. Therefore, total and complete VICTORY is His and ours. Satan is powerless and his time is limited. He is here for a season. Remember, that Satan despises us. His jealousy is like an eternal rage, fueled by an unquenchable fire. He hates and rejects every image of the Son of God. But, in the presence of the Living God "Satan trembles." Glory to God!

When God calls upon us to carry the cross for a time, remember the refreshing words of Apostle Paul, who suffered for a season but endured to the end:

> "Rejoicing in hope; patient in tribulation; continuing instant in prayer" (Romans 12:12).

Apostle Paul provides us with the clear description and prescription to our afflictions. This is excellent medicine for the soul. We cannot overdose with God's medicine. Day-by-day, moment-by-moment, let us keep our focus on our Lord and savior, Jesus Christ. Apostle Paul walked like Jesus Christ and refused to give up the blessed hope in being in the presence of the Lord. He followed God's laws and commandments and preached the gospel for all to hear. Paul speaks the truth.

Jesus Christ made it clear to Satan, in a face-to-face confrontation on earth. God was in the flesh. Satan made every attempt to persuade Christ to worship him and reject the teachings of his Father. Christ stated:

> "Then saith Jesus unto him, get thee hence, Satan: for it is written, thou shalt worship the Lord thy God, and him only shalt thou serve." (Matthew 4:10)

Jesus Christ reminded Satan of God's written word and Satan departed from the presence of our Lord. We must follow the excellent example set by Christ.

JOB REJECTS SUICIDE

Although Job's grief was very great (Job 2:13), he maintained a focus on God. He rejected his wife's foolish suggestion to curse God and die (Job 2:9-10) and gives his wife a direct statement inspired by God that she did not care to hear.

> "But he said unto her, Thou speakest as one of the foolish women speaketh. What? Shall we receive good at the hand of God, and shall we not receive evil? In all this did not Job sin with his lips."

Job did not sin with his lips. Are we willing to accept the good blessings from God, as well as the tough portions? Ask yourself this question; "What did Jesus do?" Can we drink from the same cup as our Lord?

Remember, Jesus Christ suffered the most on the cross for all of mankind. Jesus Christ restored our relationship with his Father. We are to walk the path that Jesus left for us to follow. When we are in the Belly of the Beast and face a physical ambush, we can reflect on the heavy price Christ paid on the cross. Christ paid the full ransom for our salvation.

Father I understand your mission now, have mercy, Father I trust in you Father, my Lord and savior, I have faith, Father; lend your ear to my prayers, O' heavenly Father. AMEN.

Now the true test of a man's spirit, endurance, motivation, faith and trust in the Lord comes about. Job's trauma provides insight into a man's method of evaluating God's love, compassion, mercy and judgment. It also permits a man to view the unsavory character of Satan. He's an unmerciful adversary and treacherous spirit, doomed to failure; especially when man places his earnest trust in God. He is a relentless adversary with an enormous appetite to crush a human being through sin of the flesh. Only the power of the living God can stripe him down from his swollen pride.

WHY NOT ME?

Let's set the scenery straight before we attach ourselves to the insensitive and destructive power of Satan. The stage is set. We are about to enter some rough and bumpy terrain. The ride will be difficult, the destruction swift. Nevertheless, God's love, mercy and compassion are steady, maintaining a steadfast level. Let us keep our faith and trust in God, that He knows what is best for us. Pray in earnest that our friend, Job, will continue to travel along life's rugged terrain. As the forces of evil and wickedness attack from all sides, we pray that Job will remain anchored in the Word of God. Remember, we are not asking "why" we are saying God, "why not me Father?" We acknowledge that our blessed Father knows our limitations and will not give us a cross to carry that we cannot keep on a steady course of righteousness. With Job, are we willing to make that sacrifice in the name of God? Are we willing to kneel and submit totally to God in all situations and circumstances? God will completely surprise us. We must never be ashamed to know God. God is in the business of making us better than we are.

Let us elevate our thinking processes in order to become a God-like thinker. Let us go beyond ourselves, refusing to limit our thinking, but locating new openings in the heart, by which action we invite

God in to provide us with the wisdom and intellectual capacity to comprehend His ultimate objective. We want to say to God: O heavenly Father, bless me with the Godly tools necessary to endure the purpose of your mission. I place my trust in you. Father, forgive me, I did not see it or understand your mission at first; but, O'heavenly Father, I see it now. So, do unto me as you will Father, I submit myself to you. Father, have mercy on me. Strengthen me at all times. Teach me, Father, to glorify your name in all that I do. God, I know you will be there to help me on all accords; thereby, I will submit to do your work and your work only. In the name of Jesus Christ, our savior, AMEN.

A PERSONAL ANECDOTE

I had an illness over a six-month period that baffled the medical authorities of an eminent hospital. After lengthy examination, the most noted physicians concluded that I was suffering from dehydration. I spent several nights in the emergency room over a period of six months. The medical machinery used for diagnosis was elaborate. The doctors and nurses administered every test imaginable before reaching their conclusion. I expressed my confidence in the doctors for their excellent service and professionalism. I departed from each visit thinking they were the best on the planet. I concluded that they knew everything about curing my illness. I placed my faith and trust in the highly-educated medical personnel. I consumed the prescription medication, expecting to eliminate the pain in my right side and to lower a body temperature of 103 degrees. I was perspiring pools of sweat, my vision became blurred, and I lost my sense of taste, appetite, and experienced constant, intense pain in the right side. I was losing weight daily and lacked power or strength to do anything.

The pain was so intense that I did not sleep for a six-month period. The doctors continued to increase the medicine and no improvement resulted. I attempted to lift a bar of soap to take a bath and it seemed to weigh a hundred pounds. Due to the intensity of pain it took me over an hour merely to get dressed every morning. My wife telephoned the doctors so often that the nurses became irritated and unprofessional. They felt we were bothering them. "Keep taking the medicine as prescribed," the nurses responded. I followed those instructions over a six-month period, to no avail. The highly regarded physicians advised me to continue to stretch that right side and maybe the sore muscle would *"pop."* I tried to crack that sore area in my right side every day, over a six-month period. As time passed, I lost the use of my right leg and I finally fell in my living room with no strength to lift myself. I told my wife that it was over and I was dying. I thought the end had arrived and this was my final exit. My wife made the decision to take me to another hospital for examination. She telephoned a friend to help carry me to the automobile. Upon arriving in the doctor's office, it took her less than ten minutes to conclude that poison was leaking into my body from a leaking appendix. I was in the danger zone. She immediately admitted me and demanded additional procedures. As the IV was connected to my arm, my temperature was 105 degrees and showed no signs of dropping. Several specialists came by, and I was placed in isolation. I was getting weaker and weaker. The doctors stated that I would be in the hospital for a minimum of ten days. They found an infection in my right side between my kidney and liver. If I had *"popped"* that infection I would have died immediately from the poison. Why did God allow me to live? Doctors and medical students came by to view my ailments, as if I was a practice dummy. They sent a sample tissue from my case to the Center for Disease Control and it failed to reach an accurate conclusion as to its origin. I began to pray in earnest. The second night my minister came by around midnight and prayed to God to heal me of my ailment. When he lifted his hand from my head, he remarked, "God has healed you of your ailment, prepare to leave the hospital." I felt the spirit of the Lord come over me and I prayed to God to deliver me from this sickness. I vowed to write an exposition of the Book of Job to honor, praise and glorify the Lord of Hosts. I went to sleep for the first time in six months with renewed hope in God's mercy, compassion, grace and power to heal. The doctors checked me the next morning and stated: "remarkable, I do not believe what I am viewing. This cannot be accurate. Bring the other Specialist in for further consultation." My temperature was falling into normal range, and my sense of taste returned. I ate three plates of food. God healed me of several ailments. Glory to God! The infection and my appendix "healed itself through the glory of God." The doctors remained baffled at the development and attempted to explain it in earthly medical terminology. I told them the healing was only through the grace and power of God. I suffered for a season, and I received my reward in due season according to the will and might of the Holy Father. The doctors demanded that I receive testing every month over a six-month period, to discern if my appendix would flair up. If I did not keep my vow to God to write this book, I feared a greater calamity would come. The reader is a witness that I completed what I promised the Lord. Remember, it is better not to make a vow to God, than to make a vow and not keep it. God always remembers the promises made to Him. When I looked to God to heal me instead of the medical authorities He delivered me according to His schedule. Today, I trust in God without hesitation. I believe in God without doubt. I will not be persuaded that God does not exist. I know God is a God of life. I know I am a vile person and Christ is the key to my salvation. I have excellent health today because of God. God is alive and well. When I last checked, God was still in the healing, helping and restoration business. Will you try him today?

In all challenges in life God wants us to be brave and of great courage. Let us not become a hinderance to the body of Christ but a marvelous example of blessed hope. When a righteous person suffers there is a broad range of feelings and emotions that flash through their mind. As we wrestle, tussle and struggle with the conditions and circumstances, we eventually reach a point of acceptance and understanding that all hope and comfort rests in the hands of God. Apostle Paul writes, "I can do all things through Christ which strengtheneth me" (Philippians 4:13).

If we persevere in the suffering, we acquire a renewed intimacy with the Lord. This new familiarity with the Lord propels us to a new loving and endearing relationship with Jesus Christ. Our closeness to Christ gives us a clear picture of God's meaning and purpose in our life. We have redemption through the blood of Christ. When we become a target for pain God's sovereignty is revealed through grace. Therefore, when the beast desires to inflict us for a season, we understand that through faith and trust in the Lord we will endure the battle. And the devil cannot stomach that the blood of Christ is more powerful than any venom he can spew on the landscape.

When the flood waters and dark clouds recede and the majesty power and beauty of God is revealed, joy consumes us. As the door of Heaven opens up and the shinning face of Christ is exposed, our understanding returns and we recognize one important factor "God laid the earth's foundations."

CHAPTER 3

DON'T GET BITTER, GET BETTER

"Beloved, think it not strange concerning the fiery trial which is to try you, as though some strange thing happened unto you: But rejoice, inasmuch as ye are partakers of Christ's sufferings; that, when his glory shall be revealed, ye may be glad also with exceeding joy" – I Peter 4:12,13

Bitterness creeps up on us when we feel we have been wronged. It can happen suddenly like the death of a loved one when we immediately react and conclude that God has done us wrong. It can impact us when a husband or wife divorces. It rises up when a son or daughter engages in inappropriate behavior. It happens when a dear friend betrays us. There are volumes of encyclopedias filled with situations where people have been wronged and bitterness raises its ugly head for revenge.

Bitterness is rooted in hate. Hatred and bitterness are a peculiar mixture. Blended together the end result can only be sickness. There is a certain danger in clinging to the luxury of bitterness. Bitterness is part of the enemy's arsenal to keep us separate from God. In the end, bitterness creates a life of misery.

The Apostle Paul writes in Ephesians 4:31, "Let all bitterness, and wrath, and anger, and clamour, and evil speaking, be put away from you, with all malice." Paul encourages us to set aside every degree of anger and wrath that may surface when we are harmed wrongly. It seems difficult when we feel someone has performed an injustice against us. It stings like salt poured in an open wound. It burns like an intense flame. It puts on the appearance of embarrassment in the community and we feel the appropriate reaction to reach out and make that person pay. What price are they paying? Is the price worth it? Can happiness be achieved by taking out wrath on the person who wronged us? Is getting even the best response to being wronged?

WHY DO BAD THINGS HAPPEN TO GOOD PEOPLE?

The newspaper stories appear to leap off the page. There seems to be tragedy on every page. Someone, somewhere in the world had to confront a tragedy that impacted their daily lives in a negative way. Bitterness, resentment, and anger seemed to be the remedy of the day. The stories seem to get more gruesome on each passing moment. A question surfaces: Why do bad things happen to good people?

A 45-year-old school caretaker in New York is brutally murdered by a 14-year-old teenager. Under the picture of the grieving mother was written, "Why did this have to happen?" A sympathetic crowd gathered around the mother to offer support.

An 80-year-old grandmother, confined to a wheel chair was brutally raped, robbed and strangled to death. The murdering thief got only twenty-five dollars. Again, the community cries, "why?"

A tragic, three-car accident kills 21 people, including 11 teenagers. A child enters the world "still born." The parents weep and cry out: "God, why us?"

A few years ago, due to the pressure of sports competition, Tanya Harding (champion skater) and her accomplice attacked Nancy Kerrigan physically and Nancy Kerrigan cried out *"Why? Why? Why?"*

A man finds out he has contracted AIDS and goes on a killing spree against other innocent people and commits suicide. The family cries, "Why me? Why me?"

A mother goes to the sentencing hearing to express her feeling about the convicted rapist and murderer of her 6-year-old daughter. The tone of her voice is that of pain, anguish, depression and anger towards the killer. At the end of her speech, she says, "And I hope your soul burns in hell for what you did to my little girl."

A father's son drowns in the city pool. The father weeps, "Why? Why did this have to happen to my son?"

After being drafted number one in the NBA draft, a star athlete celebrates with cocaine and dies. Another star athlete uses pounds of cocaine and other drugs, but is given another chance to redeem himself. Society cries out, "Why this person and not this other person? It's just not right."

A gang member for no apparent reason kills a 17-year-old high school star athlete in Chicago, Illinois with over 250 colleges after his abilities. The community cries, "Why?"

A minister running a homeless shelter feeding 300-500 hungry citizens a day is senselessly killed by an angry homeless person for no good reason. The community cries out: "Why this beloved man?"

Adolph Hitler, the architect of the Nazi Third Reich in Germany during World War II, killed over six million Jews, tortured millions more, and left scars for many generations. "Why?" "For what reason?" "For what purpose?" "What was his motivation?" Why do bad things happen to good people?

During the Stalin regime in Russia, over 15,000 bodies are unearthed from a dirt tomb. Innocent lives were destroyed for no apparent reason. Families and historians ask, "Why?"

A hurricane, earthquake, tornado, or flood destroys an entire community. The survivors cry out "Why?" Where is God? Why did God let this happen?

A minister devoted to helping change the lives of young people, dies when the wood on a truck breaks away and crushes him. The church members ask, "Why?" Why such a good man? A man doing something to help society, not contaminate it. A man that was cleaning up the garbage of society.

More recently, John F. Kennedy, Jr., his wife and his wife's sister died tragically in a plane crash. The Kennedy family had experienced a history of unexpected deaths. The world cried out, "Why this young man, his wife, and sister-n-law? Why another Kennedy tragedy?" The world questions, "Is there a curse on this family?"

We could go on and on about how life, death, calamity, and mayhem confront us on a daily basis. What do we do to restrain ourselves from wrath? How do we deal with death? How do we deal with the challenges and struggles of life's situations and circumstances? Why do the happenings and "goings on" of this life surprise us? Why does it appear that the "good" suffer more than the "bad"? Why must the sun shine on our enemy, as well as us?

Job was faced with similar conditions and circumstances of a quick and substantial nature. How did he cope? How did he deal with it? Did he panic? Did he threaten? Did he curse? Did he gather a posse to go after the Sabeans and Chaldeans who stole his cattle and killed his servants? (Job 1:15, 17) Did he charge God foolishly? Job 5:2 says, "For wrath killeth the foolish man, and envy slayeth the silly one."

We face calamity regularly and the face of death challenges us in some capacity every day of our lives. From the time we are born, the clock of death is ticking. However, what about the clock of life? Should we not focus more on living than on death? Is death not an extension of life? Jesus Christ said, "Let the dead, bury the dead." Many have died for the glory of God, but how many will live for this glory, with the same passion?

The death of a loved one can be challenging to the spirit. No matter what the circumstance or cause of death, it can at times be most challenging to the soul. It is a mystery why God permits one person to die and another to live. It lies far beyond the scope and depth of our understanding. The decision rests in the Almighty mind of God.

God has permitted challenges of this magnitude to make us stronger, to make us humble. In addition, such challenges inspire us to look to Him for all things, even for understanding, on the death of a loved one. We must diligently pursue the wisdom of God to teach us greater understanding.

God has clearly stated that it is placed upon a man to die once. We know not the hour or how it will happen. Satan is convinced, in his assessment of man, that we fear death to such a degree that we will "curse God to his face." He sold himself on the idea that the patriarch Job would become so broken that he would verbally assault God. Satan is convinced that man enjoys the pleasures of this world such that he would deny God and permanently separate himself from Him. God is the solution. God is the answer. God will not allow us to suffer more than what we can endure. We can endure much when we are enamored with the shield of faith. Satan's mission is to influence us to be bitter with our brother and God when calamity strikes.

The most important point to remember is that Jesus Christ, God Incarnate, conquered death and every form of bitterness. By the Son of God conquering death, we are free of death's stranglehold. Satan cannot intimidate us with the temptation of death. He lost his sting.

Remember, Christ descended into Satan's domain, went face-to-face with him, preached the gospel, and received the Victory. Therefore, man is free of any death hold. After our departure from this physical world, we can accept victory in God's kingdom through our mediator Jesus Christ. Let us not get bitter with God; we are better because of God.

Charlton Heston, the legendary actor who portrayed Moses in the film, *The Ten Commandments,* wrestled with the agony of Alzheimer's disease prior to his death. When confronted with the fight of his life he said, "I must reconcile courage and surrender in equal measure."

It is easy to get bitter when confronted with a crisis. Sometimes the atmosphere of bitterness is a comfort zone, used by some to acquaint themselves with guilt, revenge or vengeance against themselves or another. God has established a firm doctrine against revenge. Revenge belongs in the hands of the Lord. He will handle it appropriately. There is no better judge on the circumstances of life than our Lord. Our Lord is an instrument of peace, not violence. Once violence has been established, where does it leave us? Empty. The cup is not full; only God can fill our cup to "overflow." God designed us, so He knows what's best for us. God knows how much of a load we can carry. God knows how much pressure and stress we can take before He intervenes. We, as soldiers and warriors for Christ, must not forget our mission. Our mission is solely to obey Christ and carry the cross until God states: "Enough my Son, come home now!" Proverbs 10:12 says, "Hatred stirreth up strifes, but love covereth all sins."

We must not allow ourselves to reach such a low point in our lives that we feel the only way out is to take out revenge against another. Ego and pride are dangerous tools when placed in the wrong hands. I Thessalonians says, "Abstain from all evil."

God created life from His hands. He said everything He designed was "good." We have created nothing. We can only use the things that God has created for our purposes. God is the Originator. For example, suicide is a direct effort by which some allows their situation in life to become so "self-absorbed" and so "self-centered" that they believe, through the mirror of sadness, rejection and depression, their circumstances are insurmountable. They believe that no one can solve their problems or deliver them from the total 'engulfing-ness' of their situation. Guilt is another reason why we might destroy ourselves through an act of suicide. It represents our inability to forgive ourselves for our wrongdoing. Failure to forgive ourselves is a form of bitterness that we carry around. This is heavy baggage that we carry around and refuse to let go. Once God has forgiven us of our sins, He will not toss it in our face ever again. We become new in Christ. Evil thoughts against ourselves are eliminated and we can rejoice in the thought that God truly loves us with an everlasting love. The Apostle Paul writes in Acts 8:22, "Repent therefore of this thy wickedness, and pray God, if perhaps the thought of thine heart may be forgiven thee."

I interviewed a female client that had suffered years of incest (from the age of five) from her father. She was 32 years-old at the time, and married, but was having serious problems fulfilling her responsibilities to her husband. Normally, this would be a problem in many marriages, but she was blessed with a husband who possessed great patience and understanding. Through several therapeutic sessions, she was able to improve and strengthen herself to the point where she requested to meet one-on-one with her father. The father agreed to the session. The father was in prison at the time for this terrible act upon his daughter. She was able to reach a point where she could say to her father: "Dad, I forgive you for what you did to me; I no longer have anger at you and I look upon you as my father. I love you." The woman and her husband continued on to have a fruitful life. The father was shocked that his daughter was capable of forgiving him for this crime and committed suicide due to the burden of guilt he placed upon himself and his inability to accept his daughters 'forgiveness' as reality. Satan wants us to think that God has not forgiven us for our sins. Satan wants us to doubt God. Satan wants us to believe that our crimes against God are so embarrassing and hurtful that He would never forgive us for such "heinous crimes." Satan is absolutely wrong.

We must have the faith and confidence in a Supreme Lordship, that when God has forgiven us, He has done just that. Remember, God keeps His word. We must trust in God that he means what he says: "heaven and earth shall pass away, my words shall not pass away" (Matthew 24:35). God means it. God cannot lie. We must strengthen ourselves against the persuasive tactics of Satan. When God forgives us for our sins, He drops that sin into the deepest part of the ocean, never to be revisited. God will not confront us about our old ways once He has erased it from the record. The past is dead. The poet, Longfellow, states in his poem "The Psalm of Life:"

"Let the dead past bury its dead"

We always bring up the past to make one feel guilty about one's failures. Every man has fallen short of the glory of God. No man is qualified to render judgment against the other. If the Son of God refused to render judgment against us, then what is man to accomplish by making judgment against another? Man is not qualified to render judgment against anything (I Corinthians 4:3). Man is a product of sin. He comes into the world full of sin and is filled with the thought of corruption until his heart is filled with the glory of God. God's grace is a mighty thing to have. Jesus Christ says in Matthew 6:14, "For if we forgive men their trespasses, your heavenly Father will also forgive you." Christ makes an even more powerful statement in verse 15, "But if ye forgive not men their trespasses, neither will your Father forgive your trespasses." These words are pivotal in how we live our lives today. When we forgive our brother, we elevate ourselves to a position to receive the blessing from God. Forgiveness is a prime ingredient of love. Forgiveness makes us better, not bitter.

Jesus Christ approached a crowd of community misfits attempting to stone a woman to death. She was caught in the act of adultery. Jesus Christ, the Master builder speaks with the mercy, compassion, and love of God:

> "He that is without sin among you, let him first cast a
> stone at her" (John 8:7).

The tone of the crowd was filled with bitterness in their eagerness to fulfill the law. Fulfill the law? On the other hand, fulfill their selfish urges? In the end, Christ forgave her and advised her to go and sin no more. This is prime indication of God's eternal mercy and compassion. And we must illustrate the identical love to our brother.

Jesus Christ gave the perfect example on how to deal with our earthly problems. Rather than making the circumstance dependent upon us and us depending on the earthly and limited decision-making processes of our own brains, Jesus Christ taught us to be totally, completely, and absolutely dependent on our Lord and savior. We are to have total faith and confidence that God will deliver us from our circumstances. When we are persecuted by our enemies we simply place it in the hands of God. He will take it from there and, in time, one will see the results of God's work.

King David cried out to God when his friends turned against him. He was surrounded by enemies. He was pressed daily by harm, threats and danger. Yet, David continued to look to "the hills" for his strength and protection:

> "Lord, how are they increased that trouble me! Many are they that rise up against me. Many there be which say of my soul, There is no help for him in God. Selah. But thou, O Lord, art a shield for me; my glory and the lifter up of mine head. I cried unto the Lord with my voice, and he heard me out of his holy hill. Selah. I laid me down and slept; I awaked; for the Lord sustained me. I will not be afraid of ten thousands of people, that have set themselves against me round about. Arise, O Lord; save me, O my God: for thou has smitten all mine enemies upon the cheekbone; thou hast broken the teeth of the ungodly. Salvation belongeth upon the Lord: thy blessing is upon thy people. Selah" (Psalms 3:1-8)

David was surrounded by a lot of bitter people seeking to destroy him. He fully understood that God was his shield of protection. He cried out to the Lord for help. He did not rely on himself against his enemies. And God heard his cry. This identical God will hear our cry when we reach up to Him. He will not deny us if we place our complete faith, trust, and confidence in Him.

The Book of Job is so important for us today. Job recognized Christ while in the midst of his suffering. Job said, "For I know my redeemer liveth, and that he shall stand at the latter day upon the earth" (Job 19:25). Today, who is our Redeemer? Throughout the New Testament it is candidly revealed that Jesus Christ is our Redeemer. Job's acknowledgment of his Redeemer is important for us in modern times. If we can accept the patience of Job as an example to follow, why can't we accept his belief in his Redeemer? In addition, Job expresses confidence his Redeemer setting foot on earth. This remarkable statement is essential for us today. We must have the faith and confidence that Christ is going to return. We must believe that Christ is going to return to earth to set up a perfect form of government and will rule forever and ever.

We have our Redeemer, our Advocate seated on the right hand of the Father in heaven. Our Advocate paid the ultimate price on earth, death on the cross, that we may have a direct relationship with God. Christ set the perfect example for us to follow. Our Advocate received the VICTORY over the grave. Our savior rejected sin. Christ lived a sinless life. I Peter 2:22 says, "Who did no sin, neither was guile found in his mouth." How was Christ able to live a sinless life? He was tempted by man and Satan. Satan took it upon himself to tempt the Lord and failed at every corner. Christ was able to live a perfect life because He was the Son of God. He was born of the Holy Spirit. "Who his own self bare our sins in his own body on the tree, that we, being dead to sins, should live unto righteousnesss: by whose stripes we are healed" (I Peter 2:24). Christ had every opportunity while on the Cross to step down and say "forget us." Even as he was suffered on the Cross, enduring the worst of punishments, nails in his feet and hands, a sword placed in his side and all the sins of man placed upon Him. Jesus Christ stated: "Forgive them for they know not what they do" (Luke 24:34). Christ did not go to the grave with any bitterness towards man. He illustrated perfect love through forgiveness. And that is the example set for us to follow; to forgive one another as Christ forgave us.

He went to the Cross willingly to show the world the glory of His Father. Picture it today, visualize our savior on the Cross feeling pain beyond the ability of a human being to imagine, and hearing the insults and curses from the people he was dying for. Our savior endured a tremendous amount of agony and torment to complete the ransom demand. The suffering and pain was so severe that Christ cried out to his Father in heaven:

> "My God, my God why hast thou forsaken me?" (Mark 24:34)

There on the Cross was God's only Son, whom He loved deeply. The Son was a good and faithful servant of the Father. Can a father stand to view his Son in this condition? Could the angels in heaven stand to view their Master suffer in this condition? Imagine Satan lingering around the Cross, whispering temptations in the ear of Christ as he wrestled and tussled with the sins of man; seeking to persuade Christ to give up at his weakest point. It sends a chill over the body to consider for a moment, the agony and trial Christ was feeling on the Cross. We thank God for His perfection in Christ because there was not a drop of bitterness in Him.

O' Father, we know not the level of pain that our Lord and savior, Jesus Christ, experienced on the Cross and we know we could not have endured the minutest portion of his suffering. However, Father, we are so thankful that your Son paid this price for us. We are so blessed, Father, to have you because you know exactly what we needed in order to maintain a relationship with you. O' Father, we humbly submit ourselves at your footstool. We are unknowing, sinful, and unclean, without wisdom and filled with iniquity. We need you, heavenly Father. Glorified is thy name and with honor we glorify your Son, Jesus, who paid for it all. Father, I realize I cannot live up to your Son's standards, but I do accept your Son as the Son of the Living God. He died on the Cross for my salvation. I do believe that, Father. Accept me, Father, unto thine Kingdom, forgive me for my sins, have mercy on me, teach me thy way, protect me and insulate me from the temptations of this world. Come into my life and make me better than the weakling that I am. Teach me to pray to Thee, always glorifying your name in all that I do. Father, teach me in all of my actions to stop first and ask myself, "how does it profit God?" rather than, "how does it profit me?" Thank you, Father, for all your blessings, but most of all thank you for your Son, Jesus, paying the ultimate price, the ultimate answer, and the ultimate solution for us. Father, blessed is Thine holy name. And these blessings we humbly submit at thine footstool, in the name of our Lord and savior, Jesus Christ. AMEN.

We examine the position of Jesus Christ in I Peter 3:22, "Who is gone into Heaven, and is on the right hand of God; angels and authorities and powers being made subject unto him."

Job suffered according to God's plan and strategy. No one knew the outcome of God's policy but God. Job did not know. The council members in heaven did not know. We, the readers, did not know. Satan had no knowledge of the outcome. Only God knew the outcome. As always, God is right and on time.

Job did not get bitter with God, although he stepped into areas where he did not belong. He acknowledged before God his error in judgment and submitted himself to God to be made better than he was. Job became better as a result of his suffering. He maintained patience and placed his trust in God through it all. Let us be reminded, of God's direct statement to Satan at the Supreme Council Meeting: "although thou movedst me against him, to destroy him without cause" (Job 2:3). Job 1:22 says, "In all this Job sinned not, nor charged God foolishly." God knew it was unjust to punish Job. In addition, for Job's obedience, God rewarded him with a tremendous increase:

> "So the Lord blessed the latter end of Job more than his beginning, for he had fourteen thousand sheep, and six thousand camels, and a thousand yoke of oxen, and a thousand she asses. He had also seven sons and three daughters" (Job 42:12, 13).

The bible records in Job 2:10, "In all this did not Job sin with his lips." Job did not voice bitterness towards anyone, especially God. Job got better, and his increase is a direct reflection that God rewards his good and faithful servants. God speaks about bitterness: "See to it that no bitter root grows up to cause trouble and defile many" (Heb. 12:15). May God add a blessing to the reading of His word for the good, sanctification, and edification of our souls.

No matter what your circumstance or situation in life may be it will get better. No one stays down forever. There is always a period of resurrection. We will get better. We cannot permit bitterness to occupy any space in our heart. Bitterness only delays our just reward. Colossians 3:13 says, "For bearing one another and forgiving one another, if any man have a quarrel against any; even as Christ forgave you, so also do ye."

Job humbled himself before God, acknowledging that God was All-knowing and All-Powerful. When God confronted him, Job admitted his mistake and humbled himself to God. Job said, "Behold, I am vile; what shall I answer thee? I will lay mine hand upon my mouth" (Job 40:4). Job elaborates, "Who is he that hideth counsel without knowledge? Therefore have I uttered that I understood not; things too wonderful for me, which I knew not" (Job 42:3).

King David states it best in Psalms 19:14, "Let the words of my mouth, and the meditation of my heart, be acceptable in thy sight, O' Lord, my strength, and my redeemer."

With the words of King David firmly planted in our hearts; let us recognize that bitterness only serves the deceiver. When we harbor bitterness towards ourselves, friends, and enemies we depart from the temple of God and embrace a consuming fire of hell. The Lord said, "That we may be the children of your Father which is in heaven: for he maketh his sun to rise on the evil and on the good, and sendeth rain on the just and on the unjust" (Matthew 5:45). The sun will shine and the rain will fall on our enemies as well as us." Let us pray that we will improve as a direct result of God's intervention. Christ showed us how to reject the arrows of the devil. He showed us how to live a sinless life. We do not have to become a servant of sin.

Bitterness can never be a proper forum to distribute our hate for another or ourselves. When we reflect on the marvelous work Christ performed on the Cross, our hate evaporates and blessed hope is restored. Keep bitterness out of your life. Become dependent on God for all things and your life will "increase." Endure trials with patience, and faith, considering that compassion and forgiveness are excellent tools in the Kingdom of God. Don't get bitter, get better. All of us are in need of some renovation. So let us become better as a result of our trials and tribulations. And we can rejoice in the congregation of our Lord and praise His holy name.

CHAPTER 4

JOB – THE PERFECT FAMILY MAN

"Man is God's marvelous creation crowned with glory and
honor, and because of this you can't quite hem him in."
– Reverend Dr. Martin Luther King, Jr.
(The Measure of a Man)

Throughout the dimensions of time, the family has surfaced as the primary element necessary for human survival. God has exemplified to us that He will not abandon us under any circumstance. God states to King Solomon in 2 Chronicles 7:16, "For now have I chosen and sanctified this house, that my name may be there forever: and mine eyes and mine heart shall be there perpetually." God is clearly stating that his "eyes and heart" will be there forever. God is in position to look after His family throughout time. Will we be there with our eyes and hearts for our families?

I am reminded, as I was growing up in my family, my mother would say, "You can have fun on the playground but don't travel beyond my eye sight." In other words, my mother was in constant lookout over us. She did not place us in a daycare center or appoint a babysitter. She was the only babysitter that we ever had. She had her eyes and heart on us. She did not fail in "looking out" for her family. My mother felt she was the best comforter for us as a family. I recollect the fear we had as children when Our Lord sent a thunderstorm. She would gather us closely together in the living room and while in constant prayer, tell us to "Be quiet while the Lord is doing His work." As I look back in time, I realize my mother had a humble respect and fear of our Lord and savior. When we faced challenging conditions or circumstances, my mother would pray, read the Bible and praise God. She encouraged us and provided us with hope to carry on with faith and trust in God. My mother kept us together as a family. We did not yearn or miss out on anything. She taught her seven sons and daughters the way to go. She was a strong woman. She seemed to have an understanding of what worked and pleased God.

In 2 Chronicles 16:9, God uses his eyes to reinforce his presence throughout the whole earth: "For the eyes of the Lord run to and fro throughout the whole earth, to shew himself strong in the behalf of them whose heart is perfect toward him." The Almighty God travels across all terrain seeking the heart that is perfect toward him. God has a personal stake in His family. Are we prepared to lead and direct our family according to God's masterful plan? Are we ready to teach and encourage our children to be God-like?

ABRAHAM AND FAMILY LIFE

Abraham was a great prophet of God. His wife, Sarah, illustrates the godly role of a woman in marriage. Titus 2:5 describes how a woman should conduct herself, "To be discreet, chaste, keepers at home, good, obedient to their own husbands, that the word of God be not blasphemed." The wife of Abraham set the prime example of how a wife submits to the rulership of her husband. I Peter 3:6 says, "Even as Sarah obeyed Abraham, calling him lord: whose daughters ye are, as long as ye do well, and are not afraid with any amazement." Sarah is portrayed as the ultimate woman in a marriage. Verse 6 reveals this lineage to all women, "whose daughters ye are." Sarah set the standard by which a woman of honor, kindness, respect, love, and graciousness behaved in the sacred marriage covenant. The latter verse also states that Sarah "obeyed Abraham." When obey is used in modern society it turns on an alarm. Obey does not mean slavery. Obey is not granting permission to demean or assault the integrity and character of a woman. The woman is not to be held in bondage. Abraham was a great man of God. He did not misuse, disrespect, or abuse his wife. He held his wife up with high regards. And obey does not grant a man permission to treat his wife in an inhuman manner. Abraham treated his wife with dignity, honor, and love. God would not tolerate one of His servants abusing his wife.

Let us take a deeper perspective of Abraham and Sa'rai's relationship. In Genesis 17:15 God commands Abraham to no longer call his wife Sa'rai but to call her Sarah. Now, in Hebrew, Sarah means "Princess." In other words, she was the princess of the house. That's a powerful position to hold. Sarah may have called Abraham lord but he is calling her "Princess." That is not lowering a woman but elevating her status within the marriage and family. Sarah was a woman who possessed extraordinary beauty. People admired her beauty. She was stunning in appearance. She was the "crown" of her husband. God smiled upon her. Although the scriptures reveal that a wife is to "obey" her husband, this does not mean like obedience to God. It does not mean submission to the husband. Why? Because we are to obey God, be obedient to God and submit to Him. We cannot serve two Masters. In Genesis 21:12 God commands Abraham "in all that Sarah hath said unto thee, hearken unto her voice." Hearken unto her voice simply means "obey her voice." In other words, God is showing us that the woman is not some submissive creature without a brain. Whenever a woman and man walks upright with God, they are blessed with kindness, wisdom, and gentleness. In the case of Sarah and Abraham there is mutual respect. God commands Abraham to listen to his wife and obey her voice. How often do we fail to listen to our wives because we feel we know all the answers? That's not how a marriage works under God. God did not design marriage to function in this manner. Like God's love for us, we are to hold our wives up as "Princess" because "daughters of Sarah ye are."

Abraham loved Sarah with a deep passion. Abraham provided for his wife and family. God blessed him with tremendous riches. Sarah lived a very comfortable life through the grace and will of God. Her husband did not neglect her. Every man today can be educated by the example Abraham sets for the quality of being a man of God. God blessed Sarah with extraordinary beauty and Abraham adored her. He did not place her above God, and she humbled herself before him and called him "lord" because he was a godly man with great integrity and character. And Abraham humbled himself before his wife and called her "Princess." He set the example allowing his wife to have total faith and trust in him. And Abraham had total faith and trust in her as well.

Abraham feared God and was obedient to Him. It is a blessing from God when a man is given a woman of honor, kindness and grace. Those are the qualities of a virtuous woman. And Abraham provided for his wife and treated her with the respect, dignity and love that she deserved. And this is clear evidence of how men and women should be today. God is the head of the family and everything in a marriage should reflect the image of God's eternal love. It's not a man's duty to punish and treat his wife with cruelty. God does not smile upon such ugliness. A man should love his wife as Christ loves the Church. The scriptures command a man to treat his wife with the highest degree of decorum. And a woman should hold her husband with reverence. God has ordained the marital relationship. No man or woman can change what God has set in concrete. When it comes to our family, love is the centerpiece.

JOB AND THE FAMILY

The Bible describes Job as "the greatest of all men of the east" (Job 1:3). This is a huge description of a man. Imagine, there was not another man as great as Job. How did he get to this position? The Bible also says he had a great family. In other words he had a wonderful wife and children.

God characterizes Job as "perfect and upright, and one that feared God, and eschewed evil." This is a glorified statement in describing an earthly man. Job was a real man and he conducted himself as a man in all phases of his life. In the family structure, like Abraham, he was a perfect father and husband. Job's behavior shows us how a man maintains the leadership role in the family. There is one important point to make about the character of Job: he possessed spiritual integrity and character. Job was a strong man that looked up to God for all things. Job knew God had the correct answers for all of his problems. He feared God, moreso than his wife. It's pivotal that a man stands in a leadership position in the family. But, he cannot set a leadership role if his integrity and character does not measure up with the standards of God.

There was a period in Job's marriage that his wife stood up and questioned his integrity and character. She reached a point in which she suggests, "curse God, and die." Job was at a low state and needed comfort from his wife. He needed her support and encouragement. He needed her love. We could briefly consider that the turmoil and suffering that sweep through their home was unbearable for her. She lashes out at her husband without a full understanding of what God had in store. Fortunately, Job does not submit to her request. He speaks to the love of God. He replies, "Thou speakest as one of the foolish women speaketh. What? Shall we receive good at the hand of God, and shall we not receive evil?"

Secondly, God states, "Favour is deceitful, and beauty is vain: but a woman that feareth the Lord, she shall be praised" (Proverbs 31:30). God goes further in Proverbs 31:26, "She openeth her mouth with wisdom; and in her tongue is the law of kindness." God says that wisdom and kindness should come out of the mouth of a woman, not venom. There is nothing sweeter than the tone of kindness and wisdom from the mouth of a woman. It can lift the spirit of a man while in the midst of suffering. A man can climb mountains when a woman's voice illustrates sweetness, gentleness, and kindness. A woman's wisdom fills the house with joy and comfort. She establishes the joy of the household with her patience and love. It is a picture to behold.

Job rebuked her statement by honoring the commandment of God. Job exalted his Father in Heaven. He did not become empathetic to his wife's plea merely to appease her selfish wishes. The bible advises a man how to behave when a woman speaks as Job's wife, "it is better to dwell in the wilderness, than with a contentious and an angry woman" (Proverbs 21:19). How many men today would have done as Job? Too many of us would have gone along with the woman's angry sentiment and denied God, so as to accommodate the mood of the woman, so there can be harmony in the house. In other words, the action is tolerated. Some may have lashed out with a profane laced tirade expecting they are defending God's turf.

When we read about the kindness, gentleness, and beauty of Jesus Christ in the New Testament, we are shown a man who was always respectful of women. And women respected and loved Him. As a matter of fact, in certain situations the woman showed more faith and confidence in the Lord than man. Christ always illustrated kindness, grace, mercy, and compassion. He did not dominate or berate women. He did not judge or condemn women for their weaknesses. Christ's kindness and respect of women created an atmosphere of joy and happiness. He did not take advantage of women for selfish pleasure or gain. He was kindhearted and women adored Him.

We are reminded of Christ's treatment of the prostitute caught in the act of adultery and how the angry mob motioned to stone her to death. Where was the man that was caught in the act with her? Was he immune to prosecution? The man was just as guilty (Leviticus 20:10). The mob was not following the letter of the law. But, Christ wrote in the sand and asked the mob, "He that is without sin among you, let him first cast a stone at her" (John 8:7). Christ did not condemn the woman, but showed "tender mercies." Christ was sin free but He did not toss a stone. He did not follow the hypocrisy of the scribes and Pharisees. Christ stood up and said unto her, "Woman, where are thine accusers? Hath no man condemned thee? (John 8:10). She said, "No man, Lord" (John 8:11). The Son of God said, "Neither do I condemn thee: go, and sin no more" (John 8:11). The Messiah shows us the qualities of a man. When we stand up for God against all temptations, then we are showing manly character. When we deny God over earthly circumstances, we destroy our integrity and character before the Father. In addition, our first and only mission in life as men is to obey God. And by being obedient to God we will hold up our women with esteem. We will illustrate a Christ-like atmosphere throughout our family. Because what is a family? A family consists of those who follow the will of the Lord. Men and women can only be evaluated by their relationship and identification with Jesus Christ.

REACTION OF JOB'S WIFE

Job's wife vocalizes her frustration and anger at their present condition. She does not show compassion or empathy towards her husband's suffering. Job's wife encourages him to behave as Satan had suggested to God in the Board meeting in heaven; namely, that Job would curse God to his face. In this case, she follows the directive of Satan rather than God. This same Satan is influencing women today to rise up against their husbands and "do as they feel." This same Satan is advising women to "do their own thing." This identical adversary is influencing men to abuse their wives physically and verbally. This same creature influences men and women to multiple affairs, destroying their marriages through adultery. This serpent persuades women to perform abortions and not consider it murder. This same devil has convinced women to degrade and combat men on all fields of battle. The Apostle Paul writes, in Ephesians, "Wives, submit yourselves unto your own husbands as unto the Lord" (Ephesians 5:22). Anyone who doubts the Apostle Paul's right to say what he does is attacking a saintly giant, hand-picked by the heavenly Father. The Apostle Paul would not conjure up a lie and place God's signature behind it. Paul was a true servant of God. He feared the wrath of God. Paul did not lower women to an animalistic level. When we read the life of Paul, he elevated women and ordered men in the church to hold the godly women up with dignity and honor.

A good wife should be supportive of her husband, especially when he is in the midst of the storm. Is it wise to stoop to a level of ugliness when you are in a state of misery? Where is the mercy, understanding, and compassion? A woman must show the same mercy and compassion that Christ showed when the woman was caught in the act of adultery and faced capital punishment before a cold, angry mob.

JOB'S INTEGRITY

Job exalts God throughout his ordeal. Under challenging and difficult circumstances, Job reveals strong integrity. Job continued his faith and trust in God. He did not lower God to an indecent standard. It is clear that Job loves God with a deep love. He did not extinguish his love for his heavenly Father. God loves to view us maintaining our integrity. God states to Satan, relative to His good servant Job: "and still he holdeth fast his integrity, although thou movedst me against him, to destroy him without cause" (Job 2:3). Glory to God. The essential term is "integrity." The Standard College Dictionary describes integrity as "Uprightness of character; probity; honesty. The state of being complete or undivided." The word probity is further described in the Standard College Dictionary as "Virtue or integrity tested and confirmed; strict honesty." Probity provides us with more depth in God's description of Job's character. The point that Job's integrity was tested and confirmed is evident by God's statement that Job "holdeth fast his integrity." The term "honesty" is given an expanded description by "strict honesty." Although Job had lost everything in his earthly treasures, he maintained "strict honesty" with God. This is a prime illustration of a true man of God. Job shows other men how to conduct themselves while God puts them to the test. A man does not charge God foolishly. A man stands up for God when all other men or women attack Him foolishly. This is the type of man that God created, in His image and likeness. Job will not forsake his God in order to accommodate the demands of man.

We cannot condemn Job's wife's action. Job speaks to her with tender words of faith and trust. His wife was under heavy pressure and stress. She witnessed the destruction of their luxury estate, death of their ten children, and having to witness her husband, formerly the richest man of the east, who was respected and held in high regard throughout the city and placed in a compromising position. This is the true test for all husbands and wives. When all is stripped away, is it best to strike out with negativity or seek refuge in the hills? Do we abandon those while they suffer or hang in there with confidence? When we encourage one another, we insert something in them that lifts their spirit and gives them blessed hope.

GOD'S DESIGN OF WOMEN

In Genesis 2:21-25, God describes how he designed woman for man:

> "And the Lord God caused a deep sleep to fall upon Adam, and he slept: and he took one of his ribs, and closed up the flesh instead thereof; And the rib, which the Lord God had taken from man, made he a woman, and brought her unto the man. And Adam said, this is now bone of my bones, and flesh of my flesh: she shall be called Woman, because she was taken out of Man. Therefore shall a man leave his father and his mother, and shall cleave unto his wife: and they shall be one

flesh. And they were both naked, the man and his wife, and were not ashamed."

Adam states, "This is now bone of my bones, and flesh of my flesh" (Genesis 2:23). We dare not interpret this as lowering woman, but merely stating that God designed woman to be a help meet for him, because man was lonely. Help meet does not inject slavery. It means "equal to and deemed appropriate for him." Over the centuries the term help meet has changed to help mate, but the bible does not make that claim. God elevated the woman by designing marriage between a man and woman as one. God states, in verse 23 that woman was taken out of man and in verse 24 God declares "they shall be one flesh." Remember, God states that everything He created was "very good." Further in Genesis 3:16, God commands to the woman "and thy desire shall be to thy husband and he shall rule over thee." What does God mean by rule over thee? If a man relies on earthly knowledge rather than godly wisdom and understanding he will interpret this verse to mean "dominance" over a woman. For over 6,000 years men have demonstrated an ingrained habit that the verse grants them the authority to dominate women, with a sense of rulership. This is a misguided practice. The prophetess Deborah, the wife of Lapidoth judged Israel for 40 years (Judges 4:4, 5:31). She was similar to a Prime Minister. There are numerous examples in the bible of women performing the Lord's work. We need to become more acquainted with the Word of God. We need a savior to repair the damage to our family.

The Apostle Paul writes in Ephesians 5:25, "Husbands, love your wives, even as Christ also loved the church, and gave himself for it." It is crystal clear in Paul's message that a family starts with love.

MAN'S FAMILIAL OBLIGATIONS

This injunction does not grant the husband the license to abuse and neglect his wife. Too many men use God's command for their own personal accommodation. This is not a godly attribute. A man should not abuse this holy position of authority. A man would not abuse himself, why would he abuse his wife? God instructs us to love our wives as we love ourselves. Christ Jesus loves the church and we are to love our wives in the same glorified manner (Ephesians 5:25-29)

God commands of a man in Genesis 2:24, "shall a man leave his father and his mother, and shall cleave unto his wife." God orders the man and wife to be on their own, joined together worshipping God. For example, this does not permit in-laws to intrude on what God has put together. In Matthew 19:6 Jesus Christ states, "What therefore God hath joined together, let not man put asunder." Too many marriages are destroyed because the man clings to his father or mother or vice versa. God does not command that a man cleave to his mother and father. It is clear that a man is commanded to cleave to his wife. God is also stating to the in-laws to "let go" of His property and let the son and daughter join in holy matrimony. The marriage is then "blessed," according to the original covenant with Adam and Eve. The married couple follows the Living Word of God. They are not to follow the word of in-laws attempting to govern their marriage due to their refusal to let go of a son or daughter. Man and woman did not design marriage; God did. If there are to be changes in the marriage covenant, it will have to come from God. This is not to promote dishonoring the parents or in-laws, but the couple must grow together under the rulership of God Almighty.

Marriage is sacred. God is protective of marriage. That's why no filth should intrude in a marriage. Satan is doing everything in his power to destroy the tradition of marriage. But, marriage is one of the most blessed unions that God ordained in the Garden of Eden. Anything that is contrary to God's original covenant at the start of the world is not of God. God has not changed since He performed the first marriage ceremony. Any man or woman considering anything other than what God has ordained should step back and reconsider what God has commanded in the biblical scriptures. It would be prudent to "consider" for a moment, serving earthly pleasures on earth for a season, or eternal torment in hell, with Satan as the Best Man. The mere thought of the situation brings fear. That's why it's essential that we become fully acquainted with the Bible. God is a merciful God with a heart of "tender mercies," "compassion," and "forgiveness." We must permit the Messiah to repair the damage to the family. He is a God with an awesome amount of love---agape love. The foundation of our society is marriage and family.

MAN IN THE MODERN WORLD

In modern times, the role of the man and woman has evolved to a variety of interpretations. There are role reversals and the traditional status of marriage has been assaulted. Authority in the home has taken on many different positions. Single parent households have reached record numbers. There is a crisis with the number of illegitimate births into the world. Teenage moms are raising children. Women are having babies through artificial means without the sacred commitment of a spouse. Families are hiring surrogates to have babies. A mom knows that she is the mother of a new born, but often times the father of the baby is in question, and blood test are necessary to identify the father of the baby. Same-sex unions have placed a new demand upon the family. The traditional family seems to be disappearing and a New Age agenda for marriage has surfaced. Divorce is at an alarming rate. Child support cases have skyrocketed. So many marriages are suffering due to the complex factor that "I am only here for the children." Yet, the marriage of the husband and wife suffers. Where is the joy and happiness? Where is the foundation of love?

God reveals that the children and husband will think highly of the mother/wife when she conducts herself with wisdom and kindness: "Her children arise up, and call her blessed; her husband also, and he praiseth her" (Proverbs 31:28). The inspired scripture in Proverbs 17:6, "Children's children are the crown of old men; and the glory of children are their fathers." God places man at the very core of the family structure. The father is the centerpiece of a child's development. This does not diminish the status of the mother or wife, but God established a covenant with Abraham that many generations would be blessed from his loins (Genesis 23:17, 18). Abraham is the "father of faith."

While Job's sons feasted in their houses with their three sisters, Job performed an act in honor of God to protect and insulate his children from sin: "And it was so, when the days of their feasting gone about, that Job sent and sanctified them, and rose up early in the morning, and offered burnt offerings according to the number of them all: for Job said, It may be that my sons have sinned, and cursed God in their hearts. Thus did Job continually" (Job 1:5).

Is the modern-day father in constant prayer for his sons and daughters, to protect and insulate them from the assault of Satan and his demons? Is the modern-day man on his knees worshipping God in a humble manner on behalf of his children? Job illustrates to us how a father conducts his daily affairs in his home. The identical qualities that Job demonstrated in covering his children during his time is ideal to practice in today's society. Remember, God said Job was "upright and perfect." Therefore, we gather that everything he engaged in was to "glorify, honor, and praise God." In Job 1:3, his home life is described as "and a very great household." A great household describes a family life that was "perfect" throughout. Job's home is a living example of wholesome living. Chapter one further labels Job as "this man was the greatest of all the men of the east." In other words, this man's reputation was the most sterling of all the men of the east. Job was the master in his household and is held in the highest regard by other men. In order to have a "great household," the man and woman work together under the instruction of God to grow a spiritually happy family. Job 42:15 describes the character and integrity of Job's daughters: "And in all the land were no women found so fair as the daughters of Job."

In modern-day language, Job's daughters were not having premarital sex, using alcohol, drugs or sniffing glue, staying out all night, cursing/arguing/threatening their parents, having illegitimate children, disrespecting their elders or other visitors to their household, ducking school or showing any dishonor to their parents. When a man married one of Job's daughters, he was receiving the fairest woman in all the land. Job's daughters were filled with wisdom, kindness and the fear of the Lord. This is the blessing that God will bestow upon a man that is obedient to His holy word. If a man fails to live upright, he takes the chance that his sins could follow his children. That is a mystery of life. At all times, fathers must fear and worship God. We can have perfect children if the man of the household performs according to the standards set by Job. Job is the institutional standard by which a man should govern himself within the family atmosphere.

God instructs a man to praise his wife and the children are to call her blessed when she illustrates wisdom, kindness, compassion, consideration and fear of God. God has not advised the woman to "rebel against her husband." The "doctrine of devils" is prevailing here, not the commands of God.

God commands that a man maintain his integrity and character under all trials and tribulations.

PHYSICAL ABUSE

We read about the many cases of men physically abusing their spouses, often times as a means of dominating them in an unhealthy and unholy manner. Job did not physically abuse his wife when she demanded that he curse God and die. He spoke up firmly on behalf of God. Physical and verbal abuse has no place in the marital household, especially physical abuse. God is not pleased with such behavior within the family. A large segment of the male population believes that "physical abuse" of the woman is an indication of "rulership" and "control." These are not men of God performing these indecent acts of cruelty. These are "weakling imprints" of a man that follows the "doctrine of devils." God did not give man a help meet in marriage for him to abuse. This was not designed by God. God did not design man for evil. God commanded man to love his wife.

News reports reveal that women are killing men in order to protect themselves from the onslaught. A man cannot have a "great household" like Job if he abuses his wife and children. God did not place man and woman together to destroy one another. In Colossians 3:19, "Husbands, love your wives, and be not bitter against them." God commands that a man love his wife as he loves himself. God says to refrain from hostile attacks of the wife. There should be no bitterness towards the wife. This is the command of God. A man is to cherish and love her as God loves the church. In addition, God's love for the church is beyond earthly comprehension. It is a deep love that is without limit. The church cannot be separated from God. God commands a man and his wife to exist together with the same degree of love, respect, and comfort. God knows what makes a man and a woman happy. Moreover, if we follow His prescription for marriage, it will be a success.

In Job, we find a person that demonstrates the true spiritual qualities of a genuine man. In order to comprehend Job's position we must start at the beginning. Too many men today are not in tune to what is manly in the presence of God. A man "pimping" or "prostituting" women for financial gain is not a man. Drugs and alcohol destroy the lives of men and families. How can a man lead his family if he is high on drugs or alcohol? A man engaged in fornication, homosexuality, and adultery for merriment within the confines of his marriage, has taken the opportunity to ignore the Gospel according to God. A man that is lazy and refuses to care for his family falls short of God's ultimate plan. By the example of Job's wealth, he cared for his family in excellent fashion. Job did not glorify in riches. Job said, "If I have made gold my hope, or have said to the fine gold, Thou art my confidence; If I rejoiced because my wealth was great, and because mine hand had gotten much"(Job 31:24, 25).

Job considered all forms of sex outside of marriage as a "heinous crime to be punished by the judges" (Job 31:11). Job continues, "If mine heart have been deceived by a woman, or if I have laid wait at my neighbour's door; Then let my wife grind unto another, and let others bow down upon her"(Job 31:9, 10). Job is unequivocal in his honesty about engaging in sex within the confines of his marriage.

He clearly states that his wife can have another man if he had lain in wait at his neighbor's door. Job feared that God would take away his increase. How many men today fear God when they are committing adultery, while God watches and listens in silence? Man is playing a very dangerous game that could lead to eternal damnation in hell. We are required to repent of our sins, be humble and submit to God, seek God's forgiveness and "sin no more." A moment of pleasure is not worth being in Satan's dungeon forever. Is it worth the gamble?

MODERN DAY LESSONS

We have to be stronger and more reachable within our family. We exist in a modern age of fast automobiles, ever-changing lifestyles, computers, websites, movies, Internet, cellular telephones, e-mails, beepers, and over-night delivery services throughout the world. We enjoy earthly conveniences and other comforts far beyond the families of thousands of years ago. With all of these enhancements, we continue to fail in spending constructive time with our wife, children, husband, and God. Do we love our wives as Christ loves the Church? Do the wives submit and obey their husbands with the law of kindness? Is the man a leader of his household? Is the father of the household in constant prayer to God to protect his children from their sins? Do our children honor their parents in order to achieve longevity in the land of the Lord? How do you see yourself reacting to a family crisis today? As long as there is a family on this planet, a crisis will come. Will your family face the crisis with righteous integrity? Is God the foundation of your marriage and family?

Today, the issue of family plays an important role in the evolution of mankind's development. The family function is ever-changing and the position of the man in the family is evaporating to a point of crisis. The status and stature of the man as the leader is rapidly deteriorating. Dignity and respect for the man that was once commonplace is no longer assumed as in past generations. There has been reluctance of the man to take charge of his family.

The moral fiber of the family is under attack like no other time in history. Every human being is subject to errors in judgment. It is never too late to restore our marriages and families. But, we must first seek the Kingdom of God and all of the desires of our hearts will be fulfilled. Keep in mind, that the desires of our hearts must be the desires of God as well.

Do not become disillusioned about troubling conditions and circumstances within your marriage or family. It may require work but we know that God can fix it. There are enough broken homes. Let us take the time to build up our marriages and families and restore the godly integrity and character to it. Permit God to straighten it out and the entire nation will benefit.

ON ABORTION

Based upon court rulings and societal upheavals, today's woman has decided that her body belongs to her and man has absolutely no "say so" in what she administers to it. A woman can dispose of a fetus in any manner she prefers, without any consideration of the man's feelings. This unholy agenda destroys the life that God created. God is a God of life, not death.

Satan has inserted gossip, rumors, and selfish desires at the very foundation of the marital relationship. Where is the love and caring? Where is the kindness and understanding? Where is the love of God as the centerpiece of the marriage? God "blessed" man and woman at the dawn of history to be holy representatives of His kingdom. Satan is not the governor of our marital institution. Marriage is the foundation of our family. Love and worship of God are the ingredients necessary for its survival. A man's position is at the top of the scale, not at the middle or bottom. Man is a special and unique creation of God. He cannot be mistaken for any other creature that God created. Job will illustrate for us the makeup of a "great household."

The modern-day man moreover, is turning to alcohol, drugs, verbal and physical abuse, adultery, fornication, incest, pornography, crime, and love of self, thereby assuring destruction of the family. Satan is having a field day in destroying the image of the man within the family. How can a woman look up to a man and call him "lord," as Sarah called Abraham? A man must follow the example of Jesus Christ. How can a man look upon his son or daughter and desire them for sexual pleasure? This is not a man, but some "creeping thing" that falls below the animal kingdom. We are made in the "image and likeness" of God. We cannot justify or tolerate such behavior. It destroys the family. A wife should not turn her back on such a "darkened agenda" and neglect the gift from God. Simply because such behavior is acceptable in hell, it does not belong and will NEVER be accepted in the KINGDOM OF GOD. A man cannot rule a family if he is practicing the "doctrine of devils." Any sin performed in darkness will become known to our heavenly Father. Man was created on a higher plateau than the animal kingdom. Satan laughs at us when we behave like animals with our family. Satan does not have a family. Remember, Satan attempted to destroy his Father. He tried to rule heaven when iniquity was found in him. God gave him a spiritual beating and "booted" him and his angels out of heaven. The bible clearly states that we are to "honor our mother and father." Think for a moment of the type of creature that would attempt to destroy God, the all-powerful deity with unlimited resources. This creature has neither respect nor shows mercy for man. This creature is the ultimate in evil and wickedness. Satan is not a creature to "play games" with on any level. We cannot allow ourselves to be governed by sin. The devil is a powerful force and only God can control him. We do not have the resources to battle Satan on our own. We need the complete armor of God to resist this creature. Satan recognizes that God is God and "fears God."

By citing Abraham, we will show how men of God responded, when tested. We will evaluate how Adam and Job behaved under difficult and trying conditions. We will examine how God's word has never changed. In addition, we will observe how, over 2,000 years ago, men of God conducted themselves while facing trials and tribulations. We have to make choices in life for our families. Will the modern-day father take full responsibility for what happens in his family? On the other hand, will the modern-day father hide behind his wife and avoid God? How do you see yourself behaving? We can learn valuable lessons from the example set by Abraham.

Too often, today's man focuses on his own agenda and not God's. He seems to be unaware of Satan's strategy of complete destruction of the family. Satan's angels are on a desperate mission to annihilate the family structure completely. Satan is convinced in thinking that man is weak and desires only to satisfy his earthly urges and pleasures. Satan is the wellspring of physical urges, desires and pleasures. His sole purpose is to persuade man to reject God and curse Him to his face. Will we maintain our integrity like the perfect upright citizen, Job?

IN HIS OWN IMAGE

In the beginning, God made man in a very special manner. He made man very different from all the other creatures. At the very start of creation, God placed man at a very high status in His kingdom, as witnessed in Genesis 1:25, "And God said, Let us make man in our image, after our likeness." God had created all things in heaven and earth and ended His Supreme handiwork with the creation of man. All things that God created were good in His sight. God thought so highly of man that he designed him after His own "image and likeness." No other creature or thing designed or constructed by the Supreme Architect came close to this pattern. This is the ultimate illustration of God's total love for man, to construct him in the image and likeness of Himself. In human terms, God made a "self portrait." We are a direct reflection of God. This distinguishes us from all the plants, animals, and fowl of the air and other creatures of God's creation. No other creature in heaven or earth resembles God, only man. When we examine God's Supreme craftsmanship, we are led to the conclusion that God imaged, invented, molded, conceived, shaped, and envisioned a being "exactly like Him." God copied himself in a form of divine duplication to inspire and influence us to be like the Creator that conceived us. God did not sketch us after His likeness and image to behave barbarously and reject Him. God commands that we follow His divine covenants and commandments and look to Him with faith, confidence, trust, honor, submission, and fear. God demands that all men have a total allegiance to Him. God is a jealous God. Any twisted thought process reveals the persuasive powers of man's chief adversary. The kingdom of God is not a cesspool of iniquity. God does not command a man to seek a feminine lifestyle that is based on the complete "doctrine of devils." We are reminded that Jesus Christ said, "In the beginning God made them male and female." Man is directed to accept the "commandments of God" as the official, sacred and holy word of the Almighty. Satan is the "author of confusion," not God. God is direct, precise, and honest in all His ways. God is not in the business of death and destruction. God wants us to have life more abundantly. There is no equal or substitute for our God.

Let us not overlook how Satan completely lied and fooled Eve in the Garden of Eden regarding the fruit that would provide the knowledge of good and evil. Satan was the master of deceit and confusion from the beginning of time. Satan is jealous of man, and if he is jealous of man, it is safe to conclude that he is jealous and envious of God.

Lucifer thought he was God's favorite angel. When iniquity was found in Satan, and when he started war against the Father, God banished him from His special position of authority in heaven. This being has no mercy or love for man. He desires man to behave more low-life than animal stock. Remember that man was not created after the "creeping things" that God created. Man was designed after the Living God. We were not designed after the reflection of Satan. Therefore, we are commanded to follow the conduct of the Creator, the ultimate Craftsman.

MAN'S AUTHORITY

After God created man, He placed him in a position of power and authority on earth. Genesis 1:26 continues, "and let them have dominion over the fish of the sea, and over the fowl of the air, and over the cattle, and over all the earth, and over every creeping thing that creepeth upon the earth." God granted man total influence and supervision to act upon his property. This passage is a prime indication of God's absolute love for man.

God states, "So God created man in his own image, in the image of God created he him" (Genesis 1:27). The key word in this latter verse is God's usage of "own." God establishes His absolute power and authority by stating He created man in His "own image." Only God has the full authority to perform this act. This is a Supreme act of generosity for a mere mortal that God elevated to a position "just below the angels." It is based upon God's love of man. Man did not deserve this position, but through the grace and will of God, He elevated man to a distinguished status. God did not have to seek permission from someone higher than Himself. All things in heaven and beneath heaven fall under the footstool of the heavenly Father. There is nothing above the Supreme Crown of God. God concludes verse 27 with the statement that "in the image of God created he him." It is a marvelous statement of God's true love and genuine affection for man. God states clearly that He had completed what He set out to do. He created man in a masculine gender.

Satan has used the pleasure principle from the start of time. God did not design man to fall lower than the position of authority in which He him.

When God selects or "calls" a man to represent His Gospel, that person is "changed" or "converted" from his old, sinful nature to a higher, godly nature. The person will be filled with the power of God. The Apostle Paul could not remain as Saul and represent God. He had to change and become more God-like. How can we serve God or our brother if we continue to live in sin? Sin does not move us towards perfection such as the Father's. Any minister that practices sin is a "false teacher" and does not represent God. If we are to accept this "false premise," then the scriptures are a lie and there is no need to attend church, pray, or have faith or trust in God. It is important to study, meditate, and be in constant prayer over the scriptures that God has given us. For example, God tells us in I Corinthians 3:16, 17,

> "Know ye not that ye are the temple of God, and that the Spirit of God dwelleth in you? If any man defile the temple of God, him shall God destroy; for the temple of God is holy, which temple ye are."

God is revealing to us His spiritual nature. He tells us that our bodies are temples that cannot be defiled in any fashion. God goes further in Leviticus 19:2, "Ye shall be holy: for I the Lord your God am holy." How can a man engage in iniquity that is contrary to the recorded word of God? God has commanded us to remain "holy" and glorify Him that is in us. Our failure to do so would mean "destruction," ordained by God. Do we not fear God? God reveals in 1 Corinthians 6:19-20:

> "What! Know ye not that your body is the temple of the Holy Ghost which is in you, which ye have of God, and ye are not your own? For ye are bought with a price: Therefore glorify God in your body, and in your spirit, which are God's."

GOD WILL NOT FAIL US

We have to strengthen ourselves against the power of Satan in this world. His "doctrine of devils" has invaded the churches, temples, synagogues, and various places of worship to weaken man's status before God. When we manifest God within us, Satan and his methods of confusion will not prevail, as stated in Proverbs, chapter 30, verse 5; "Every word of God is pure: he is a shield unto them that put their trust in him." Glory to Almighty God! He will not fail us even when our church leadership may fail us. Even when our mother and father may fail us. Even when our sister or brother may fail us. Even when our husband or wife will fail us. God will *NEVER* fail us. God is eternal, omnipresent, omniscient, omnipotent, unchangeable, sinless, object of worship, and superior to Men and Angels. We cannot permit the craftiness of Satan and his agents to confuse us regarding the *God* that governs over us, moment by moment. God will not allow filth to enter His holy sanctuary. One can fall prey to the earthly intellectual jargon that supports and justifies the habits of sinful pleasure. This behavior is nothing new under the sun. It existed during the days of Job. However, Job did not fall prey to Satan's doctrine. Satan threw his best ammunition against Job and Job maintained his integrity and character before God. Job did not defile the holy temple of God. Job is a living example for all times on how to elevate God under tough conditions and circumstances. We cannot let our urges and self-pleasures ruin the holy temple that God created for us. We curse God and defile our temple when we lust in sinful pleasure for a season.

HUMBLING ONE'S SELF BEFORE GOD

"Who do you fear most - God or man?" If God brought down the plagues that He placed upon Egypt, would you not fear Him? If it means eternal damnation in hell, would you not fear Him? Do you not fear the wrath of God over the urges and pleasures of man? If we fail to stand up for the integrity of God against all others then He will not recognize us on the Day of Judgment. Remember, Job stood up tall and erect for the integrity of God. Job did not permit uncleanliness to permeate into his family life. Job would label such behavior as a "heinous crime." Job would decree the punishment to be, "consumed in fire." What does it gain a man to have all the physical pleasure of the world and lose his soul on the Day of Judgment?

Job humbled himself before God and stated, "Behold, I am vile." The Standard College Dictionary defines the term "vile" as, "Morally base; shamefully wicked, despicable; vicious, disgusting, degrading, of little worth or account, unpleasant." Job acknowledged before God that he was extremely unworthy of being in the presence of God. Job presents himself as an "unclean man," one that required God's intervention to make him clean again. This is how a man humbles himself before God. A man does not arrogantly participate in sinful pleasure without any "guilt" or "fear of God." A man is required to stand before God and admit his shortcomings. God responds to Job's statement with a direct command in Job 40:7: "Gird up thy loins now like a man: I will demand of thee, and declare thou unto me." God is filled with tender mercies and compassion endures forever. God will forgive because the blood of Christ washes away all sin. When we become meek before God, like his servant Job, we become a new creature functioning in the likeness of the Almighty.

THE LIMITS OF KNOWLEDGE

God tells Job to "prepare for action like a man." God instructs him on righteousness and judgment and questions Job about his ability to "know and question so much." God questions Job in chapter 40, verse 9, "Hast thou an arm like God? Or canst thou thunder with a voice like him?" In addition, in verse 10, God makes a statement to Job that I feel is honorable and most powerful of all: "Deck thyself now with majesty and excellency; and array thyself with glory and beauty." Satan cannot perform as our God. Man cannot insist on knowledge, when he does not "know." This latter statement to Job is so strong and powerful that it leaves us stupefied when it comes to our understanding of anything. Job states it accurately; "we are vile." He becomes completely meek in Job 42:3, "therefore have I uttered that I understood not; things too wonderful for me, which I knew not." Lastly, in verse 6, Job states what God needs to hear from His servants, "Wherefore I abhor myself, and repent in dust and ashes." Glory to God! Job states clearly to God that he "detests" the way he is. He does not hide his transgressions, as Adam attempted to do. Then, Job asks God for "forgiveness and mercy." These are the endearing qualities of a man before God. Job shows us how to be humble and submit to God, then God will provide us the ultimate family decorum necessary for a successful family. Job's honesty convinces God to restore him. God blesses Job with a harvest beyond his imagination. God restored his entire family.

God performs His most important act for man and woman as revealed in the Book of Genesis, chapter 1, verse 28, "And God blessed them." God commanded that male and female be fruitful and multiply and replenish the earth (verse 28). God "sealed" His covenant with man and woman. God does not change merely to accommodate man. How can man unseal what God has put together? God confronted Job about his inability to be like God. God told Job, clearly and unambiguously, that this is His world and He is the Supreme Ruler of it all. Therefore, a man cannot pluck from the hands of God what is rightfully His and change it to accommodate the "corrupt desires of mankind." God is clear in His judgment that all He created was *good,* just as He designed it. How can man redecorate the perfect plan created by the Almighty? Genesis 1:31 says, "behold, it was very good." When man engages in sinful pleasure he is, clearly, telling God that what He designed is not "good enough" and man has a better design. This flaw dominates the integrity and character of man. Satan preys upon this weakness and consumes us like a burning flame.

In the Book of Job we find a man that God describes eloquently as "there is none like him in the earth, a perfect and an upright man, one that fearth God and escheweth evil." God illustrates to us the qualities of a real man in the life of Job. Job was a strong-willed man that yielded and knelt before God. Job maintained his complete allegiance to God. He feared being separated from God. God says this holy man "escheweth evil." It reveals to us, as men, that we should follow Job's example of "avoiding evil and evil doers on all levels of society." A man does not engage in evil. God did not design us to end up in hell. Remember that God created us to live forever in the luxurious Garden of Eden. God created hell for Satan, his angels and agents. Satan made his choice to reside in hell as ruler rather than submit to his Maker. This ignorance is projected into the mind and heart of a man that persuades him to seek sinful pleasure rather than "perfection and uprightness." Do we fear that God will take away our increase if we sin?

ADAM AND JOB'S MANLY ATTRIBUTES

What are the measurements of a man? Let us examine the conditions under which Job and Adam existed. Adam was created and lived in the perfect Garden of Eden. The proper description is "Paradise." Adam was designed after the "image and likeness" of God. God was the perfect sculptor when He molded Adam into a perfect living being. Job was the "perfect and upright" servant of God. God is the perfect artist. Adam was a beautiful man structured by the hands of God from the clay of the earth. Therefore, there was not a flaw upon his flesh. Adam was "blessed" with an excellent mind and soul. He was uninfluenced by worldly wickedness. His mind was not polluted by sin. Job also had an excellent mind and soul because he was wise enough to "fear God and escheweth evil." King David said the first sign of wisdom is to "fear God." Job avoided the earthly pollutants of sinful pleasure. Adam names all the creatures of the earth. He was knowledgeable. Job was filled with knowledge and understanding too. Job 29:21-22 says, "Unto me men gave ear, and waited, and kept silence at my counsel. After my words they spake not again; and my speech dropped upon them." The latter scriptures reveal Job's ability to give godly counsel to those in need of it. This is a form of wisdom that God blessed upon this upright man.

Adam named all the creatures of the earth. In addition, he decided the name of the female and called her "Woman" ("because she was taken out of Man"). Adam had a one-on-one relationship with God. God instructed him on the proper way of living and gave him every creature comfort imaginable. Adam lived a life of luxury under the grace of God. God loved Adam in a special way. Genesis 2:15 says, "And the Lord God took the man, and put him into the Garden of Eden to dress it and to keep it." Adam had free reign of everything in the garden except "the tree of the knowledge of good and evil, thou shalt not eat of it: for in the day that thou eatest thereof thou shalt surely die" (Gen. 2:17).

God is clear about His command to Adam. It is safe to conclude (with Adam's intellectual brainpower) that Adam understood what God advised him "not to do." God is "very specific" about the outcome, if His command is disobeyed. Did Adam not fear the command of God?

THEIR CREATURE COMFORTS

In the case of Job, he had the same creature comfort as Adam. He was the wealthiest man of the East. Just like Adam, Job was rich and holy. There were no imperfections in either individual. God propped up each man and personally served each. Job 1:3 says, "His substance also was seven thousand sheep, and three thousand camels, and five hundred yoke of oxen, and five hundred she asses." All of the creatures that Adam had named were part of Job's portfolio. Both men were humble servants to God. They had no complaints. God provided and insulated both men with His power.

We are reminded that Satan was filled with jealousy and hate when God created man "just below the angels." Man will hold a position higher than the angels for those resurrected in the bosom of Abraham. Satan concluded that man was intruding on his space. He immediately set into place his desire to embarrass man and destroy God's image and likeness. God (knowing and understanding all things) looked down from His lofty position in heaven and decided that man was lonely. God immediately solved this problem by creating a woman to comfort Adam. God was pleased and Adam was thankful for God's consideration of his condition. God "blessed" them both and there was total joy and happiness in the garden.

Job had his property, servants, maids, money, honorable children and wife. He had total joy and happiness on his compound. Both settings had to be beautiful. Even man's greatest adversary acknowledged the lovely life Job had. Satan felt Job had everything handed to him on a silver platter and if the platter was stripped from him, he would sin against God. Satan comments in Job 1:10, "Hast not thou made an hedge about him, and about his house, and about all that he hath on every side? Thou hast blessed the work of his hands, and his substance is increased in the land." Satan was jealous of God's earthly servant's rich, wholesome and spiritual lifestyle. Satan's desire and pleasure was to bring total destruction to Job and his estate. Satan did not comprehend that Job had built up treasures in heaven not on earth.

THE FALL FROM GRACE

As we travel back to the Garden of Eden, the woman is "beguiled" by the serpent to eat of the fruit of the tree of knowledge of good and evil. The serpent encourages her against God by stating in Genesis 3:5, "your eyes shall be opened, and ye shall be as gods, knowing good and evil." Up to this point, the serpent had not "beguiled" Adam to follow his lie. Satan makes an adjustment and goes after the woman with powerful craftiness and trickery. It is a classic illustration of Satan's art form, a persuasive art that is founded upon "wickedness and total evil." As with Job, Satan knew he was protected on every side by God's power. He could not penetrate Job's integrity and character to effect sin against God. One of Satan's confusing tactics is to go after someone intimately close in order to complete his mission. In Adams's case, it is the woman.

Eve presented the fruit of the tree of good and evil to Adam and he consumed it: "And the eyes of them both were opened, and they knew that they were naked; and they sewed fig leaves together, and made themselves aprons" (Gen. 3:6). God was listening and watching from His holy throne in heaven. God is an excellent observer and will intercede only when He finds it necessary. God did not react when Eve ate the fruit. It is only after Adam ate the fruit that "the voice of the Lord God walking in the garden in the cool of the day." The scriptures reveal the overwhelming power of God when his "voice walks in the garden." This achievement is beyond human comprehension. How can one perform such an act? To witness this action would bring about fear among every creature in the garden, including the deceptive serpent. Why did God wait until the cool of the day? Did God wait until His wrath was calmer? The clear fact is that Adam was afraid when God said, "Where art thou?" Lord God, please have mercy! Adam, with all his knowledge, had no idea what God was going to do to Eve and him. We can imagine that Adam was shaking with fear when he heard the "voice" of the Living God pacing through the Garden of Eden. It would be safe to assume that God was not in a good mood. Sin had fallen on the ones to whom He had shown so much love and affection. God is a jealous God!

The Bible says, "Adam and his wife hid themselves from the presence of the Lord God amongst the trees of the garden" (Genesis 3:8). How can we hide from God? What is performed in the dark will come to light. God will not permit one sin to be swept under the rug. Every sin has to be accounted for before the Lord. Keep Adam's behavior in mind, as we examine Job's behavior when God arrives on his premises as the "voice in the whirlwind." The Lord performs two different techniques with His voice but achieves the same objective.

After God's inquiry as to Adam's whereabouts, he responds, "I heard thy voice in the garden, and I was afraid, because I was naked; and I hid myself" (Genesis 2:10). What is Adam implying? Was he hiding due to his nakedness? On the other hand, was he hiding because he heard the powerful voice of God (knowing he had sinned)? How often do we sin knowingly? We can learn a lot about ourselves by observing Adam's behavior. Did Adam fully comprehend what God meant when he said, "surely die?" Alternatively, did Adam feel that his relationship with God would have brought mercy? Adam reveals his fear of the Lord when he remarks, "I was afraid." In my opinion, Adam reacts like a little boy when the parent comes home and catches him in the cookie jar. The child fears the voice of the parent and its possible outcome. In the presence of God, we are all like children. Adam rejected God's command and God arrived to confront the situation and make a final judgment of Adam's sin, "And he (God) said, who told thee that thou wast naked? Hast thou eaten of the tree, whereof I commanded thee that thou shouldest not eat?"(Genesis 3:11).

THE MEASURE OF A MAN

We understand based on God's statement that He will confront our sins. He will not allow our sins too merely "fly by", without us acknowledging our wrong. God hates sin and will discipline us "appropriately," according to His will. Remember that we cannot hide from our sins. We can hide from man our inappropriateness in the dark, but God will bring our sins to light and judge those sins at a relevant time. We have to give an accounting of every sin before God. Therefore, if we feel our sins in the dark do not count against us, it is an unjust conclusion. It is extremely important that we focus in on our examination of Adam and Job and their responses when confronted by God. In the end, we will have a clearer comprehension of the measure of a man.

Adam takes a timid and fearful posture when confronted by God in the Garden of Eden: "And the man said, The woman whom thou gavest to be with me, she gave me of the tree, and I did eat" (Genesis 3:3). What does Adam really mean? It appears that Adam is stating that if God had not given him a woman, he would not have sinned. Adam is hiding behind the apron of his wife. God does not like excuses or finger pointing when we are approached about our failures. Also, Adam seems to be blaming God for his predicament. However, we behave in a similar fashion when faced with our corruption. Do our children make excuses when confronted about their wrongdoing? When criminals go before a judge, do they not point the finger somewhere else rather than at themselves? We make up excuses when we are late for appointments or work. We make excuses as to why we cannot spend time with our children. There is an excuse why we cannot spend more time with our husband or wife. Often children make excuses as to why they fail to respect and honor their parents. Many psychologists and sociologists make excuses why criminals behave as they do. Uncommitted husbands and wives make excuses as to why the marriage must end in divorce. We make excuses why we do not attend church, temple, synagogue, or any place of worship. We make excuses why we did not help the homeless, widow, or anyone in need. We are a society laced with excuses. Did we learn this from Adam? Is Adam the excuse we will use for our sin [If Adam had not sinned, my life would be perfect]? Is Adam's failure an excuse to sin against God? What about the command that God has given us? When we follow the Word of God there is no excuse. When we witness how the saints, prophets and apostles of the bible handled various situations, we have sufficient evidence on how to live a life without sin. Did not Christ show us how to live a sinless life?

We are an excuse oriented generation. Often we point a finger rather than take full responsibility for our actions. Adam pointed a finger at his wife and God. Eve pointed a finger at the serpent. What would have transpired if Adam and Eve accepted full responsibility for their actions before the Lord and humbled themselves and asked for forgiveness? I believe God shows great mercy and compassion when we gird up our loins like a man and admit our shortcomings.

We sometime forget the three *C's* of God's kingdom; abide by His Covenants, follow His Commandments, and obey His Commands.

God gives us very specific instructions to follow. He has no desire to confuse us. Satan is the author of deception and confusion. God did not care what the woman did to Adam because His covenant was with Adam. We cannot violate our covenant with God, nor ignore His commands in order to appease man. We have to take charge and be responsible for our actions.

Remember how the father of faith Abraham followed the command of God and offered up his son as a sacrifice.

> "And he (God) said, Take now thy son, thine only son Isaac, who thou lovest, and get thee into the land of Moriah; and offer him there for a burnt offering upon one of the mountains which I will tell thee of"(Genesis 22:2).

Abraham did as the Lord God commanded him to do. Abraham took the wood and "laid it upon Isaac his son."

Abraham's obedience is revealed in Genesis 22:10,

> "And Abraham stretched forth his hand, and took the knife to slay his son." And the angel of the Lord called unto him out of heaven, and said, Abraham, Abraham: and he said, Here am I."

The angel continues in verse 12,

> "Lay not thine hand upon the lad, neither do thou any thing unto him: for now I know that thou fearest God, seeing thou hast not withheld thy son, thine only son from me."

Glory to God!

OBEYING GOD

Abraham reveals how a man of God should respond when commanded by God to perform. Abraham did not ask his wife to grant him permission to kill their only son. He placed God above his wife and himself. Any parent would have cried out not to destroy their son and that is why God did not ask the woman to perform the act. He commanded the man made in His "likeness and image." Without reservation, Abraham placed his entire faith and trust in God. God commands us to forsake all others and follow Him. This was Abraham's only son that he was willing to sacrifice to please and maintain his relationship with God. God tested Abraham with something that Abraham cared for deeply. God reveals His blessing upon the seed of Abraham as a result of his obedience: "And in thy seed shall all the nations of the earth be blessed; because thou hast obeyed my voice" (Genesis 22:18).

THE VOICE OF GOD

God's voice spoke to Adam, Abraham, and Job. Abraham received his blessing for having faith, trust, and obedience to God's "voice," the same *voice* that "walked through the Garden of Eden." This identical voice commanded Adam not to eat of the tree of good and evil. The same voice spoke out of a whirlwind to Job.

Abraham did not blame someone else; he followed the command of God. Abraham could have consulted with his wife Sarah, but he refused and obeyed God. Abraham knew what Sarah's response would have been. No mother would have allowed their husband to slay their only son. However, God's commands are not about our personal opinions, feelings, or agendas. Our lives should only concern the will of God. There will be opportunities for us to deny ourselves in order to accommodate God. There will be opportunities when we must deny our friends, associates, colleagues, and family in order to follow the Word of God. Abraham is a prime illustration of how a man of God conducts himself under the most difficult conditions and circumstances. A man places his complete faith and trust in God. A man is obedient to his Father, who provides for all his needs. Abraham is the example we should follow in being a man. He was not confused or psychologically impaired about his masculine status.

In the case of Adam, God banished him and his wife from the Garden of Eden. The Supreme Housing Judge evicted Adam and his wife. The subject property did not have housing violations, but the tenants occupying the property violated God's existing ordinances. Genesis 3:17 says,

> "And unto Adam he said, Because thou hast hearkened unto the voice of thy wife, and hast eaten of the tree, of which I commanded thee, saying, Thou shalt not eat of it: cursed is the ground for thy sake; in sorrow shalt thou eat of it all the days of thy life."

Again, God tells Adam that he adhered to the "the voice of thy wife" and not the "voice of Almighty God." God reminds Adam that He, "commanded thee" not to eat of the tree. It is wise to listen and obey the "voice of God."

Remember, when God questioned Adam about what he had done, he blamed his wife. This is not the conduct of a man. God commands us to stand before him and admit our sins, repent of our sins, and seek forgiveness for our sins before His righteous judgment seat. God commands us to be humble and submit to Him. God prefers to hear the truth, not excuses or finger pointing. He desires that we take full responsibility for our sins and submit to Him for mercy and compassion. We have to be obedient to God. God provides for us out of the goodness of His heart. When we are blessed from His treasure chest, we have found favor with God. It's His love that provides. We are not deserving of His blessings, so no man can elevate or lift himself up with importance. God states in I Samuel 2:3, "Talk no more so exceeding proudly; let not arrogancy come out of your mouth: for the Lord is a God of knowledge, and by him actions are weighted."

When we engage in sin, we separate ourselves from God. Adam and Eve did not fully understand the final judgment of their transgression. If they knew the outcome, they probably would not have sinned. However, God advised Adam that he would "surely die" if he violated His directive. There are awful consequences to deal with as a direct result of sin. Genesis 22:19 reveals God's final decree: "for dust thou art, and unto dust shalt thou return." Adam had everything at his disposal, yet he sinned. The punishment of death was God's final order.

In the case of Job, all of his wealth diminishes, ten children killed, servants murdered and boils take occupancy of his body from the crown of his head to the sole of his feet. While engulfed in a firestorm of misery, Job's wife encourages him to "curse God, and die." Where is the support and encouragement? Where is the mercy and compassion? God speaks about evil communications in I Corinthians 15:33, "Be not deceived: evil communications corrupt good manners." Remember that the Apostle Paul instructs us that a wife should love her husband and care for him, hold him with reverence. Job's wife swiftly concludes that death is the only option for Job. Yet, while under extreme pressure, Job does not relinquish his hold on righteousness. He does not permit his strength of character and integrity to sink to a demonic level. Job responds, "Thou speakest as one of the foolish woman speaketh."

Job's wife had benefited greatly from her husbands faith and obedience to God. How soon we forget. Job injects further, "What? Shall we receive good at the hand of God, and shall we not receive evil?" (Job 2:10). This is a real man expressing his love, trust, and confidence in the Almighty. Job ignores his wife's lack of compassion and devotes himself to elevating and exalting God. This is how a man responds to his wife when she attempts to interfere with the commands of God. Although we love our wives, we cannot allow Satanic influences to make us go against God. A man must be the master of his home and his wife must be a loving, caring, wise, kind help meet to her husband. She must be a Princess like Sarah. Job has lost everything and is alone in his pain and suffering. Yet, the scriptures reveal in Job 2:10, "In all this Job did not sin with his lips." Glory to God! This is the integrity of a real man. While surrounded by all the negative forces during his ordeal Job stood tall in the saddle for God. Although Job was seriously wounded, he continued to carry the cross for God. God does not want us to fall; He commands us to be committed and dependent on Him. We will receive a great blessing in due season.

Job was a man held with great respect and honor in the land of Uz. Of all the men in the kingdom, "this man (Job) was the greatest of all the men of the east" (Job 1:3). How did Job receive the title "greatest man of the east?" Job worshipped and followed the absolute word of God. Remember, God said Job was "perfect and upright and one that feared God and eschewed evil." These are the attributes of a real man of God.

Job makes a solemn protestation of his integrity in comparing his actions with Adam: "If I covered my transgressions as Adam, by hiding mine iniquity in my bosom" (Job 31:33). As opposed to Adam, with whom he compares himself, Job's own character and integrity has held up to the highest level of evaluation. Job advises God that he has not hidden his transgressions in his bosom. Job opens up regarding the moral status of his integrity and character before God. While Adam hid from God in the Garden of Eden, Job refuses to cover up any sin. He is in the open and asks for an audience with God to illustrate his obedience. He proclaims, "Let me be weighed in an even balance, that God may know mine integrity" (Job 31:6). Job presents himself before God to be judged. He is not running from any sin that he has committed. Job wants to know God's reasoning for permitting him to suffer without just cause. He feels confident that his assessment is correct and his affliction unwarranted.

Adam had every luxury that God could provide for his comfort, and yet, he sinned against God's command. Job had all of his wealth, family, servants, and friends taken away. In addition, a horrible affliction is placed upon him that disfigured his entire body and made him unrecognizable to his friends. Although Job was in a sad and depressed state, he did not sin against God. Adam followed his wife and sinned. Job rejected his wife and maintained with God.

> O Heavenly Father we kneel before thy footstool in humble submission to thou power and strength. We glorify your precious name. Father, we were shipwrecked and you lifted us up and had mercy on our souls. Father, we thank you today for insulating and shielding us from the author of jealousy and confusion. Father, we are vile servants of yours and we thank you again for granting a harvest that we are unworthy to receive. Teach us O gracious Father to walk in your ways and obey your commands against the temptation of the enemy. Precious Lord, we are weak and powerless before thee, clean us of the iniquity in our hearts. Make us your warriors to fight the battles that you see fitting for

us to defend. Father, we hope in your mercy. In the name of Christ Jesus. Amen.

JOB AND THE LESS FORTUNATE

Job cries out to God regarding his days of honor, "Did not I weep for him that was in trouble? Was not my soul grieved for the poor?"(Job 30:25). Job is revealing his days of compassion for the less fortunate. Job reached down to lift up those that suffered. Job salutes God with his most profound statement in Job 13:15, "Though he slay me, yet will I trust in him." Job's latter words have power. He places his total dependency on God. While in the midst of the storm and flooding waters, he finds the strength to seek out the heavens. God enjoys a faithful servant. Can you see the angels in heavens leaping and shouting for joy when they heard Job's words? Job is willing to accept whatever fate God has in store for him. This is the faith God commands from a man in his heart. A man must trust God under all conditions. A man does not turn away from God when calamity comes. A man does not curse God because his wife suggests it. A man does not "pass the buck" and blame someone else for his sins. In Job 40:7 God orders Job to, "Gird up thy lions now like a man." God demands that we stand up like a man, address him honestly, and submit to His overwhelming power, knowledge, understanding and wisdom. A man is required to be truthful before God, not a liar. We take our sins to God and admit to God our shortcomings, repent of sin and acknowledge God for His Supreme mercy. The Apostle Paul instructs us in Romans, 2:4, "not knowing that the goodness of God leadeth thee to repentance?" Without God's mercy, patience, and compassion for us we would receive His wrath far more often. Job admits to God that he is vile and he "abhors himself and repents in dust and ashes." Since God is in the renovation business and not the destruction business, Job is prepared to be reshaped for God's purposes. Paul instructs us properly on our conduct before the holy Father in Ephesians 3:14, 15, "For this cause I bow my knees unto the Father of our Lord Jesus Christ, Of whom the whole family in heaven and earth is named."

How many men tell God on a daily basis that they "abhor themselves?" Do you truly detest the way you are as a man? Do you repent in dust and ashes? Every man in modern society would benefit from the example of Job. A just harvest will come, according to God's will. In due season we will see and feel the impact of God's blessing upon our family. We have to maintain our love and devotion to our Lord and savior. King David writes in Psalm 33:13, "The Lord looketh from heaven; he beholdeth all the sons of men."

God created the family through marriage as the greatest resource for human development. He blessed the union of man and woman as one with God. God blessed the union of man and woman and commanded them to be fruitful and multiply. A man is to love his wife as Christ loves the Church. The position in the marriage for the man is to be the leader. The woman holds her husband with reverence. The woman and man do not undermine the others position of authority in the family. Job had a "great household," because God resided in the center of his family. Sin did not occupy his dwelling.

The family is the foundation of society. God designed marriage for total joy, love, and happiness between the man and woman. Job revealed to us, through his actions, that we have to obey the commandments of God in order to have a perfect family life. In addition, Job classified any sinful pleasure within the marriage covenant as a "heinous crime." Job rejected adultery on all corners. He did not seek pleasure in knowing other women. He feared the wrath of God. Job did not permit his selfish desires and urges to violate his covenant with God. Are we following the example set by Job? Do we permit the burning desire for pleasure to intrude on our marriage in violation of God's commandments? God has made it clear that fornication and adultery have no place in the marriage covenant. The following scriptures provide us with clear doctrine for our edification regarding sex within the sacred marriage covenant:

> "Moreover thou shalt not lie carnally with thy neighbour's wife, to defile thyself with her" (Lev. 18:20).

Jesus Christ states:

> "Thou knowest the commandments, do not commit adultery" (Mark 10:19).

King Solomon writes:

> "And why wilt thou, my son, be ravished with a strange woman, and embrace the bosom of a stranger?"(Proverbs 5:20)

King Solomon continues:

> "Such is the way of an adulterous woman; she eateth, and wipeth her mouth and saith, I have done no wickedness" (Proverbs 30:20).

Although we live in an ungodly world, we can live a life filled with the Holiness of God. We can use common sense in a lot of our decision making, but the ultimate purpose is to take a divine perspective to our decision making. What may appear to be the "right" thing to do may not be the "righteous" thing to do. Same-sex marriage or unions may seem like the "right" thing to do, but is it the "righteous" thing to do? Engaging in fornication or adultery may appear justified in the flesh, but is it the "righteous" thing to participate in? Would God ordained this action? As Job shows us, adultery and lying in wait at your neighbor's house for the widow in moaning are part of a "devilish doctrine." Such behavior violates all the commandments of God. A man requires constant prayer with his Father in heaven. He will become strengthened and more powerful in the word of God in order to reject the temptation of Satan. The Apostle Paul gives us inspired scripture to persuade us, "Nevertheless let every one of you in particular so love his wife even as himself; and the wife see that she reverence her husband"(Ephesians 5:33). Glory to God! The great Apostle Paul directs us regarding the proper mannerisms of a man and woman in the marriage. Paul states further that a man is to love his wife as he loves his own body. God's marriage to the church is spotless, wrinkle free, holy and without blemish. This is the picture of a perfect marriage. The Apostle Paul does not suggest, nor hint, that a woman is the head over the man or family. The man is described as the head, "even as Christ is the head of the church." Keep in mind, the word of Paul is an honest word. The Apostle Paul is a true witness to Christ. He heard his voice while traveling to perform evil upon God's people. He gives us clear evidence, straight from the Father, as to the official conduct of a successful family. Jesus Christ instructed Paul on the way to go. Paul was a strong leader for the Church of God. He loved and obeyed God without reservation. The inspired scriptures of the Apostle Paul guides us. Paul is convincing in his delivery because he unselfishly directs us in the proper manner to achieve wholesome, sin-free living within the family. Living a righteous life pleases God. Paul states, "Now the things which I write unto you, behold, before God, I lie not" (Gal. 1:20). Truth prevails here. Glory to Almighty God!

If a man loves himself, then he will not abuse his wife. If a man loves his wife he will not violate the marriage covenant to satisfy a darkened appetite of earthly pleasure. Adultery and fornication have no place in a marriage. Incest and pornography are not part of a divine marriage in the kingdom of God. "They which do such things shall not inherit the kingdom of God" (Gal. 5:21). God commands that a man present himself as a strong, masculine representative of His divine nature. The Apostle Paul states in Galatians 5:24, 25, "And they that are Christ's have crucified the flesh with the affections and lusts. If we live in the Spirit, let us also walk in the Spirit."

Paul states in Ephesians 6:10, "Finally, my brethen, be strong in the Lord, and in the power in his might." In Ephesians 5:16 Paul reveals the prescription for a perfect life: "Walk in the Spirit, and ye shall not fulfill the lust of the flesh."

Job set the saintly example and did not fall prey to the lust of the flesh. Job relates in Job 29:14, "I put on righteousness, and it clothed me: my judgment was as a robe and a diadem." Keep in focus that Job was always in prayer for his children. Every man would benefit from Job's humble submission to the Father. As a "perfect servant" of God, Job is insulated in all corners from the wrath of Satan. Satan could not get to his family and create havoc. Job's children were the best mannered children in all the land. In other words, they "honored their mother and father." This is the command of God. Children cannot violate this commandment and expect their days to be long upon the land which God has given thee. God did not design the family for children to dishonor their parents. However, in order to have a "great household" a man must pray like Job to protect his children from the temptation of the devil. The Bible states that Job prayed continuously. Job placed a protective covering over his children when he prayed to God for their sins.

Today, we live in an unsafe and violent world. Evil men and women kidnap our children, rape, abuse and murder them. Wicked acts are performed on children beyond our imagination. We have to be on our knees praying to God to permit His glory to manifest itself in our daily lives. Men have to protect their families and the foundation of protection starts with God. Will we give in to God today? Husbands, will you love your wife as Christ loves the Church? Wives, will you submit yourselves to your own husbands as unto the Lord? Children, will you honor your mother and father so your days will be long upon the land that God giveth thee? Men, will you follow the holy example of Job and reap the harvest that God has in store for your family? Remember, we are full-pledged members of God's family.

THREE MEN OF GOD

In this chapter, we have observed the actions and reactions of three men of God, Job, Adam and Abraham. Each faced a different type of challenge within the confines of their respective families. Job was concerned and loved his family deeply. When Job's children partied he made sacrifices and prayed to God for their protection, insulation, and forgiveness of sins. He did not permit his children to travel along the highway of life without God's absolute protection. Satan acknowledged to God in heaven that Job had a hedge around him. It was only after God pulled away His protection that Satan was granted permission to set foot on the premises.

Job was considerate of his children. He placed their "possible" sins in the hands of God. Is the modern day father making sacrifices and prayers for his children? The scriptures reveal that Job's daughters were the "fairest in the land." Job's children "honored their mother and father." Job had a "great household." Although Job was the richest man in the land of Uz, he took time out for his family. Job was a strong-willed and strong-minded person. When Satan kills all ten of his children, he refuses to "curse God." He kneels and praises God to the highest. He did not condemn or blaspheme God. He humbles and submits himself before God. When Job is deformed with a disease from hell by the hands of Satan, he stands firm on his integrity. The unsightliness caused his friends to "lift up their voice and wept; and they rent every one his mantle, and sprinkled dust upon their heads toward heaven." This disfigurement placed upon Job comes directly from the compartment of hell. Job's condition was an apparent eyesore to his friends. Consider for a moment: this is a small peek at what hell is like, from its chief governor, Satan. This ghastly picture of Job provides us with the ungodly horror that awaits those that prefer hell to heaven. Satan hates us like an intense flame in an oven. If he treats us like Job, what would he do to us if we had permanent residency in hell? Do you think he would provide us comfort and beauty like God did for Adam and Eve in the Garden of Eden? One can imagine that the torment would be beyond human comprehension. God encourages us to walk upright and worship Him and not become a servant of sin.

Do you ever wonder why Satan never talks about his residence? Satan is on a twenty-four hour a day mission to destroy us. He desires to erase every image of Christ. His prime objective is to have us as his permanent guest in hell. Is it not strange that scripture does not record what hell is like from the lips of our chief adversary? However, God provides a clear picture of the beauty of heaven that awaits us if we remain obedient to Him. God also tells us that hell is not a place for any of His children to visit. God does not want anyone to perish. Jesus Christ wants to introduce all of us to His Father. God remains patient with us, giving us more than sufficient time to repent of our sins and join Him in His holy sanctuary. Will time run out before you receive the glory of God? Paul writes, "According as he hath chosen us in him before the foundation of the world, that we should be holy and without blame before him in love" (Ephesians 1:4). Paul continues in Ephesians 1:7, "In whom we have redemption through his blood, the forgiveness of sins, according to the riches of his grace."

In the case of Adam in the Garden of Eden, his wife encourages him to eat of the fruit of the tree of "knowledge." This is contrary to the command of God. Adam listens to the "voice of his wife" rather than the "voice of God." When Adam is confronted with his transgression, he hides in the trees of the Garden. He uses his wife as an excuse for failure. He refuses to stand before God and acknowledge his sin. In addition, he does not humble himself and submit to God. Adam and his wife receive a punishment of banishment from the Garden of Eden forever. Adam's sin also included the punishment of death. God warned Adam that if he ate of the fruit he would, "surely die." All of mankind lives under that penalty.

God instructs Abraham to sacrifice his son. Abraham follows God's order without question or challenge. He successfully passes the test. Today, Abraham is considered the "father of faith." He set such a high example of integrity and character as a man and husband that his wife humbled herself before him and called him "lord." God blessed Abraham with a "tremendous increase." When we are obedient to God, we receive our reward in due season, according to His grace. Abraham's wife, Sarah, was a woman of gentleness, kindness and love of God. She was a virtuous woman. Every woman today is the daughter of Sarah. She set the supreme example of how a woman should conduct herself as a wife. Are the women of today following the example of Sarah?

Job lost everything, yet he remained obedient to God. Adam rejected God and received a just punishment according to God's will and power. God's mercy and love of Adam and his wife suppressed His anger. Praise God for His mercy!

All were not lost due to the original sin of Adam. God developed a plan for salvation before the foundation of the world (Ephesians 1:4). The Chief Architect of civilization had designed a masterful "blueprint" to save man. He knew man would be lost without Him. Throughout the Old Testament, God's blueprint slowly unfolds. God kept it a secret. Satan did not know the plan. The great prophets and judges did not fully comprehend His blueprint. God's secret was foreordained prior to creation of the world. For believers, Jesus Christ said, "Unto you it is given to know the mystery of the kingdom of God."

God revealed His secret in the fullness of Jesus Christ. God sacrificed His only Son to pay the ransom. The Cross represents the holy sacrifice made by the Son of God. We cannot be confused by the position we have in the eye, mind, and heart of God. God's Son was the ultimate Man. Jesus Christ honored, respected, worshipped, loved, and elevated His Father. He set the example for every child of God to follow. The Apostle Paul amplifies the significance of the secret, "Even the mystery which hath been hid from ages and from generations, but now is made manifest to his saints: To whom God would make known what is the riches of the glory of this mystery among the Gentiles; which is Christ in you, the hope of glory" (Colossians 1:26, 27).

Jesus Christ was sin-free. He has ascended unto the Father to prepare a place for His family. He will return to receive His bride. Will you be ready? Will you love your wife as Christ loves the Church?

We have choices to make. Will our wives conduct themselves as Job's wife, or Adam's? On the other hand, will our wives behave like the adorable Sarah? Will the wife salute her husband as "lord?" Men, will you cherish your wife and children like Job and Abraham? Men, will you keep God as the centerpiece of your family? Peter writes, "giving honour unto the wife" (I Peter 3:7).

God is the Supreme authority over all things in heaven and beneath heaven. Every man is required to position himself to be a reflection of the likeness of Christ. We were purchased for a price. And upon the head of every man is the glory of God. It is essential that we seek God for "all things." God is the centerpiece of the family. Remember, God is watching and listening. The same "voice" that instructed Adam, Abraham, and Job is the identical "voice" that will instruct us today. God has not changed. He is the same today, yesterday and forever. Paul reminds us to be watchful, "Beware lest any man spoil you through philosophy and vain deceit, after the tradition of men, after the rudiments of the world, and not after Christ" (Colossians 2:8).

Christ is the substance of it all. The entire ministry of God was placed on the shoulders of Jesus Christ. "For in him dwelleth all the fullness of the Godhead bodily" (Colossians 2:9). The full secret was uncovered with The Christ. We need not expect another. Everything was completed by Him for Him. There is no other. Christ is the only one to present us blameless before His Father (Colossians 2:22). He has full power and authority in heaven and earth. Paul writes, "Grace be to you and peace from God the Father, and from our Lord Jesus Christ. Who gave himself for our sins, that he might deliver us from this presence evil world, According to the will of God and our Father. To whom be glory forever and ever. Amen." (Galatians 1:3, 4).

The words of the prophet Joshua ring true today. He told the people to, "choose you this day whom ye will serve" (Joshua 24:15). He encourages us further in verse 14, "Now therefore fear the LORD, and serve him in sincerity and in truth."

God is the Supreme Head of our family. We have decisions to make. Joshua shares with us the blueprint for success with our family. He writes, "but as for me and my house, we will serve the LORD" (Joshua 24:15). Today, that is the only decision that we can conclude. Will you follow the examples of Joshua and Job?

CHAPTER 5

WHAT IS 'BEING UPRIGHT'?

*"Be ye therefore perfect, Even as your Father
which is In heaven is perfect." – Matthew 5:48*

ON BEING UPRIGHT

When does it mean to be "upright?" Not leaning? Does it mean perfect posture, erect or vertical to the floor? Does God speak of dimensions of geometry or morality?

God describes Job as; "perfect and upright, and one that feared God, and eschewed evil" (Job 1:1).

In verse 8, God questions Satan,

> "And the Lord said unto Satan, hast thou considered my servant Job, that there is none like him in the earth, a perfect and an upright man, one that feareth God, and escheweth evil?"

In Job 2:3, God questions Satan a second time:

> And the Lord said unto Satan, "Hast thou considered my servant Job, that there is none like him in the earth, a perfect and an upright man, one that feareth God, and escheweth evil? And still he holdeth fast his integrity, although thou movedeth me against him, to destroy him without cause."

Webster's dictionary defines "upright" as: "in accord with what is right: upright dealings; adhering to rectitude; righteous, honest, or just: an upright person."

Webster's dictionary defines "rectitude" as: "rightness of princi-pal or practice; moral virtue: The rectitude of his motives, correct-ness, rectitude of judgment, straightness."

In simple terms, Job was not "shady" in anything in which he par-ticipated. Since he was a man of extreme wealth, he dealt 'honestly' in all transactions. In his family relationship, especially with his wife, he did not engage in adultery, pornography, fornication, incest or any other corruptible sexual activity outside of marriage. He raised his children in a manner consistent with the mental images and concepts of godly ambition; teaching his children to meet and resolve difficulties and use resourcefulness. Most of all, he gave them the godly commandments at an early age which was tradition at that time. Sometimes we cannot view ourselves in Job's position because of our own personal annoyance, pride and so-called "I made it" syndrome. Often we take for granted from whence we come, failing to examine the downfall of Job in a serious manner. When all of it is taken under serious consideration, we recognize that we are only a nanosecond from being tested like Job. It could happen suddenly like Job. We will have to ask ourselves, will I curse God and die?

Satan did not take away Job's integrity. Job had his integrity to fall back on. God granted Satan the authority to take Job's children, wealth, servants, health, and friends. Lastly, he influenced his wife to inject foolish comments to encourage him to quit. Job stood firm on his integrity and maintained his uprightness throughout the saga.

Uprightness gives us the option of swaying into the direction of Satan or maintaining in the presence of God. Do we trust God, Satan, or ourselves? Bildad speaks of God's Justice and uprightness in Job 8:1-6:

> "Then answered Bil-dad the Shu-hite, and said, How long wilt thou speak these things? And how long shall the words of thy mouth be like a strong wind? Doth God pervert judgment? or doth the Almighty pervert justice? If thy children have sinned against him, and he have cast them away for their transgression; if thou wouldest seek unto God betimes, and make thy supplication to the Almighty; if thou wert pure and upright; surely now he would awake for thee, and make the habitation of thy righteousness prosperous."

We expect our friends to provide words of comfort while suffering in the pit of pain and suffering. We prefer to hear words of support and encouragement; not self-righteousness spewed across the landscape. When we are confronted by an attack from the enemy, we expect our friends to shelter us with heartfelt understanding and a voice of compassion. Can you depend on a friend to be there with words of comfort if you experience sickness or other troubling circumstance?

Today, if friends or family members fail to deliver comfort, we have to reflect on the action of King David who sought refuge in "the hills." We have to awaken our imagination and consider that God is the only being that we can absolutely depend on when the flood waters rise around us. When we are awakening to the true holiness of God, we recognize that God is all we need. We cannot permit our thinking to become dull.

How a person handles suffering reveals a lot about the person. In addition, a lot is revealed to the person. We can handle suffering with dignity, placing all faith and confidence in God, or we can curse God and die. Can we embrace suffering like we embrace the fun and joy of life? It is possible if we knew the deadline date for sufferings exit, we could embrace it more readily? But, God never gives us the outcome while in the midst of the battle. But, when we place our total faith and trust in God we are convinced that the outcome will be in His favor. We want everything laid out before us, so we can know what the outcome will be. We do not want to experience any pain along the way. We want every angle covered for our benefit. Sorry, God does not work that way. We limit ourselves to such a degree that we never enjoy the true fruits of what God has in store for us when we suffer for Him. Do we completely trust God, like Job? Faith is a part of our integrity. Faith is a part of our uprightness. Do you trust and believe that God will deliver you from any trial or tribulation? Trust is a part of our integrity. Trust is a part of our uprightness. Faith and trust work hand and hand with each other. Faith and God's grace rule over all things. Remember, God's grace is sufficient.

THE ROLE OF FAITH

We have nothing without faith. Strong faith brings about marvelous results. How can God please us if our faith is weak? We must be anchored in faith. Job trusted God while in his crisis. Hebrews 11:1 clearly defines faith:

> "Now faith is the substance of things hoped for, the evidence of things not seen."

Apostle Paul addresses the proper dress code in I Thessalonians 5:8,

> "But let us, who are of the day, be sober, putting on the breastplate of faith and love; and for an helmet, the hope of salvation."

Paul writes that "faith is the substance of things hoped for." Paul advises us to wear the breastplate of faith and love and for a helmet, the hope of salvation. This is strong spiritual armor. Our chief Adversary cannot penetrate this protection. Being a prisoner of Jesus Christ produces tested faith, self-discipline, love, blessed hope which become visible in our good works, because every good work comes from God.

How can we have faith in the heavenly Father if we do not love Him? How can we say that we love God and hate our neighbor? It is impossible to have faith without love. Faith and love work hand-in-hand in order for us to receive "the evidence of things not seen." Glory to God!

EXAMPLES OF FAITH

Paul provides us with examples of faith in Hebrews 11:3-5, 7, 11, 17, 20: (The author strongly encourages the reader to review the entire Chapter of Hebrew 11, verses 1-40 to have a clear comprehension of the Lord's view of faith. The reading of his holy word will bring about a blessing).

> "Through faith we understand that the worlds were framed by the word of God, so that things which are seen were not made of things which do appear. By faith Abel offered unto God a more excellent sacrifice than

Cain, by which he obtained witness that he was righteous, God testifying of his gifts: and by it he being dead
yet speaketh. By faith Enoch was translated that he
should not see death; and was not found, because God
had translated him: for before his translation he had
this testimony, that he pleased God. By faith Noah, being
warned of God of things not seen as yet, moved with
fear, prepared an ark to the saving of his house; by the
which he condemned the world, and became heir of the
righteousness which is by faith. Through faith also Sara
herself received strength to conceive seed, and was delivered of a child when she was past age, because she
judged him faithful who had promised. By faith Abraham, when he was tried, offered up Isaac: and he that
had received the promises offered up his only begotten
son, By faith Jacob, when he was a dying, blessed both
the sons of Joseph; and worshipped, leaning upon the
top of his staff."

We have been provided with both the definition of faith and
prime examples of faith. Now, God will advise us of the results
without faith. Hebrews 11:6 says,

"But without faith it is impossible to please him: for he
that cometh to God must believe that he is, and that he
is a rewarder of them that diligently seek him."

Being upright involves complete faith, trust and love of God. This
is the blessed hope of the believer. Being upright involves denying
self and carrying the payload for Christ. When we suffer in the Name
of our Lord, we will reign with Him. Uprightness involves facing a
terrible act and firmly believing that it will turn out for the best. This
is accepting the will and power of the Living God. We place our trust

that God is "all knowing" and will insulate us from any attack from man or Satan. Man may destroy the physical but we must fear the One who controls the physical and spiritual. Remember, God will reward for uprightness.

King David writes in Psalm 25:8,

> "Good and upright is the Lord: therefore will he teach sinners in the way."

King David continues in Psalm 17:30, 32,

> "As for God, his way is perfect: the word of the Lord is tried: he is a buckler to all those that trust in him. It is God that girdeth me with strength, and maketh my way perfect."

King David gives us the prescription for uprightness when he asks God to "teach" and "lead" him into the path of righteousness in Psalm 143:10,

> "Teach me to do thy will: for thou art my God: thy spirit is good; lead me into the land of uprightness."

God is invisible but forever present in us. Because what resides in us is better than what is in the world. Today, we have perfection through Jesus Christ. Christ carried the entire payload for the world. The foundation of the Church is anchored in Christ. He is the chief cornerstone. Every day that we are awake brings praises and thanks to God for His masterful blueprint for our salvation. We exalt God for keeping this mystery a secret until the actual appearance of Christ in the flesh. Our hope for glory is the Christ in us (Colossians 1:27). When we walk step and step with Christ we pace ourselves into the "land of uprightness."

King David reveals the pleasures of God in Psalm 143:11,

> "The Lord taketh pleasure in them that fear him in those
> that hope in his mercy."

The glory that God placed on the head of man is manifested through Jesus Christ. Paul writes in II Thessalonians 1:12,

> "That the name of our Lord Jesus Christ may be glorified
> in you, and ye in him, according to the grace of our God
> and the Lord Jesus Christ."

There is a lot of filth in the world. At times our thoughts can be troubling. It's the flesh that eats at us. Christ did not have these concerns because He was born of the Holy Ghost. But, I find that reading of the scriptures provides the rich treasures of the mind of God. When we neglect the scriptures we open our mind and heart up to heresies and areas of wonderment that dilute sound reasoning. We develop an earthly intellect that fails to measure up to the spiritual nature of God. Today, there are many images that proclaim to reflect the embodiment of Christ. There are great orators who proclaim to know God but when challenged with the scriptures fail to measure up. When we compose our self and focus on the living waters of God, we set a different course to our lives. The biblical scriptures give us deeper understanding, knowledge and wisdom to the works of God. We develop a zeal for good works and the fruits of holiness. When we are wrapped in holiness, we no longer are tempted by the passion of this world and our desires are no longer controlled by earthly images, but by the image of Jesus Christ. Be strengthened by the reading of the Lord's Word. The Word of God restores our uprightness and builds up our integrity, our Godly integrity.

CURSE GOD AND DIE

The Bible does not tell us what happened to Job's wife after she suggested that he curse God and die. Would it be safe to conclude that Job's righteousness saved her? Did Job pray for her as he did his friends Eliphaz, Bildad and Zophar? If we accept the premise that God's "tender mercies endureth forever," maybe she was saved from a final exit. These are opinions from the author and not based on any factual evidence. Whatever the outcome, we believe that it worked out in God's favor.

Job's wife's statement suggests abandonment, anger and frustration at all the events happening around them. She witnessed the loss of their children and the total destruction of the estate. It would cause any human being to lash out and make a knee jerk comment like she made. How often have we lashed out at a wife, husband, son or daughter, brother or sister, mother or father, friend or co-worker and said words that inflicted hurt?

It's amazing that she repeats the exact words that Satan communicated to God in heaven. It illustrates that Satan is not an angel of mercy or compassion. He is a demon of destruction and reserves no empathy or sympathy for man. He gets swelling pleasure in creating confusion and chaos. His sole mission in this world is to persuade man to dismiss God. He wants to fill hell to overflow with souls. That's why God does not desire that any should go to hell. God does not want us to spend eternity in a dungeon of torture and torment. Satan would be a brutal warden in hell. God wants us in the presence of His everlasting light.

Satan influenced Job's wife to assist in his mission. This is a consistent attribute of Satan, to attack those close to us. Psychologically, she was suffering from the destruction of the estate, death of their ten children and servants and the embarrassment of walking into the city of Uz and hearing all the gossip and rumors about the demise of her husband. This could wreck the confidence of any person. It could shatter the faith and trust in some who are not completely anchored in the Lord. Job was at a low point in his life he needed the love and tenderness of his wife, not the poison of her tongue. Based on his wife's words, it would be safe to assume that she was angry. She seems prideful when she inquires, "Dost thou still retain thine integrity?" (Job 2:9). We may inquire how could she look upon her husband's suffering and make such an utterance? In this instance Job's wife did not place her husband above her own desires and emotions. We could conclude that she wanted to have her husband out of his misery and death seemed the only option. Did she desire to get rid of her husband immediately? We can speculate on what she was thinking, but one point is clear: she did not offer support, encouragement, or prayer for her husband. That is what happens to us as human beings. We are so easy and quick to give up on each other when confronted with an earthly trial or tribulation. We are quick to condemn, rather than to show mercy and compassion. Our heavenly Father is extremely patient with us; slow to anger and always forgiving us. But we fail in our dealings with one another. We are quick to abandon our neighbor. How, then, can we say we love and worship God, whom we have never seen, and hate our neighbor? How can we say we love God and refuse to give our brother water to quench his thirst? How can we say we love God and fail to give food to a hungry neighbor? We cannot slip anything by God. We cannot get over on Him. God will shine light upon our darkness. He hears and watches all. We cannot fool God.

When we elevate our thinking to a godly platform, we get a better focus on Job's wife's comment of "curse God and die." This is a cruel statement. Nevertheless, there is more to this statement for our modern-day evaluation. This statement is clearly based on the observation of Job's physical appearance, not his spiritual nature. We often look at a sick person based solely on their physical appearance. Often times we fail to search out the heart and soul of a person prior to rendering judgment. We may fail to understand a person's commitment to God. We may say, "O' they are in such pain." "O I wish the Lord would end their suffering." "O' it is so painful to see them in that condition." "I hope the Lord will just take him or her and relinquish them of the pain and suffering." "He or she suffered so badly at the end." "I could not stand to see them in such pain; I wish I could do something to ease their pain and suffering." "I didn't visit them because I wanted to remember them the way they were." "O they suffered enough. I'm glad God took them." "He or she deserved everything they got at the end for how they treated people." "He or she was a bad person anyway and that's why they suffered at the end." "I told you the Lord was going to put something on them before they left this planet." "All the bad stuff you did in life, you are lucky the Lord didn't put more on you." "That's nothing for what you did to other folks."

Are those utterances from the lips of an upright person? Have you heard any of those comments? Do we know the heart or soul of a person? Why are we always evaluating the flesh? Is there a righteous judge among us? Remember, God is spirit. The flesh cannot go face-to-face with God. Why do we witness upon the "physicalness" of a person's condition rather than the spiritual? If we view only the physicalness of Christ's work on the Cross, we will miss out on the true purposes of His mission to earth. We can look upon the ugliness of Christ's damaged body on the Cross and immediately conclude that it was horrible. But, if we search deeper in the spirit, we will recognize the beauty of Christ's work on the Cross and sing praises of merriment to the Lord for this impeccable work for mankind. Indeed, Christ suffered terribly in the physical sense of things; but when He said, "Father, forgive them; for they know not what they do" He was demonstrating mercy, compassion and love in its highest form. This was coming from the heart and soul of Christ. If Christ had looked upon man solely on the physicalness of His pain and suffering, He would have come down from the Cross. But, the spirit that lived in Him refused to permit Him to come down, because He understood that the ransom had to be paid. He understood the depth of His mission. The Spirit of His Father dwelled in Him and provided the necessary strength to complete the journey. At the end, Christ cried with a loud voice, "Father, into thy hands I commend my spirit" (Luke 23:46). We are enriched by the crucifixion of Jesus Christ, His resurrection and ascension into heaven.

Satan takes advantage of every available resource to destroy Job. He uses his wife to discourage him. She did not say to her husband, "I know how you feel," or "I am here for you." King Solomon writes in Proverbs 18:21,

> "Death and life are in the Power of the tongue: and they
> that love it shall eat the fruit thereof."

Job's wife does not employ wisdom. Her statement is a clear indication that Satan is alive and well and attempting to destroy the last meaningful thing in Job's life, his wife. To turn her against him leaves Job with absolutely nothing. In earthly terminology, we can safely conclude, "Job lost everything." Satan governed over this destruction. God is not in the destruction business. God is in the restoration business, always making situations and circumstances better. Remember, Jesus Christ came to earth as a carpenter, a builder of

Men. He came to save man from total destruction at the hands of Satan. Remember, this is the Satan, formerly known as Lucifer, who attempted to overthrow God. Lucifer wanted to be like the Most High. The following scripture in Isaiah 14:12-15 describes Lucifer's desires and what ultimately happens to him:

> "How art thou fallen from heaven. O Lucifer, son of the morning! How art thou cut down to the ground, which didst weaken the nations! For thou hast said in thine heart, I will ascend into heaven, I will exalt my throne above the stars of God: I will sit also upon the mount of the congregation, in the sides of the north: I will ascend above the heights of the clouds; I will be like the most High. Yet thou shalt be brought down to hell, to the sides of the pit."

Lucifer envisioned himself sitting on God's throne. He wanted to remove God by force. Lucifer had walked in the presence of the glory of God but was not satisfied. He desired to have it all. After his defeat in heaven God designed a permanent hellhole to deposit him in. The angel Michael slammed Satan into a dark bottomless pit of nightmarish proportions. Pride, jealousy, and envy surfaced in Lucifer. He continues to inject his venom in every aspect of our society today. He remains the author of confusion and negativity. Satan has been soundly defeated and is no longer welcomed in heaven. Therefore, we should not welcome him into our daily lives. He was soundly whipped in heaven and God has the victory.

Job's wife challenges his integrity in a belittling manner. She questions his uprightness, faith, trust and love of God. The Bible does not provide us with Job's wife's name. Satan has influenced Job's wife against him, like he did with Eve in the Garden of Eden. But, Job does not fall prey to this temptation and cries out a salute to God; "What?

Shall we receive good at the hand of God, and shall we not receive evil?"(Job 2:10). It takes a true man of God to make the latter utterance. Job's words were not a simple task. His delivery is the expression of man dedicated to the will of the Father. His words illustrate the total commitment of a man of faith. Deeply embedded in Job is a commitment to only please God. His statement is made with power and authority. There is not a crack in Job's armor. There is no doubt that he believes in the Lord and remains obedient to the will of God.

Job's wife did not offer support, encouragement, hope, or prayer to her husband. She merely encourages him to give up, to quit. It appears that she simply wanted him out of his misery. Remember, Job's misery was great.

Let us take a humanistic assessment of the real content of Job's wife's dialogue. What she is relating to her husband is much deeper and elaborate than what is stated on the surface.

Job's wife is apparently saying, "Get yourself out of this misery Job." She is also saying, "I'm tired of dealing with your belief in this man called God. I do not believe you any more Job. I do not believe anything anymore Job. Job you told me God was a just God, a fair God, and a God of high-esteem. Well why is he doing this to you, to me, to us? Why Job? This is your reward Job for all your uprightness? Where is your integrity Job? Job, for all these years you put this God before the kids and me. Look at yourself Job; we have lost everything. I no longer have my children; I lost all my servants; we have no money. All of my friends look at me in shame. I am embarrassed when I go to the market place. You have been made to look less than a man before your so-called high and mighty God, Job curse your God and die."

None of us is in a position to condemn Job's wife for her words. Remember those elder friends of Job tossed fire on him with their tongues as well. Of course we wish that Job's wife would have shown more compassion, but here actions are a reflection of our self. In our world today, we read and hear of stories of abandonment in the midst of crisis. We hear of marriages destroyed because of a spouses transgressions. Every husband and wife wants their spouse to hang in there through the thick and thin. Isn't that the foundation of marriage? Adam didn't have anything but the clothes on his back when he and his wife were evicted from the Garden of Eden. Yet, they stayed together and were fruitful and multiplied. Adam took care of his family.

Job was suffering mightily. He needed his wife's mercy and compassion. He needed the loving touch of his wife. Job needed to hear, "Honey I'm here for you and will remain here for you. Honey, you have been a faithful man to God, and served him well. You have done nothing wrong in the presence of God, and may God have mercy on us. May God lift you up from this disgrace and make you the man that you were. I love you, Job. I love you more now that I have ever loved you. May God strengthen us both as we face this challenge. Always remember that I am here to do as you need. I will pray for you, asking the Lord to deliver you from this misery and return you to greatness." That's what Job needed to hear. Those are words of uprightness. Those are words that would shake the foundation of heaven as angels leap for joy.

Remember, Job was the wealthiest man of the east. He was the most admired man in Uz. He was respected throughout the kingdom. He was popular and looked up to by princes and commanding officers of the military. He was a man of power and authority. And due to his blessed prosperity, Job's wife enjoyed all the trappings of riches and power that came along with his position. We can imagine that she was a house wife, highly respected among women's groups.

Women would seek her out for advice about life and marriage. She had numerous servants, and the children were the best in Uz, respectful of their parents and community. She was looked upon as a "pillar of the community"; performing acts of charity. But once hard times hit, she rose up against her husband, failing to fear the Lord her God. Even the evilness of Satan had to acknowledge before God Job's total and complete insulation from wrong doings. Satan states to God in Job 1:10,

> "Hast not thou made a hedge about him, and about his house, and about all that he hath on every side? Thou hast blessed the work of his hands, and his substance is increased in the land."

How often do we abandon a husband or wife due to a loss of riches? Do we show mercy and understanding and strive harder to work things out? In most cases today, divorce would be the answer to a situation similar to Job's. The first thing our friends and neighbors would say, "Hey, he doesn't have any money. He lost his job. He's bankrupt. Girlfriend, you better leave him and find you another man with money. He can't take care of you the way you are accustomed." Do you know someone who has repeated those words? Those are not words of wisdom. Simply because a husband or wife is facing a major trial or tribulation is not sufficient reason to abandon a marriage. God has the power and authority to restore everything that is lost. If we manifest patience, faith and endure until the end, we will witness a marvelous work from the Lord.

Satan acknowledges that Job has a hedge around him on all sides. What an acknowledgment by Satan to God's mighty power and authority. In other words, Satan could not place his hands on God's servant. Job is well insulated from the hands of Satan and his demons. Satan's admission reveals that he can do nothing without the consent of God. Also, it reveals that those who walk upright with the Lord and resist the devil are protected from his wickedness. Sin not and follow the words of our Lord and savior. Fear God, not Satan. Praise God's holy name, not Satan's. Worship God, not Satan. Keep in mind one thing about Satan: he is only about absolute, total, and complete destruction of man. Satan is not in the replacement or rebuilding business. He leaves a path of total annihilation and destruction.

God blesses those that maintain their integrity and walk upright. We will not fall and worship the creature, only the Creator (Romans 1:25).

MERCY KILLING AND EUTHANASIA

To curse God and die could mean an immediate, permanent and eternal reservation in hell. To curse God and die invites the "seducing spirits and doctrines of devils" (I Timothy 4:1). For example; euthanasia, mercy killing, suicide, and assisted-suicide fall under the "doctrines of devils." There will be great argumentation regarding this labeling. Many medical professionals, scholars, intellectuals and theologians will justify the killing of another person due to their pain or illness as proper to eliminate intense suffering. Is assisting someone to kill themselves due to an illness acceptable to God?

When Dr. Jack Kervokian assists a client to die with his medieval contraption due to what he perceives is undue pain and suffering; what is he inviting into the room? Would God endorse his actions? The patient and family members feel the suicide doctor is fulfilling a need, a desire to place patients experiencing intense pain in a state of permanent comfort. For those patients who have been informed by their doctor that there is no hope, Dr. Kervokian delivers a chemical mixture to ease their suffering through death. For the patient, family members and Dr. Kervokian, this may appear on the surface to be a sound doctrine. It may seem like the "right" thing to do. But, is it the "righteous" thing to do? Does the behavior curse God to His face? Where is the fear of God?

Today, we are faced with decisions regarding life and death. There is a lot of mess on the landscape. And it is easy for human beings to be influenced by experts who value their opinions, research, and assessments better than the spiritual care of a patient. Of course, pain and suffering can be difficult, but how can we take a life that does not belong to us? I Corinthians 6:19, 20 says, "You are not your own. Therefore honor God with your body." A ransom was paid for us. A heavy price was paid by the "spotless blood of Christ." When we grab control of our desires and passions and seek the passion of Christ, we develop a higher form of thinking. The answer to pain, suffering, hopelessness, and despair is God. Christ promised, "Come to me, all you who are weary and burdened, and I will give you rest" (Matthew 11:28). Christ did not say that we give ourselves rest. We are not equipped to make that decision. God has plans to prosper and not to harm you, plans to give you hope and a future (Jeremiah 29:11). We cannot give up hope because the world feels it's stylish and fashionable. Even in suffering God has a bigger plan. We have to remain patient and wait on the Lord. Every decision in life should be made based on the Word of God. We cannot rely on confusion and deception to assist us in making the right decision on life and death. Satan's entire mission is to create havoc. He is a demon of destruction. His plan is to deliver you to hell for his pleasure. John 8:44 says, Satan is a "murderer" and the "father of lies." He has his agents throughout society delivering lies as truth. Remember, he attempted to fool Christ in the wilderness and failed miserably.

Remember the story Christ told about the rich man and the poor man Lazarus. Lazarus, full of sores, merely wanted to be fed the crumbs from the rich man's table. Like Job, the dogs licked his wounds. The rich man feasted while a sick man sat starving at the gate. The bible says the poor man was "carried by the angels into Abraham's bosom" (Luke 16:22). The rich man died and was buried, but awoke in hell. The rich man lifted up his eyes, being in torments, and cried to Abraham to have Lazarus bring him a drop of water to cool his tongue. The rich man continues to give orders even in hell. One wonders if he had learned his lesson. At this stage, his wealthy is meaningless. Abraham rejected his request. Abraham reminded him about the good things he had in this life but the poor man was now in comfort in paradise. It appears that the rich man's pride was still alive because he wanted Lazarus to serve him. But, the rich man begged Abraham to send Lazarus back to tell his five brothers "lest they also come into this place of torment" (Luke 16:19-31). Abraham rejected his request again and said "They have Moses and the prophets; let them hear them." Today, we have the Moses, the prophets and word from our savior to live by. Christ has illustrated to us on how to live a perfect life. Hell is a real place and the decisions we make in this world must reflect the divinity of Christ, not our own imagination. Our strength is to resist the desires and passions of this world and keep our thoughts lifted up in the heavens. Wealth and social status in this world are no guarantee into heaven. Job was rich, yet righteous. The bible says "Abram was very rich in cattle, in silver, and in gold" (Genesis 13:2). Yet, he was righteous before the Lord. The poor and downtrodden should never be oppressed.

Satan has a variety of methods to persuade us that our thinking and reasoning have a certain amount of wisdom. He misleads us to think that we can solve our own problems. He wants us to believe that God does not exist and we are the center of the universe and that we can solve our problems. It forces many in our world today to believe in doctrines that have no foundation with God. It is based on human knowledge and not heavenly wisdom and understanding. Divine wisdom and understanding can only come from God.

Do we quit and give up because the struggle seems a mighty one? Do we blaspheme the Name of the Living God because society pressures us? Do we endorse a program that assaults the integrity and character of God? We are God's creations. Man did not create us. Our Lord would never endorse such a program. Euthanasia, mercy killing, suicide or assisted-suicide (or the practices of Dr. Kervokian) does not glorify God. Dr. Kervokian is practicing death. Our God is a God of life. By practicing death, one is attempting to taint the name of our savior, who gave us Life and conquered death with the Supreme Victory. There is no 'mercy' in mercy killing. There is only 'killing,' and God's commandment clearly states: "Thou Shall Not Kill." How can one 'assist' someone in suicide? There is no assisted-suicide. If you are a participant in an assisted-suicide matter, you are assisting in murder, and murder falls under the same commandment, "Thou Shall Not Kill." If a physician assists in such an action, he is committing murder and murder is contrary to God's teachings on Life. Where is our faith? Where is our renewed hope in Jesus Christ? Why can't we wait patiently on the Lord to come? We do not know how long a sick and suffering person must carry the Cross. Only God knows that. Remember, the spirit is not damaged, only the flesh is damaged. When we take our focus off the flesh and stand firm in the spirit, we comprehend the blessed hope of the Lord. We must keep hope alive.

I reflect upon my father's last months fighting, wrestling and tussling with incurable cancer. When the rages of cancer had taken over his body, my wife and I cared for him in our home. He had 24-hour nursing care and the best treatment that could be provided for his condition. The doctors set me down and advised me that there was no cure and my father would exit any day. My father was in extreme pain. His suffering was intense. My father was suffering deeply. He was in and out of consciousness. To watch the suffering made me break down in tears; crying out to the Lord for His "tender mercies." I prayed daily for the Lord to bring healing to his body. Towards the end of his life, my father awakened and said to me: "Son, I haven't given up, my body has given out." When I watched him sit up in bed and scream out his deceased father's name as if he could see him, I knew the time was near. A few days later he died. Throughout most of my father's life he did not believe in God. He felt his God was money. That was amazing because he was raised in a godly home. His father, my grandfather was a noted North Carolina Baptist preacher. But as the end drew near a schoolmate of my father's came to visit. He was a preacher. When I told him that my father did not believe in God or preachers, amazingly my father overheard the discussion and whispered, "Please son send him in." Hours later the preacher exited the room, looked me in the eyes and said, "Your father received Christ." Glory to God!

Days later, I reflected on my father's last words before he died. His words were quite profound. My father was saying the flesh was destroyed but his spirit had not given up. I thought: "His spirit is in top shape, because of our Lord and savior Jesus Christ, but his temporary shell of flesh was completely worn out." My father's heart, soul and spirit were maintaining but the flesh had seen its last days and was slowly deteriorating from the bone. Jesus states in Mark 14:38, "The Spirit truly is ready, but the flesh is weak."

The Apostle Paul writes in II Corinthians 4:16,

> "For which cause we faint not; but though our outward man perish, yet the inward man is renewed day by day."

MODERN-DAY PRESCRIPTIONS

There are many modern-day doctrines that are influenced by devils and seducing spirits. It seems that many people are searching for that higher form of deity that they can touch and feel. Hope and faith in an invisible God appears lacking from the elite of our society. There are challenging issues facing our generation. There are so many religions around the globe to choose from, each celebrating its own form of deity. There is a lot of confusion as to what is right versus what is righteous. Many people are being guided into doctrines of seducing spirits which can lead only to a world of torment. There is temptation all about. Preachers, ministers, prophets, and saints are working overtime in prayer and supplication to God to rid our world of its problems. God continues to have His hand on the pulse of things. He is a righteous judge and will soon rid the world of its problems.

When faced with a serious choice today, we have to pause and inquire: "How would Jesus Christ behave in such a situation?" Secondly, we should question: "How will my actions profit God?" You will find out every time that God's doctrine is the best medicine. Man consistently develops foolish procedures and doctrines to accommodate the 'urges' of man. Satan inspires many of these doctrines for the full benefit of Satan and his angels. That's why man has difficulty solving modern-day issues. There is a large amount of accommodation, so as not to offend any group of people with a set agenda, but is the holiness of God being manifested in those decisions? Man creates problems and man feels he can solve his own problems. Where is God? Throughout the bible, noted followers of God received effective solutions to all of their problems by first seeking out God. Why not look at God first? God has all the answers. He created us. Would not the Creator know more about His creations? It seems quite simple to call on God rather than to dally with man's limited knowledge. God has infinite knowledge and wisdom. Satan, on the other hand, has one answer to everything--total destruction of mankind. Man looks to "pop psychology" to pacify the desires, emotions, pleasures, and urges of man. If the desire or urge is demanded or commanded frequently, consistently and loud enough, man will develop a system of accommodation, even if the doctrine is contrary to God's Laws.

Often times, ministers of the cloth have compromised their position by accommodating issues that are contrary to the commandments of God. How can you accommodate something that is totally and completely contrary to God's Law? It appears that what is godly is wrong and what is wrong is godly.

God has not changed his commandments or covenants since the beginning of time. Like a rock, his laws are firmly planted for us to follow. There are no adjustments to God's Laws, no temptation to comply with men's simple pleasures or desires. God wants us to be "upright and perfect, one that feareth God, and escheweth evil." King David has warned us that the "fear of our Lord" is the very foundation of wisdom. King David maintained a lofty position with our Lord; therefore, why would we challenge the warning of such a man? God found great favor with King David. His advice is worth lending an ear too.

Man destroys the flesh, yet the spirit lives on with God. The flesh bothers man. We focus a lot of attention on the flesh. We forget that the flesh (the physical) is temporary. Its final resting place is the soil of the earth. Dust back to dust.

THE CASE OF DR. KERVOKIAN

Let us take the case of Dr. Kervokian, the assisted-suicide doctor. First, there is no such thing as assisting a suicide. Simply stated, this is murder. Some may call it mercy killing. There is no mercy in killing someone. A patient decides to kill himself or herself due to the intense pain and suffering from an illness or incurable disease. This suicide, simply stated, is self-murder. Euthanasia's foundation is contrary to God's principle. But, simply put, it is murder. Murder is murder. We can adjust the language and dialogue to accommodate society but it serves no worthwhile purpose but to destroy mankind. It opens the doors of hell for Satan to walk in and plant his heinous crimes upon the crown of man. Wickedness is prevailing in our society.

Relative to suicide, the person that speaks most clearly, on the record, is God's Son, Jesus Christ. Jesus Christ had many audiences with his Father in heaven before coming to earth to save mankind. Jesus' information is directly from the mouth of the Father. John 8:44 reveals the status of Satan and those that follow him:

> "Ye are of your father the devil, and the lusts of your father ye will do. He was a murderer from the beginning, and abode not in the truth, because there is no truth in him. When he speaketh a lie, he speaketh of his own: for he is a liar, and the father of it."

152

Christ reveals that Satan is the architect of deception. God is not about murderer. God is not about death. God is a god of *LIFE*.

When we engage in death-related tactics like euthanasia, assisted-suicide, suicide, or mercy killing due to the physical pain of an ailment, we are engaged in an "abomination in the sight of God." Murder is death. Satan is the father of murder. He was formerly in charge of death, but Christ took the keys back to His Father. Christ conquered death. Our Lord entered the gates of hell and preached the gospel and Satan and his demons could not contain Him. Jesus proclaims in Matthew 22:32,

> "I am the God of Abraham, and the God of Isaac, and the God of Jacob? God is not the God of the dead, but of the living."

God is all about living. Satan's agenda is death and mayhem. His devices are deeply entrenched in formulating euthanasia, suicide, and mercy killing as useful tools of engagement. We are placing our focus on death and destruction. Satan's uses these tools to carry out his ministry. God has firmly established that his Son received the VICTORY over the grave. Death lost its sting. Therefore, to perform these 'heinous crimes' in the name of God takes away God's glory. In addition, God will not stand for it. Robbing God of his glory is a form of thievery. Satan is the director of theft and stealing. It is astonishing that we would perform these acts in the name of God. Christ explains the results of those ministers who proclaim His kingdom in a negative manner:

> "Not every one that saith unto me, Lord, Lord, shall enter into the kingdom of heaven; but he that doeth the will of my Father which is in heaven. Many will say to me in that day, Lord, Lord, have we not prophesied in

thy name? And in thy name have cast out devils? And in
thy name done many wonderful works? And then will I
profess unto them, I never knew you, depart from me,
ye that work iniquity" (Mat.7-21-23).

Our Lord and savior will not recognize evil and wicked works
done in His Name. Christ states, "I never knew you; depart from me,
ye that work iniquity." Praise Jesus! When we rob God of his glory,
we are robbing God of life.

There is no mercy in mercy-killing. God forbids it. Man defiles
himself when he engages in assisted murder of any type. The goal of
life is not death. Death is a non-issue because the Son of Man conquered death. Death has no sting.

The doctrine of Satan is a non-healing doctrine. If those people
that have died from the hands of euthanasia-assisted-suicide,
suicide, or mercy killing could contact us today, they would have
regrets over ever participating in such a "heinous crime." They
would want to warn us against such activity, but God will not allow
that warning. The warning is there in the form of the words laid
down by our Lord and savior, Jesus Christ and other prophets of the
bible. God's doctrine is firmly established.

Jesus Christ told Satan in their face-to-face encounter that there
is only One God that we should bow to. In Luke 4:8,

"And Jesus answered and said unto him, get thee behind
me, Satan: for it is written, Thou shalt worship the Lord
thy God, and him only shalt thou serve."

Job never considered quitting during his torment. He did not
consider suicide or assisted-suicide to solve his problem. He demanded an audience with the Lord to plea his case for correction and
restoration. In our modern day crisis, we cannot give up hope due to

the intensity of our pain and suffering. We cannot permit Satan to influence us that euthanasia, assisted-suicide, suicide and mercy killing are devices of God. God does not design devices of this nature. Only Satan's lab in hell can design such instruments to influence man. We can glorify God through suffering, if we endure. We do not glorify God when we use devices designed by Satan to destroy what God has created. Assisted-suicide may seem like the "right" thing to do in certain conditions and circumstances, but it is not the "righteous" thing to do. It does not serve God. It does not manifest the Christ in us.

The problem is solved. Wickedness cannot prevail when we glorify, honor, and praise God for his Grace. Jesus Christ states:

> "Likewise, I say unto you, there is joy in the presence of the angels of God over one sinner that repenteth" (Luke 15:10).

Glory to God! Our Advocate in heaven has paved the way for us to maintain favor with the Holy Father. Let us not be tormented by Satan's doctrine of destruction, but elevate our thinking to a godly plane, refusing to defile ourselves in fleshly matters, and endorsing preferring spiritual matters. Apostle Paul writes,

> "Teaching us that, denying ungodliness and worldly lusts, we should live soberly, righteously, and Godly, in this present world; Looking for that blessed hope, and the glorious appearing of The Great God and our Savior Jesus Christ, who gave himself to us, that he might redeem us from all iniquity, and purify unto himself a peculiar people, zealous of good works" (Titus 2:12-14).

The practice of uprightness should be a part of our daily regiment. It is our duty and responsibility to dismiss all forms of ungodliness. God commands us to walk in holiness. Jesus Christ set an excellent example of how our daily walk should be. Christ was the perfect role model. He walked upright every day while on earth. He was sinless.

When we are faced with pain and suffering Apostle Paul reveals to us in II Corinthians 4:17, 18,

> "For our light affliction, which is but for a moment, worketh for us a far more exceeding and eternal weight of glory. While we look at the things which are seen, but at the things which are not seen: for the things which are temporal: but the things which are not seen are eternal."

Paul reveals to us that the battle is not of flesh and blood, but of the spirit. We have to keep our focus on the unseen, the invisible and glorify the precious Name of the Lord. We possess eternal glory by the invisible. We may groan in the flesh, waiting on our pain-free environment in heaven. God is on the premises, quietly and silently watching us. Strong and powerful is our Lord. God is the healer. God can eliminate all pain and suffering when we live upright and maintain our faith, trust and love in Him. King David writes in Psalm 19:7,

> "The law of the Lord is perfect, converting the soul: the testimony of the Lord is sure, making wise the simple."

On the battlefield of life we need the doctrine of God, not the doctrine of devils. Being upright pleases God. Strive for perfection in all that you do. AMEN.

CHAPTER 6

WITH FRIENDS LIKE THESE WHO NEEDS ENEMIES

"There is no greater loan than a sympathetic ear."
– Frank Tyger

My mother made certain we were in Sunday School and Church every Sunday. But not only Sunday School and Church but also every Revival and Vacation Bible School. She would not permit us to watch television, have a friend visit, go outside or play at the park if we failed to attend Church. As I reached my teenage years attending church was deeply indwelled in me and mother did not have to threaten me with the wrath of God if I failed to attend. Today, I am thankful to my mother for instilling this discipline in me. And she did not stop there; there were the in-house prayers and scripture readings at home. Outside of the spankings I can always reflect on my mother constantly in prayer over the smallest thing. She was always praising God for the simplest things. In modern times, I fully understand why she did it.

But, one thought came to mind when I attended church. There was a special hymn that the choir would sing called, "What a friend we have in Jesus." My spirit praised God when the choir sung that hymn. It was uplifting, and I felt that Jesus was always a friend, a friend that I could truly count on. Today, as I look back on my life, it is clearer today that Jesus has truly been a friend. He has always been a person I could converse with, reveal my problems to and get an honest answer. I could not hide my deepest secrets from Him. He would uncover the slightest form of iniquity in the darkest corner of my heart. I trusted Him not to reveal my weaknesses to others. He always encouraged me to come to Him with all of my problems and issues. He was never in a rush to do other things. He gave me His undivided attention, love and support. He showed patience, understanding and knowledge of my misery. He did not condemn me for my stupidity. He strengthened me through grace and forgiveness. He stood in my shoes and understood my feelings. He gave me power to overcome with His mercy and compassion. In addition, His answers were always correct and true. Even when I failed to listen to Him, He showed me love and embraced me. He did not toss me away like a filthy rag. I could depend on Jesus to deliver. He never failed me as a friend. He is the type of friend you always wanted. Jesus Christ is a friend that knows everything about life's situations and circumstances. He never promoted the wrong advice. Jesus Christ is a friend that is not intimidated by the intensity of the consequences. He is a friend that laid His life down for me.

JOB'S FRIENDS

In Job's case, three of his friends, elders of the church heard of his ordeal. They heard that Job was terribly ill and they about a visit. Job was suffering from a terrible affliction, as described in Job 2:11, 12,

> "Now when Job's three friends heard of all this evil that was come upon him, they came everyone from his own

place; Eliphaz the Tenanite, and Bildad the Shahite, and Zophar the Naamathite: for they had made an appointment together to come to mourn with him and to comfort him. And when they lifted up their eyes afar off, and knew him not, they lifted up their voice, and wept: and they rent every one his mantle, and sprinkled dust upon their heads toward heaven."

One would expect a friend to visit in a time of need, especially when you are suffering from a potentially deadly illness. We would look for friends to mourn with us, get low with us and comfort us to the best of their ability. A friend would not condemn us for our condition or circumstance. A friend would look upon us with mercy, compassion, prayer, and confidence. A true friend would bring along encouragement and comfort. He would be a good, keen listener, both verbally and non-verbally. A friend would have a good picture of what you are about and would do everything in his or her power to make you comfortable. A friend would pray in earnest for God to have mercy and compassion for us. He or she would inquire of God for healing and greater courage over our illness or troubling circumstance. Those are the ingredients of a friend, a true friend. Simply stated, we look for a friend to be there for us. We would never expect a friend to be inconsiderate, insensitive, condescending, condemning, self-righteous, unkind, or judgmental. In our affliction, we need understanding, mercy, compassion, meditation, and prayer. We need to be encouraged that God's grace is at hand. At times, we need simple quietness and silence. We need to feel an air of comfort.

Do you have a person you can call a friend? What is your criterion for a friend? Can this friend be counted on through the thick and thin of life's difficulties?

Job felt he had three friends in whom he could place his trust. The elder friends arrive on the premises as Job 13:2 describes:

> "So they sat down with him upon the ground seven days and seven nights, and none spoke a word unto him: for they saw that **his** grief was very great."

Seven days and seven nights the friends sat with Job, without an utterance. The three friends took notice of his physical condition and were horrified with grief. The elders witness a body infected with despicable boils from the crown of his head to his feet. The elders, "knew him not" (Job 12:2). Job's body had to be so painfully disfigured for the elders' inability to recognize him. He had a smelly, disgusting appearance. Satan's desire was to inflict as much physical damage as possible within the mandate God had given him. Satan's goal was to make the physical appearance of Job so appalling to his friends, wife, business associates, servants or passers-by that Job would curse God to his face and die. Remember, Job's wife had suggested earlier that he perform such an act. Seemingly, she was fed up looking at his disgusting appearance. As we re-call, Job immediately dismisses her remarks as that of a foolish woman speaking. After this exchange Job praised the good and bad portions of life.

After seven days and night of quietness, Job speaks. He immediately "cursed his day" (Job 3:1). Due to the anguish of his physical condition, Job curses the day he was born. He wanted his birth stricken from the record. He wanted the memory of his conception dismissed from memory. He demanded that his original be like the blackness of the day and the shadows of death stain it (Job 3:3-6). It is clear that Job is hurt, sad, angry and determined to lay down the framework to justify that he was not deserving of this suffering. Job's misery is extremely difficult and challenging because he is convinced that he has been a good and faithful servant to the Lord. He is so depressed that he desires that his entire life be erased from the Book of Life. Job knew he had lived an upright life and feared the wrath of God. Life has become meaningless to Job. Job needs strong support, understanding, compassion, mercy, prayer, and encouragement from his friends. He can only get worse as he continues to ventilate about his present physical condition, loss of his children, and assets. Job feels broken in all arenas. He is attempting to rationalize his present condition. Job says, "For the thing which I greatly feared is come upon me, and that which I was afraid of is come unto me" (Job 3:25).

THE DIMENSIONS OF FRIENDSHIP

Now, this is where a true friend or wife steps in to bring comfort to a troubled, depressed soul. At this stage Job needs encouragement, support, and understanding. More importantly, he needs prayer. James writes, "Is any sick among you? Let him call on the elders of the church; and let them pray over him, anointing him with oil in the name of the Lord" (James 5:14). We will soon find out if these elders perform this righteous act.

Knowing that Job's grief is very great, a gentle, caring, and kind approach would work. Every attempt should be made to illustrate mercy and compassion when a person is drowning in a sea of misery. Love and patience should be at the center. Often times, merely being a good, keen, and understanding listener can do much for the wounded soul. An expression of sincerity in the most kind and caring manner goes a long way in placing a sick person at peace. When we step into the patient's moccasins for deeper understanding of their plight, we are embracing them with heartfelt understanding and blessed hope for recovery. Every person experiencing a state of pain and sorrow wants to feel that hope is alive. "And the prayer of faith shall save the sick, and the Lord shall raise him up; and if he have committed sins, they shall be forgiven him" (James 5:15).

When we view someone's afflicted with a disease or ailment, do we only look at the 'physicalness' of their affliction? The flesh can sometimes fool us about the true condition of the patient. We have to look deeper and concern ourselves with the spiritual component of the person. As stated earlier, the flesh returns to the dust from which it originated. God is primarily concerned about our spirit. Man or Satan may kill the flesh, but our fear should concern us about our Father in heaven, who can destroy flesh and spirit. Therefore, it is important that we give the suffering person all of our "lovingkindness," offering encouragement to hang on and prayer to sustain them. We should not offer encouragement of a foolish nature as if the sickness is non-existent; instead, we must offer the type of encouragement that gives the person hope. Jeremiah advises on denial of the inevitable.

> "They have healed also the hurt of the daughter of my people slightly, saying, Peace, peace; when there is no peace" (Jeremiah 6:14).

We have to be honest and realistic with Job, not self-righteous, condescending, condemning or charging God foolishly. Sometimes a person's silence is sufficient to carry on. However, always pray in earnest for anyone that is ill; pray that the person will receive God's mercy, compassion, and wellness. In addition, we must do what we can to service the sick. We must provide for their needs as much as we can. We should never make fun of their condition, but be a strong rock that the sick person can lean and depend on.

Job's friends consistently condemn him for his righteousness. The friends place him in a position to defend his integrity and character. This was not necessary. A friend should not be placed in a position to defend themselves against accusations of sin when none are righteous, not one amongst men. God states that we fall short of His glory. Therefore, no one is perfect enough to render judgment on another. Jesus Christ did not render judgment on us. He was sinless, yet showed mercy and compassion to the sinner.

Suffering and afflictions come in many forms. It takes shape and unveils itself when we carry the Cross. It's a test of our commitment to God. It's only a test. We may have to take the test over and over again in order to pass, but through faith and patience we can win. It is not necessary for us to understand God's full purpose for us. It is necessary for us to trust Him as the Teacher with full knowledge of how the outcome will be. If Job did not possess the brainpower to understand the Lord's mission fully, then what do we understand? Throughout the test process God receives the glory that He justly deserves. It is safe to conclude that all suffering is not a result of sin. But, we can receive growth and nourishment in suffering as God slowly uncovers his true mission. That's why we shout "glory" when God's healing power brings us back better than we were. It's an amazing mystery as to why suffering comes upon us, seemingly at a surprising hour, but we have to be ready and prepared through prayer and supplication to face the Lord and all of His majesty and justice. He is a righteous judge with plenty of patience, mercy, compassion, and love. Adversity is meant to bring us closer to God. Suffering places us in a position to understand that there is only one power in heaven and earth. And in the affairs of man that Higher Power rests in the hands of Christ Jesus. He showed us how far He would go as a friend when He gave up His life on the Cross. The price He paid took us out of bondage.

God singles us out to suffer in His name to decide who will reign with Him. When we suffer in His Name, we receive the victory over Satan and his demons. God knows how much we can endure. God knows our endurance level. God knows our maximum capacity. God knows us.

STANDING IN THE NEED OF PRAYER

Job occupies a seat of misery and despair. He has complained about the cruelty of his friend's behavior. They have shown a lack of empathy while Job suffers in a pit of affliction. Job is so down on himself that the following scripture provides us with a small indication of Job's wide range of emotions:

> "He hath destroyed me on every side, and I am gone: and mine hope hath He removed like a tree" (Job 9:10).

Job is losing hope of a cure for his present illness. This is where a friend offers encouragement of a sincere nature. A true friend, noticing Job's anguish, would ask God in prayer for mercy:

> "Bless our friend with the power and will, Father, to endure and serve you according to your will. Father lift this burden from the shoulders of our friend. By doing so, it glorifies you Father. O' heavenly Father have mercy on Job; strengthen him to keep you near and that you will arrive on time. This we believe Father. In Jesus name, we pray. AMEN."

Society offers up a consistent question. Why do bad things happen to good people? Why do good people suffer and bad people appear to prosper in their wickedness? King Solomon, a man of great wisdom, stated that righteous people die all the time, some at a young age, and the wicked will live long with their wickedness, suffering throughout that period. Solomon encourages us to be godly in an ungodly world. Throughout his words of wisdom as he assesses daily living, he instructs us to use more than common sense in our travels through the turmoil of life, but take the divine perspective. "God overthroweth the wicked for their wickedness" (Proverbs 21:12). Remember, in the book of Genesis, Cain killed Abel, but God punished Cain for a long time, as a vagabond. Abel died young, but Cain lived a long life of pure misery (Genesis 4:12-14).

Jesus Christ provides us the best modern-day answer to the question of why certain people suffer in John 9:2, 3,

"Who sinned, this man or his parents, that he was born blind? Neither this man nor his parents sinned.... but this happened so that the work of God might be displayed in his life."

Christ's divine perspective reveals a higher understanding of the purposes of God. God wants His mighty works revealed to illustrate His mastery over all things in heaven and earth. All things are under the control and jurisdiction of God. All things in heaven and beneath heaven fall under the direction of God. Our suffering is under the full supervision of God. Isn't it satisfying to glorify God in all things? God is the Supreme Master over life. Even in our most dreaded affliction, God commands us to seek His power and authority and not dwell on the condition, but focus on the marvelous outcome God has in store for those who endure. Christ instructs us that all suffering is not a result of sin, but to manifest the overwhelming presence of God. This is the secret that's concealed in the mind of God.

God gives us grace. If you are chosen to carry the cross for Jesus, carry it with the supreme confidence that God will not let you fall, that God will restore and make you strong, firm and steadfast (I Peter 5:10). He will make you a living sacrifice for His glory. Never charge God foolishly about that which you do not understand. Maintain your faith in God. He knows the outcome is ALWAYS in his hands. In addition, we ALWAYS benefit from God's favor (gifts).

Do not be fooled by man and Satan's doctrine as to the type of person God is. God is Holy. God is our exalted Father, the Most High. There is no one higher than God. Remember one thing about life: "you always have a friend in Jesus."

Glory to God. Rejoice that the Most High is with us today. Praise God! Praise God! There is no one like our holy and sacred Father, a trusted Father as friend that we can ALWAYS count on to be there for us, no matter what the condition, situation or circumstance. ***God is on point.***

God is watching. Remember, Jesus Christ provides us with daily bread for our consumption. Develop an appetite to partake of the Lord's delicious food, as reflected in Mark 8:38,

> "Whosoever therefore shall be ashamed of me and of my words in this adulterous and sinful generation: of him also shall the Son of man be ashamed, when he cometh in the glory of his Father with the holy angels."

We need not be ashamed to know Christ. Through Christ all things are possible with His Father. We have a trustworthy friend in Jesus. Welcome the Most High back into your life. Do not take another breath without accepting Jesus Christ as your Savior. Establish a new friendship, a new divine relationship with God. Deny yourself and trust in our Lord and Savior. We must maintain our relationship, our friendship, our love, our faith, and our trust in God at all times. God is real. Reverence Him. Allow no man to advise you differently. Remember, if a man teaches contrary to God's commandments and covenants, he or she is teaching the "doctrine of devils." Do not get caught up in that cesspool of iniquity. "When you have nothing left but God, you become aware that God is enough" (Guideposts).

Through Job, Satan has accurately illustrated that he will DESTROY you if given the opportunity. Praise God for Job's illustration of how to maintain our integrity and character under the most troubling of conditions. Satan's mission is to inflict unbearable pain to persuade us to give up, to lose our faith and trust in the Most High. He will go to any extreme to inject pain. He is a creature without mercy and compassion. He is soulless. Deceit and confusion are parts of his awesome arsenal. The battle is not of flesh and blood; the war is of the spirit. As believers in the Word: "If we live in the Spirit, let us also walk in the Spirit" (Galatians 5:25).

When we labor for Christ, it is always a labor of love. In time, Christ will give us rest from our labor.

ILLUSTRATIONS OF GOD'S POWER

We have clear evidence of the destructive power of Satan. Therefore, we must not fall prey to his tactics. We cannot battle Satan alone, we need God. God is overpowering. God has the Holy Power to control and manage Satan. We do not want to serve Satan's agenda, only God's. Do not become a servant of sin. When suffering comes, and it will come, do not seek the outcome before the start of the mission. Simply, accept and trust in God that He will do us right, that He will be just, that He will not destroy us, but restore us to greatness and make us better than we were. Do Not Get Bitter, Get Better. Do not become the servant of sin. Do not be deceived when you are tempted with sin. Stop for a moment and ask yourself a question, "What would Jesus Christ do in this situation?" The answer is right at your door. The Spirit is talking to you. Listen to God. God is watching and listening. In addition, if anyone questions the power of God in this world, remember the following three examples that Jesus illustrated when he walked among us in the flesh. The first is from Matthew 8:24-27,

> "And, behold, there arose a great tempest in the sea, insomuch that the ship was covered with the waves but he was asleep. And his disciples came to him, and awoke him, saying, Lord, save us: we perish. And he said unto them, why are ye fearful, O ye of little faith? Then he arose, and rebuked the winds and the sea; and there was a great calm."

What did Christ show us when He rebuked the winds and the sea? The disciple's reaction in verse 27 places it all is perspective:

> "But the men marveled, saying, What manner of man is this, that even the winds and the sea obey him!"

The disciples were astonished by the power and authority of the Living God. Their question, "What manner of man is this?" reveals that the men had never witnessed anything like the power illustrated by Christ. They had never seen a man born of woman command the winds and sea to obey him. They witnessed a form of power that had never been demonstrated on earth. The disciples were convinced that Christ was truly the Son of the Most High.

The disciples witnessed the overwhelming power and authority of God. You have a decision to make. Do you serve God in heaven or the architect of sin, Satan? You cannot serve God and mammon (Mat. 6:24). Are you not in awe of this God, the only true God, and the God above all gods? What awesome power? We must fear the Son of Man.

"Seeing then that we have a great high priest, that is passed into the heavens, Jesus the Son of God, let us hold fast our profession" (Hebrews 4:14). Let us not be misled, Satan understands the power of the Living God and 'trembles.'

Another example of Jesus' marvelous work is illustrated in Matthew 9:35,

> "And Jesus went about all the cities and villages, teaching in their synagogues, and preaching the gospel of the kingdom, and healing every sickness and every disease among the people."

There is no limit to the power of our heavenly Father. There He is, curing every form of sickness and disease. Now you understand why Satan is jealous and hates our Father. This is great stuff to live by. Honor and glory to the Most High. Job need not question God, challenge God or demand an audience with God. God can heal any sickness or disease. Remember, Satan is not in the healing business, only the demolition business. God is a Carpenter, a Builder of strong men. There is no doubt this is the God we must serve.

In Matthew 14:25-31, a third example of the awesomeness of God's power is revealed:

> "And in the fourth watch of the night Jesus went unto them, walking on the sea. And when the disciples saw him walking on the sea, they were troubled, saying, It is a spirit; and they cried out for fear. But straightway Jesus spoke unto them, saying, Be of good cheer; it is I, be not afraid. And Peter answered him and said, Lord, if it be thou, bid me come unto thee on the water. And he said Come. And when Peter was come down out of the ship, he walked on the water, to go to Jesus. But when

he saw the wind boisterous, he was afraid; and beginning to sink, he cried, saying, Lord save me. And immediately Jesus stretched forth his hand, and caught him, and said unto him, O thou of little faith, wherefore didst thou doubt?"

The disciples witness another startling event in the life of Christ, walking on water. What matter of man is this? They had never seen a man walk on water. The mere thought of it was inconceivable. Peter was so moved by the event that he wanted to mimic Christ. He wanted to go to Christ. He attempted to mimic Christ and fell slightly short, but Christ was there with a helping hand.

We cannot permit ourselves to be defiled by false prophets, deceptively proclaiming the Kingdom of God. Jesus Christ is the true and only Son of the Most High. He died for us, so we can have a permanent relationship with His Father.

Our Lord and Savior have total command of all the elements. This is our God walking on water. Walking on water? Think about it. Who can compare to Him? Who can measure up to Him? Will you serve this God? We need not serve the evil master of wickedness. Our Father is the architect of "Goodness." There is none good but the Father. Notice that Peter had faith for a moment and walked on water. When he needed help, he cried out to Christ. There was our Father with an outstretched hand to help him make it. God always has his hand out to help us. We need not worry. God loves us in a special way. Notice how Jesus inquired of Peter "wherefore didst thou doubt?" In other words, "keep the faith." God is a living God, with all the power of the universe. Jesus is saying, "There is no need to fear. I am here. Do not lose faith in me. You can do as I do. Something greater than the temple is here."

Those were only three examples selected from the New Testament. Jesus Christ gave so many examples of his Father's power while on earth that it would take volumes to record. Jesus Christ also gave us the proper illustration of what a true friend does, "stretches forth his hand" to help a friend in need. Those are the ingredients of a true friend. Let us be more of a friend with one another, always remembering that our ultimate friend is God.

A FRIEND IN JESUS

The hymn that rang in my ears as a child still rings true today. The lyrics cried out, "What a friend we have in Jesus." Jesus reveals to us, "Ye are my friends, if ye do whatsoever I command you. Henceforth I call you not servants; for the servant knoweth not what his lord doeth: but I have called you friends; for all things that I have heard of my Father I have made known unto you"(John 15:14, 15).

Peace is with you and your friends. May the Lord add a blessing to the reading of his Holy word for the good, edification and sanctification of our souls. Thank you, Father, for being a special friend to us. Father, we will obey your command, as your way is the best way. Help us to be a true friend while our neighbor suffers according to your will. Father, have mercy on us. Teach us to reach out and help a friend in need. We recognize your Word is quick and powerful (Hebrews 4:12). Father, we come boldly before your throne of grace, that we may obtain mercy, and find grace to help in time of need (Hebrews 4:16). We will remain in good cheer and seek the covering of the blood of Christ when called upon to suffer in His Name. And when pain and suffering arrive on our doorstep, we will embrace it, knowing that your purposes are beyond our limited, human reasoning. We will trust that your arms will keep us safe and secure. That your mighty word will strengthen us and we will rejoice when the healing season comes. O Lord, our faith is with you. Let your tender mercies prevail. In Jesus' Name, we pray. AMEN.

CHAPTER 7

WISDOM FROM THE MOUTH OF BABES

*"To give subtlety to the simple,
to the young man knowledge and discretion"
– Proverbs I: 4*

It's often assumed that age brings about knowledge, understanding, and wisdom. Age does not constitute wisdom and understanding. Even elders can evaluate, judge, rationalize, and condemn falsely. The three elders visiting Job do not accurately illustrate a passion for mercy, compassion, and heartfelt understanding. Wisdom was lacking in their words. The elders Eliphaz the Temanite, Bildad the Shuhite, and Zophar the Naamathite are friends of Job. The elders were there to mourn and comfort him in his grief (Job 2:11). Instead, they become "miserable comforters" (Job 16:2).

The elders consistently pointed a righteous finger at Job. They wanted to press down on him as a hypocrite. They amplified his misery and fail to bring comfort to a wounded soul. While blood was pouring out of his wounds, the elders continued to inflict additional wounds through their communications. Can we see ourselves in Job's shoes? Can we see ourselves in the elders' shoes?

JOB'S CHALLENGE TO HIS FRIENDS

The impact of the elders' lack of sensitivity to Job's plight is revealed in Job 12:3,

> "But I have understanding as well as you: I am not inferior to you: yes, who knoweth not such things as these?"

Remember, when a friend is experiencing discomfort our prime mission is to show care; a sense of empathy. There must be an inner satisfaction in giving. This is not the time or place for judgment or condemnation. This is a time for the elders of the temple to point us to God. We must become cheerleaders of patience. It is not wise to torture an injured soul while they suffer in pain and sorrow. Job directs his frustration with his friends in Job 16:2-4,

> "I have heard many such things: miserable comforters are ye all. Shall vain words have an end? Or what emboldeneth thee that thou answerest? I also could speak as ye do: if your soul were in my soul's stead, I could keep up words against you, and shake mine head at you. My friends scorn me: but mine eye poweth out tears unto God."

Job continues to complain of his friends' cruelty in Job 19:2-5,

> "How long will ye vex my soul, and break me in pieces with words? These ten times have ye reproached me: ye are not ashamed that ye make yourselves strange to me. And be it indeed that I have erred, mine error remainth

with myself. If indeed ye will magnify yourselves against me, and plead against me my reproach."

Job is quite challenging to his three friends, who have arrived to comfort him during his hour of affliction. They fail to bring comfort, but offer up a plate of steaming conceit and condemnation. Job states that the elders "magnify yourselves against me." As the story unfolds, the Lord shows us how a friend should not be. How can we serve God, whom no man has seen, yet treat our neighbor inhumanly? Here is a servant of God in the midst of a mighty struggle between saint, serpent, and servant. Job's suffering is a mystery. And the elders fail to show "that the excellency of the power may be of God, and not of us" (II Corinthians 4:7). Job's friends lack true empathy, mercy, and compassion in their meeting. Job is in a pitiful state of mind. He has lost everything. His wife has requested that he deny God and die. His kinfolk have ignored him and his friends have forgotten him. He is an alien in the sight of his maids. Job receives no response when he calls upon his servants. Job's breath is strange to his wife. Young children despise him and speak against him. Those whom he loved have turned against him (Job 18:14-19).

The Book of Job is a perfect prescription for us today. Job's struggle and the elders righteous judgments of clear indicators of our unrighteous nature. We can visualize our own faults and righteous condemnation against each other. How often have you been stabbed in the back by a friend? How often have you been left out in the cold when you depended on someone to come through? When you needed support or encouragement, how did we feel when a friend promised but failed to deliver? What sparked an outcry when a friend failed to offer a crumb of comfort? All of us have been a witness to the crushing effects of criticism and backroom whispers.

But, the story of Job grants us a clear picture on how to perform an introspection of self and look to the heavens and attach ourselves to the "holiness of God." We are guilty of similar transgressions and fall short of the glory of God. Just like the elders, we need to change and encourage a wounded spirit to carry on. We need to offer up prayer for a troubled soul and devote ourselves to a higher cause. Galatians 6:2 says, "Bear ye one another's burdens and so fulfill the law of Christ."

Job cries out to his friends in Job 19:21,

> "Have pity upon me, have pity upon me, O' ye my friends: for the hand of God hath touched me."

Job wants an audience with God to pour out the good things he had accomplished in life, especially his commitment to the Lord. He wants to present his case to the ultimate Judge. In the midst of his misery, it should have been the duty of the elders to remind Job of the eternal mercy and love of God. Job reminded them that their words were breaking him into pieces. Job needed a sympathetic ear. When the friends failed to provide the comfort that he needed, his understanding returns and he recognizes that God is the only answer to his pity.

All of us are sinners and only Jesus Christ was sinless. Glorified is His name in heaven and earth. We must be careful what we ask for. If we demanded and audience with God, what would we say? Would we confront God? Would we submit a list of all the good works we had performed for others? Would we submit a financial report of our tithes and offerings to the church? Or would we become humble and submit to the divinity of God, crying with thanks and praises for the mercy and compassion He has shown?

SUBMITTING OURSELVES TO GOD

King David writes in Psalm 25:14, 15,

> "The secret of the Lord is with them that fear him; and
> he will show them his covenant. Look upon mine afflic-
> tion and my pain; and forgive all my sins."

As we suffer, our total focus should remain on our Savior; not on ourselves. We should maintain our confidence and faith in God throughout the ordeal. We place our focus on the tender mercies of God; stripping our mind of self is pivotal in the holy dimensions of God. God knows our hearts and rejects a heart filled with pride. When we submit to the power and authority of the Most High, we can now engage in a healthy discussion with God. Throughout the Old Testament God asks the question, "Can we reason together?" If God is willing to come off His mighty throne in heaven and visit with us for a conversation, it should reveal the true nature of the Holy One. God did not come down from heaven to condemn us. When He visited us for a season, He offered love and salvation. He healed the sick and shut-in. He raised the dead. He lifted up the heart of men. That's why it's important when we visit the sick or suffering, our heart should be a heart of meekness, kindness and gentleness, reflecting the likeness of Christ.

King David made it a daily ritual to exalt and magnify the Lord. Even in the midst of attack from the enemy he cried out to the Lord for strength and healing. We can feel the impact of David's faith and trust in the Lord in Psalm 30:1-5,

> "I will extol thee, O'Lord; for thou hast lifted me up, and
> hast not made my foes to rejoice over me. O'Lord my
> God, I cried unto thee, and thou hast healed me. O'Lord,

thou hast brought up my soul from the grave: thou hast kept me alive, that I should not go down to the pit. Sing unto the Lord, O ye saints of his, and give thanks at the remembrance of his holiness. For his anger endureth but a moment; in his favour is life: weeping may endure for a night, but joy cometh in the morning."

King David's example makes it clear that God will deliver us. We are all his children. The same God that delivered King David is the same God that will deliver Job and us today. Our God has not changed. Our God has a deep love for us. We must maintain our love, faith, and trust in Him.

Job and his three friends have questioned, made accusations, condemned, demanded, and challenged God. In most of their statements, there has been a lack of empathy and a refusal to submit to God's high principles and standards. We normally expect our elders to have a reasonable degree of knowledge, understanding and wisdom due to their age, experience, and general observations of the human condition. We expect them to deliver an honest and mature opinion regarding life's circumstances; however, that is not always true. Note what our Father's Son stated when He walked on earth in the flesh, as He praised and gave thanks to his Father in heaven for revealing the gospel to the simple, (Mat. 11:25):

"At that time Jesus answered and said, I thank thee, O Father, Lord of heaven and earth, because thou hast hid these things from the wise and prudent, and hast revealed them unto babes."

A BABE AMONG ELDERS

The babe among the elders, Elihu surfaced in a humbled fashion to address his elders and Job. The youth has listened attentively to their complaints and frequent acknowledgment of themselves, rather than God. He has observed their elevation of self and refusal to glorify the holy name of God. The elders had reached their limit in condemnation of Job. They are fed up as Job 32:1 reveals,

> "So these three men ceased to answer Job, because he was righteous in his own eyes."

Elihu speaks for God. He places the entire focus on the "divinity of God." The following scriptures regard the babe's observation of the elders' self-righteousness and condemnation of Job. It includes the elder's failure to praise God:

> "Thou was kindled the wrath of Elihu the son of Barachel the Buzite, of the kindred of Ram: against Job was his wrath kindled, because he justified himself rather than God. Also against his three friends was his wrath kindled, because they had found no answer, and yet had condemned Job" (Job 32:2-3)

Initially, Elihu followed tradition in his respect for his elders, because of his age. However, it became clear that wisdom does not necessarily come with age, as illustrated in verse 6:

> "And Elihu the son of Barachel the Buzite answered and said, I am young, and ye are very old; wherefore I was afraid, and durst not shew you mine opinion."

Elihu continues to educate the elders and Job regarding the essence of age and its relationship to wisdom. Age and experience should demonstrate wisdom, but that is not often the case. Elihu expounds in Job 32:7-9,

> "I said, Days should speak, and multitude of years should teach wisdom. But there is a spirit in man: and the inspiration of the Almighty giveth them understanding. Great man are not always wise: neither do the aged understand judgment."

Elihu's words are words of wisdom to Job and the elders. Elihu's words are godly-inspired. Elihu advises the men that a man's title and position are insignificant and to exalt a man would be foolish in the eyes of God. Elihu continues in Job 32:21, 22,

> "Let me not, I pray you, accept any man's person, neither let me give flattering titles unto man. For I know not to give flattering titles; in so doing my maker would soon take me away."

Elihu feared the wrath of God. He is firm in explaining that no man can measure up with the majesty of God and he would not look upon any man with favor. This young man illustrates a righteous demeanor that's not often found in men of his age. Elihu's opinions are accurate and filled with the spirit of the Lord. The elders and Job listen to the young man with amazement (Job 32:15).

ELIHU POINTS OUT THE ERROR OF HIS WAYS

In Job 34, Elihu charges Job with wrongly accusing God of injustice against him during his period of affliction. Elihu explains that God does not have to justify himself before man. God is free of errors or mistakes. God has never made a wrong choice. He points out that there is only one with righteousness, God. And in the shackles of affliction one can only look to the heavens for answers because God is righteous in all things. Elihu advises in Job 34:5,

> "For Job hath said, I am righteous: and God hath taken away my judgment."

Elihu is angry at Job's self-righteousness before the Father. Job is wrong to inquire that God is not listening or watching, simply because he has not responded to Job's demands. Elihu explains that God soars high and is a witness to all of man's doings. He explains in Job 34:21,

> "For his eyes are upon the ways of man, and he seeth all his goings."

God is everywhere. Although your neighbor may not know what you do in darkness, God knows. We cannot hide our sins from God. God will expose sin to the light as he explains in the following scripture:

> "There is no darkness, nor shadow of death, where the workers of iniquity may hide themselves" (Job 34:22).

Elihu advises them that no man can expound upon his earthly works to God and expect favor. How can man elevate himself regarding his "good works"? God will strike such wickedness down. He will destroy it because it is baseless. Man fails in not following God's way of life. Elihu confronts Job further regarding his lack of understanding of the ways of the Lord:

> "Job hath spoken without knowledge, and his words were without wisdom. My desire is that Job may be tried unto the end because of his answers for wicked

men. For he addeth rebellion unto his sin, he clappeth his hands among us, and multiplieth his words against God" (Job 34:35-37).

Elihu reveals that we must be extremely careful what we say to God. Do we want to add rebellion unto our sin? Do we want to multiply our words against God? God is always watching and listening. God does not need a rest. He is in tune to us. In addition, God does not enjoy hearing His name used inappropriately, especially from a lack of knowledge and understanding. Remember, King David said the first step to wisdom is to fear God. The Son of God was in constant praise to His Father. Jesus Christ never elevated himself over His Father before man. He was humble and in constant submission to His Father. Jesus Christ never challenged his Father. He elevated his Father by always denying himself. Christ often spoke that his Father would receive the glory through the works of the Son.

Jesus Christ states in Matthew 10:38,

"And he that taketh not his cross, and followeth after me, is not worthy of me."

We are not worthy or deserving of God's blessings. It is only through His grace that we stand. We cannot bargain with God. God is holy. We are sinners. There is no comparison. But, through God's grace and the sacrifice of His Son, we can achieve perfection through the One who is truly Prefect, the Son of the Most High. When we place our full faith and trust in God, knowing that the outcome will be in His favor, we set the foundation for His grace to shower down from heaven like a storm.

JOB'S VANITY REVEALED

Is there a sniff of vanity in Job? Elihu strongly questions Job about his lack of understanding regarding the holy mind of God in Job 35:13-16,

> "Surely God will not hear vanity, neither will the Almighty regard it. Therefore doth Job open his mouth in vain; he multiplieth words without knowledge."

Here, Elihu points out clearly to Job that his vain remarks will be met with quietness from the Lord, that God will not hear vain statements based on self-praise or self-admiration. We cannot make ourselves the center of anything. God is the centerpiece of all things on earth and in heaven. Elihu advises that God will turn His ear away from vanity. Man is not in a position to elevate himself. Any elevation from man is similar to the swollen ego of Lucifer when he desired to be like the Most High. His pride sent him to the bottomless pit for eternity. Remember, Jesus Christ said, "deny yourself" first. When we seek the Supremacy of God first, we place our misery in a position to be heard by the mighty ear of the Lord. There is nothing in this life or life to come more important than God. We love our children, but they cannot come before God. We love our parents, but they cannot come before God. Our love for our jobs cannot come before God. Christ makes an important point in the universal system of the Kingdom of God in Matthew 10:37,

> "He that loveth father or mother more than me is not worthy of me: and he that loveth son or daughter more than me is not worthy of me."

Everything in heaven and beneath heaven was created from the hands of the Almighty. We cannot place anything created by God for our pleasure above Him. God is a jealous God and for any person to prop himself up in vanity is a violation of the commandments of God.

Elihu continues to bless and honor God's work. Elihu acknowledges God's strength, knowledge and wisdom in Job 36:3-5,

> "I will fetch my knowledge from afar, and will ascribe righteousness to my Maker. For truly my words shall not be false: he that is perfect in knowledge is with thee. Behold, God is mighty, and despiseth not any: he is mighty in strength and wisdom."

OBEY GOD'S COMANDMENTS

Elihu reveals the necessities for a life eternal in the Kingdom of God in Job 36:11, 12,

> "If they obey and serve him, they shall spend their days in prosperity, and their years in pleasure. But if they obey not, they shall perish by the sword, and they shall die without knowledge."

Those of us that obey God's commandments and covenants will have a life of abundance. Those that disobey and fail to serve God will die without receiving full knowledge of the Kingdom of God. They will perish without reaching the apogee of God's complete knowledge.

Every person has a choice to make. Obey God or follow the doctrine of devils. Do we fear the wrath of our Savior? Will we carry the cross for God when called to serve? Is man's law more important than God's law? When God puts us to the test will we do like Abraham and be prepared to sacrifice our son at the request of God? When affliction visits, will we complete the mission that God has for us? On the other hand, will we quit and seek out the devils doctrine of suicide, assisted-suicide, euthanasia, or mercy killing? God does not place us in a position to quit. Remember that the physicalness of our affliction cannot destroy our spirit. We must elevate our thinking. God is spirit. We do not want to live in this dusty body forever. Let this body return to the earth from which it came. We do not need it. It is not as important as the spirit within. We want to embrace the spiritual things of life. We want to gain the full knowledge of the Kingdom of God. Let us remember and accept what our Savior, Jesus Christ, said in Matthew 10:28,

> "And fear not them which kill the body, but are not able to kill the soul: but rather fear him which is able to destroy both soul and body in hell."

Remember God is BEAUTIFUL in every department. God should be feared, due to the great blessings He has showered upon us. He demonstrated His eternal love by sacrificing His Only Son on the Cross. We need not know every secret of God. Whatever God allows us to know, we should be pleased and thankful because God knows what we need to know and when we should know it. But, for those who follow Christ, every mystery will be revealed in due season. Let us not be like Job and speak on areas in which we have absolutely no knowledge. It's not wise of us to speculate in areas where our knowledge is limited or non-existent:

> "Touching the Almighty, we cannot find him out: he is excellent in power, and in judgment, and in plenty of justice: he will not afflict." (Job 37:23).

"God will not afflict." God is for us. He will protect us from harm. "For no one can anticipate the time of disaster" (Ecclesiastes 9:11). If danger surfaces, God is equipped with the power to handle it. If we place our attention or focus on the suffering, we will lose. But, when we maintain our focus on heaven in the midst of our suffering, we gain wisdom and our calamity becomes secondary to the glory of God. God is excellent in power and judgment, as noted in Job 37:5,

> "God thundereth marvelously with his voice; great things doeth he, which we cannot comprehend."

Praise God! God's servant, Elihu, has delivered the perfect message to Job and the elders Eliphaz, Bildad and Zophar. God will deal with each one when He appears on the premises. We will believe and trust that, "No one will curse God to his face." Believe, trust, and have faith in God and we will learn and gain knowledge and wisdom with understanding.

We cannot make the mistake that Adam and Eve made in the Book of Genesis. The serpent led Eve to believe that knowledge would be gained by eating the fruit from the forbidden tree. God said, "ye shall not eat of it, neither shall ye touch it, lest ye die" (Gen. 3:3). Did Adam or Eve gain knowledge or wisdom as the serpent had promised? Adam and Eve failed the test. They did not receive the full lesson from God. Their disobedience got them kicked out of the Garden of Eden. Their actions set the stage for God's ultimate blueprint for man. Adam and Eve received a strong judgment from God, along with Satan. As a result, man was separated from God.

We fail when we rely on human knowledge and reasoning. We fail when we rely on human intellect. God knew we needed a Savior and He laid out a plan of action to return man to his rightful place. The prophets of old did not fully comprehend the plan. Satan did not understand the plan. No one understood the secret, the mystery. The blueprint was established prior to creation of the world. This was done through the marvelous mind of God. God made up His mind to send a Savior into the world to save man. He sent a babe from the womb of the Virgin Mary named Jesus, the Christ. Christ paid the ransom and saved the lost. This babe's death, burial, and resurrection fulfill the divine perspective of God that was preordained prior to creation. This is our glorious inheritance that awaits us in heaven. Praise God! AMEN.

CHAPTER 8

THE HIGH TOWERING PRESENCE OF GOD

Towering Presence of God
"For the Lord is great, and greatly
to be praised, he is to be feared above all gods."
– Psalms 96:4

How do you measure God? Are there any man-made instruments to provide an adequate indication of the power of God? How do we measure the will of God? How do we measure the 'love' of God? How do we measure the mercy or compassion of God? How do we measure the 'grace' of God? Is there one among us, dead or alive, that can be an effective judge of God? Is there an effective evaluator of God? Some of you may nominate Moses, Isaiah, Elijah, Apostle Paul, Noah, King David, Abraham, or the great psychotherapist C. L. Jung, or, perhaps, our upright and perfect servant Job? We could go on and on and include many modern-day evangelists, preachers, rabbi, bishops or popes in the above list. Who is duly qualified to judge God? Can God's only Son, Jesus Christ, and the only non-sinner that ever lived on this earth, one with the Father, be the ultimate judge of God? We encourage you to think about this now. All of the men of the bible were great men, sent here to fulfill a specific objective for our Lord and savior. But, who is equipped to measure God? Who can stand before God and say, "Father you have wronged this man Job. You made a mistake. God you need to rethink this situation here. God, maybe you need to take a break and re-evaluate your status as God." These are challenging questions to place before the Almighty. Who will make those utterances? Who will step forward and judge God?

In John 8:15, 16, 18 Christ speaks to the Pharisees regarding his Father's doctrine:

> "Ye judge after the flesh; I judge no man. And yet if I judge, my judgment is true: for I am not alone, but I and the Father that sent me. I am one that bear witness of myself, and the Father that sent me beareth witness of me."

Jesus Christ continues to reveal the teaching of His Father. Christ is in a position to judge man, but due to the mission His Father sent Him to perform; He reframes from judging man and elevates the wisdom of His Father. In John 8:26 Christ reveals,

> "I have many things to say and to judge of you, but he that sent me is true; and I speak to the world those things which I have heard of him."

Christ was always lifting up His Father. He gave His Father credit for everything. He is God's only Son speaking the things that his Father taught him. In other words, Jesus Christ is repeating the things "which I have heard of him."

Jesus Christ exalts his Father in Heaven by denying self. This is the example we must follow on behalf of the Father. We must deny self and carry the cross for Christ.

Jesus acknowledges in Verse 15 that man "judges after the flesh." Man is unequipped and unqualified to be an evaluator, or a judge of God. This clearly means: "No man can judge God."

WHO CAN JUDGE THE FATHER?

Is the Son greater than the Father? Is the Son holier than the Father? Can the Creator be less than what He has created? We may marvel at the things God created throughout the universe–the stars, planets, moons, and earth. We may be impressed with all that God created in the heavens. But, none of it measures up to God. None of the wonders in the heavens can be exalted over God. Remember, God reigns over all things. Nothing can compete with God. There is no challenge to God. There is no comparison to God. God is God. Our heavenly Father is so sacred and holy that we simply cannot picture it in our own minds. It is difficult to express in any human terms. We gain wisdom by listening to the One that has been in the presence of God, who can repeat verbatim God's exact words. That person is his Son, Jesus Christ. As we have noted, Jesus Christ elevated His Father. Christ humbled himself and praised His Father. Jesus Christ always looked up to His Father for all things.

Christ continues to elevate the supreme importance of His Father. He elevates and magnifies Him. He describes who sent Him and how He desires to please His Father:

> "Then said Jesus unto them, when ye have lifted up the
> Son of man, then shall ye know that I am he, and that I
> do nothing of myself, but as my Father hath taught me, I

speak these things. And he that sent me is with me, the Father hath not left me alone; for I do always those things that please him" (John 7:28-29).

Christ's mission was in "pleasing his Father." He exhibited total dedication to completing the mission his Father sent him to do. Therefore, knowing that Jesus Christ was without sin, does this qualify him as the ultimate judge of God? The Godhead consist of three Members: the Father, Son, and Holy Spirit. They function as one within 3 separate parts. This connection is beyond human comprehension. It is a mystery. Yet, no one in heaven or beneath heaven is in a position to judge God. God is above all. This is not lowering Christ. He and the Father are one. They are one in accord on all matters. Christ is seated on the right hand of the Father with full power and authority. Remember, the son is never greater than the father. Christ said that only His Father was "good." When we assemble all the facts and mediate on the scriptures, we can safely conclude that God is God and no being made by God can judge Him.

JESUS EXALTS THE FATHER

In John 8:54; Jesus Christ continues to honor his Father in heaven in deed and in words.

> "Jesus answered, If I honour myself, my honour is nothing: it is my Father that honoureth me; of whom ye say that he is your God."

Jesus Christ continues to exalt his Father and their sacred relationship in John 10:25, 29-30, 32, 37-38,

"Jesus answered them, I told you, and ye believed not: The works that I do in my Fathers name, they bear witness of me. My Father, which gave them me, is greater than all; and no man is able to pluck them out of my Father's hand. I and my Father are one. Jesus answered them, Many good works have I showed you from my Father; for which of those works do ye stone me? If I do not the works of my Father, believe me not. But if I do, though ye believe not me believe the works: that ye may know, and believe, that the Father is in me, and I in him."

Prior to raising Lazarus from the dead, Jesus thanks His Father and acknowledges Him before the people:

"Father, I thank thee that thou hast heard me. And I know that thou hearest me always: but because of the people which stand by I said it, that they may believe that thou hast sent me" (John 11:41-42).

Jesus Christ continues to exalt his Father and their relationship. Jesus humbles himself and states the following:

"Ye have heard how I said unto you, I go away, and come again unto you. If ye loved me, ye would rejoice, because I said, I go unto the Father: for my Father is greater than I" (John 14:28).

Jesus Christ acknowledges that the Father is greater than the Son. There is no argument here regarding the relative status of the Son and Father. There is no confusion on the subject. Jesus honored His Father. Christ was never disobedient and never worked against his Father. He fully supported the mission of His Father, frequenting exalting Him before man. God was pleased with His good and faithful servant. God is glorified and magnified through the Son.

There is no other person living, dead, or yet to be born that can advise us better on God than his perfect Son, Jesus Christ. Jesus Christ has sat in the presence of the Father. He has listened and absorbed the full teaching of His Father. There is no better example regarding the holiness, power, will, and towering presence of God than the examples set by the Son of God. If we believe in God, we are required to believe in Jesus Christ. There is no separation; God and the Son are one. Jesus speaks in John 14:1,

> "Let not your heart be troubled: ye believe in God, believe also in me."

The Son of Man clearly states that He and God are on the same page. There are those in our midst today that may advise that we do not need Jesus Christ. There are those that say Jesus Christ does not exist; Jesus Christ is dead; Jesus Christ has never been on earth for a time, or my God would never die on a cross. The fairy tales go on and on about our Lord and Savior.

Nevertheless, I state clearly for the record that Jesus Christ is our Savior. The biblical scriptures provide us with more than sufficient eyewitness evidence and testimony. There are eye witness accounts that Jesus Christ preached the gospel according to his Father, healed the sick, died on the cross and was resurrected on the third day as prophesized. Jesus Christ went into Satan's den, preached the gospel, and received Victory over the grave. Jesus Christ ascended into heaven where He sits on the right hand of the Father. He continues His presence in our daily lives, rescuing us from the fangs of the devil. Christ in us is greater than he who is in the world.

There are intellectuals and scholars that proclaim that believing in Christ is nonsense. I encourage doubters to pray and read the scriptures on their own to establish a personal relationship with

Christ. Jesus Christ was perfect in every way. **He was sin-free**. Just like God, his Son cannot lie or fabricate a story. In John 14:6 Christ reveals His position:

> "Jesus said unto him, I am the way, the truth, and the life: no man cometh unto the Father, but by me."

When we meditate over the latter verse from Christ, we find out that the only way to God is through Jesus Christ. This is a powerful and commanding verse. Jesus makes it crystal clear that His way is the only way. The only way to the Father is through the Son. The Son has laid it out on the record, without hesitation. The order is there. The command has been voiced. How can you challenge such a statement? Anyone preaching contrary to this doctrine is preaching the doctrine of the Anti-Christ. Do not be fooled by the earthly doctrine of identifying with the universe in order to get to God. The scriptures are clear; Jesus Christ is the only answer. Christ has paved the way for us to return to the Father. We cannot permit Satan to persuade us that Christ remains in some unmarked grave. Jesus Christ paid the price and qualified himself to make such a statement. God has given him the power. We have salvation because of one person, Jesus Christ. You have a decision to make on how you will live your life.

This same Jesus Christ was there with God when He created the world. This identical Jesus Christ made the first man, Adam, in His image. This same Jesus was with Noah at the destruction of this world by water. This same Jesus Christ guided man and the Jews out of bondage and into the Promised Land. This same Jesus Christ is the Father of Abraham, Isaac, and Jacob. This is the same Jesus Christ that will return to rid this world of sin and firmly establish His Kingdom on earth.

GOD IS SPIRIT

Jesus Christ was overseeing the struggle of Job yet His presence was not revealed. Christ was part of the decision-making possess in lifting the trials and tribulations from Job. Job does not give up His search for God. He cries out to be in the presence of God, to sit at His footstool to justify himself at the throne of grace. Job desires to present his case before the Judge of man. In Job 23:3, he cries,

> "Oh that I knew where I might find him! that I might come even to his seat!"

Job continues, in verses 4-6 on how he would present his case before God; namely, that he is innocent of all charges and acknowledges God's great power and his own weakness.

> "I would order my cause before him, and fill my mouth with arguments. I would know the words which he would answer me, and understand what he would say unto me. Will he plead against me with his great power? No; but he would put strength in me."

I find the most important argument in Job's decree to be, "he would put strength in me." That point registers stronger than any other comment by Job. Even in his misery he acknowledges that God will provide strength. In each passage of scripture Job continues to grow. Every statement signals out his request to meet with God. He maintains his focus on God. His arguments may be on the edge of collapsing, due to the pain and suffering; he proves he is not a quitter and will not give up without an audience with the Father.

King David was always seeking an audience with God. He was after the heart of God. When King David fell short of the glory of God, he returned to the source of all fulfillments in life, God. He searched the hills for His Father. David writes in Psalm 103:3, 4,

> "Who forgiveth all thine iniquities; who healeth all thy diseases. Who redeemeth thy life from destruction; who crowneth thee with loving kindness and tender mercies."

Job searches far and near for the Lord. He does not give up as he continues in Job 23:8, 9,

> "I go forward, but he is not there; and backward, but I cannot perceive him. On the left hand, where he doth work, but I cannot behold him: he hideth himself on the right hand, that I cannot see him."

How often do we misinterpret God's presence because He is silent? In the Book of Esther God is silent, quiet throughout the story, but His Almighty presence is felt throughout. This is the marvelous work that God performs with us. Of course, we would love to sit down at the table and break bread with God and discuss our problems, like Moses did in the tent. But, God does not need to reveal Himself physically in order for us to know that He is there. God reveals His power and authority through man in many different ways. His mighty hand continues to direct all situations in heaven and earth. For the believer, the presence of God is known and cannot be disputed. This invisible God is "in-tune" to all activity in heaven and earth. God is on full alert; constantly watching, listening and seeking out those that are worthy of His kingdom. Job acknowledges the wisdom and understanding of God in Job 23:10,

> "But he kneweth the way that I take, when he hath tried me, I shall come forth as gold."

Job exhibits wisdom in Job 23:15, 16, relative to his fear of God:

"Therefore am I troubled at his presence: when I consider, I am afraid of him. For God maketh my heart soft and the Almighty troubleth me:"

King David spoke clearly and profoundly in Psalm 25:14 regarding fear of the Lord:

"The secret of the Lord **is** with them that fear him; and he will show them his covenant."

When King David was afflicted and his heart swollen in trouble, he placed his confidence in *prayer* to God. Psalm 25:15-21 says,

"Mine eyes are ever toward the Lord; for he shall pluck my feet out of the net: turn thee unto me, and have mercy upon me; for I am desolate and afflicted. The troubles of my heart are enlarged: O bring thou me out of my distresses. Look upon mine affliction and my pain; and forgive my sins. Consider mine enemies; for they are many; and they hate me with cruel hatred. O keep my soul, and deliver me: let me not be ashamed; for I put my trust in thee. Let integrity and uprightness preserve me: for I wait on thee."

GOD'S HIGH-TOWERING PRESENCE

King David knew the right direction to go and all of us can learn by his example.

In King David's Psalms, we read scripture that will empower and strengthen us. As servants of Christ, the foundation of everything in our lives rest on the shoulders of Jesus Christ, the Just One. We lived a life of defeat at the hands of the enemy prior to the arrival of Jesus

Christ. Our blessed hope was restored through the birth, death, and resurrection of Jesus Christ. Even the prophets of old acknowledged that one was coming to save the world from the darts of our chief Adversary. The high-towering presence of God was revealed in Jesus Christ.

When we speak of God and His high-towering presence, we must acknowledge that God is exalted above all things; that God can only participate in "goodness." Also, God's word is perfect, clearly understood, never wrong, accurate 100% of the time, and un-challenged throughout time. King David writes about the purity of God in Psalm 33:4, 5,

> "For the word of the Lord is right; and all his works are done in truth. He loveth righteousness and judgment: the earth is full of the goodness of the Lord."

God is perfect. King David gives us clear words to guide us through life and how to exalt our holy Father. God is not prone to error. How can man measure up to such righteousness? How can man challenge God's truthfulness? We are so unjust, so unfair with one another that our behavior erodes at God's principles. We are poison, as compared to God's holy doctrine. King David acknowledges that, throughout the earth, the goodness of the Lord is evident in full form. We continue to settle for the lower position of life. This is the evil and wickedness of life: the belly of life rather than the high principles sent down by our glorified Father. Be joyful in our Lord.

After his affliction -- and in spite of his physical ailments -- Job continued, a consistent forum of praising God and recording his own good works throughout his life. He reminds us of his days of prosperity, integrity and uprightness. Job expounds on his philosophies about death and the grave. He is confident in God's mercy, the 'uncharitable spirit' of Bildad, and his own honor.

O MAJESTY OF GOD!

When we walk in sin, we track in a pathway of unrighteousness. Sin is a "cesspool of iniquity." God hates sin and all its devices. God is a righteous God. He is a God of Supreme Holiness. Only God is Holy.

When our feet are muddled in unrighteousness, we become unclean. We become a dwelling place for the spirit of demons. God cannot reside in the same residence as Satan. Any dwelling occupied by the devil, the occupant becomes a member of the Synagogue of Satan. He no longer belongs to the Church of Christ. Satan shouts with a howl every time a sinner embraces his tactics, techniques, tools, and devices. He craftfully designs these instruments to attack man and bring him down to a subterranean level. But, when a sinner is restored into the Body of Christ, the angels in heaven leap and shout with joy and their heavenly voices sing the Songs of Moses.

God is a patient God. He designed patience. And Job is an beautiful illustration of God's patience with us. But, God has a limit. His wrath can be immediate if He so desires. His punishment can be swift and severe. God will destroy a nation in order for us to recognize that the source of ALL power rests in Him. And He will save an entire nation from His wrath on the back of one righteous person. Do we re-call God's destruction of Sodom and Gomorrah? God showed His authority and Almighty power in the destruction of those cities. Satan has power but he does not have almighty power. He is limited by the almighty hand of God.

God will give us warnings. And when the warnings come we must be prepared to REPENT under the blessed footstool of Jesus

Christ. Christ will speak up and stand up on our behalf when we follow Him. God will show mercy and compassion for any sinner that accepts Jesus Christ as their savior and repents of their sins. God promises forgiveness of sins and eternal life with Him to all who receive, by grace through faith, Jesus Christ as Savior (John 1:12; John 3:16; Acts 16;31). Christ redeemed us from the Law. All power and authority rest with Christ. Colossians 2:8 says, "Beware lest any man spoil you through philosophy and vain deceit, after the tradition of men, after the rudiments of the world, and after Christ." The Apostle Paul says, "But we believe that through the grace of the Lord Jesus Christ we shall be saved, even as they" (Acts 15:11). While Paul was in prison the Philippian jailer inquired, "What must I do to be saved?" Paul replied, "Believe on the Lord Jesus Christ, and thou shalt be saved, and thy house" (Acts 16:30, 31).

Are we prepared to meet God? In the book of Amos, God sent many plagues to get the peoples attention. The people rejected every warning sent by God. God sent famine, drought, death and destruction and the people refused to worship the Lord. Greed and injustice was running rampant throughout the land. True worship was ignored and false religions grew and the presence of God was dismissed across the land. The prophet Amos warns the people that divine justice would soon come. Amos warns, "The Lord God hath sworn by his holiness, that, lo, the days shall come upon you, that he will take you away with hooks, and your posterity with fishhooks" (Amos 4:2). Amos gives a strong warning to the people that the day of reckoning will soon arrive if they do not repent of their transgressions. God reaches an ultimate point: "Therefore thus I will do to you, O Israel, because I will do this unto you, prepare to meet your God O Israel" (Amos 4:12). The tone in which the Lord announces the warning provokes fear. God continues, "Behold, the eyes of the Lord

God are upon the sinful kingdom, and I will destroy it from off the face of the earth" (Amos 9:8). The mere statement has a chilling effect. In the end, God's "tender mercies" shine through. After releasing His anger upon the sinners, God says, "And I will bring again the captivity of my people of Israel, and they shall build the waste cities, and inhabit them; and they shall plant vineyards, and drink the wine thereof" (Amos 9:14). God is always "reminded" of His eternal love for His people. He turns an awful situation into a land of milk and honey.

We know what sin resembles. We have tasted its bitter fruits. But, when we tasted the sweet fruit from the "vine of the Lamb" we became new creatures under the covenant of God. The "blood of the Lamb," cleansed us. We cannot forget or limit the impact of Christ's beautiful work on the Cross. His sacrifice delivered us from the shackles of hell. We must continue our strengthening in the Word of God, praying and fasting for deliverance from temptation. Let us put on the helmet of salvation and the breastplate of faith. Now, we are properly armored to resist the darts of the enemy.

When God commanded Job to gird up his loins like a man, He questioned him regarding his limited knowledge and understanding of heavenly and earthly matters. Job did not have the answers. God makes a pivotal point in Job 40:10, "Deck thyself now with majesty and excellency; and array thyself with glory and beauty."

Let us continue to shout praises to the Most High. Let us embrace the workings of Christ like no other period in history. When we keep our focus up high and not below, we begin to recognize the steadfast love our God, through Christ Jesus. O Majesty of God!

WHY NOT ME?

Job reflects on his works during his days of prosperity in Job 29:12, 13, 15, 16, 21, 25,

> "Because I delivered the poor that cried, And the fatherless, and him that had none to help him. The blessing of him that was ready to perish came upon me: and I caused the widow's heart to sing for joy. I was eyes to the blind, and feet was I for the lame. I was a father to the poor: and the cause which I knew not I searched out. Unto me men gave ear, and waited, and kept silence at my counsel. I chose out their way, and sat chief, and dwelt as a king in the army, as one that comforteth the mourners."

Job proclaims his compassion for the poor in Job 30:25,

> "Did not I weep for him that was in trouble? Was not my soul grieved for the poor?"

Job references his works at the seat of judgment. He makes it clear that he never ignored the poor, that he gave sound advice to those in needs. Job points out that he has been upright throughout his life. Job stands firm about his integrity and character. Although Job cannot locate God, God is watching and listening. Job feels the Lord has neglected him. He laments in Job 30:20,

> "I cry unto thee, and thou dost not hear me: I stand up, and thou regardest me not."

Quietness makes a pointed impact on us when we are in the pit of suffering. But, does Job speak truth about God? He responds as any of us would response while in the midst of a destructive surgical procedure performed by the hands of the enemy. Job is crying out to the Lord. Being in a state of misery can make a dramatic impression on how we perceive God. We desire His immediate attention and God will often times sit on His throne of glory and watch and listen. He will decide when to lend an ear to our cry. In Job's case, he wants to feel the presence of the Lord. He is not rejecting the Lord. He wants an audience with God to present his case for release from the shackles of hell. God will respond, but only on His time. God's appearance is perfect timing. God is never late; He is always on His time.

Job continues to cry out in Job 31:4,

> "Doth not he see my ways, and count all my steps?"

God's appearance draws near. Job has been demanding a direct conversation with the ultimate Judge. Job has related that he has prepared his case for a formal presentation before the Lord. Let us tune in to his questions in Job 31:14,

> "What then shall I do when God riseth up? and when he visiteth, what shall I answer him?"

We must be careful what we ask for. Here Job questions himself. How would we perform in the presence of the Living God? Would we confront Him about His judgments?

FIRST STEP TOWARDS REDEMPTION

In order to prepare properly for God's holy entrance onto Job's premises, let us examine the words of King David in his magnificence description of God's majesty, power, grace and strength in Psalm 33: 6-9, 18-20,

"By the word of the Lord were the heavens made; and all the host of them by the breath of his mouth. He gathered the waters of the sea together as a heap: he layeth up the depth in storehouses. Let all the earth fear the Lord: let all the inhabitants of the world stand in awe of him. For he spoke, and it was done; he commanded, and it stood fast. Behold, the eye of the Lord is upon them that fear him, upon them that hope is his mercy; To deliver their soul from death, and to keep them alive in famine. Our soul waiteth for the Lord: he is our help and our shield."

GOD CONFRONTS JOB

David presents a clear case on the power and will of God. Words fail to express all the loveliness our Savior possesses. Ready yourself for the appearance of Our Lord through a whirlwind. God performs delicate surgery on Job's lack of knowledge in heavenly and earthly matters.

God has set on His throne of glory in heaven and watched and listened to all the participants in the Job saga. God is a patient and merciful God. He has His own agenda and will set His schedule according to His own testament. Neither man nor Satan can tempt or influence God.

God appears on the premises in the form of a whirlwind to confront Job about this new found knowledge and understanding. God will confront the servant that wished he had died in the womb of his mother. God heard every single word. On the Day of Judgment we have to give an accounting of every word and action undertaken by us while on earth. God states the following to the prophet Jeremiah in Jeremiah 1:5, "Before I formed thee in the belly I knew thee; and before thou comest forth out of the womb I sanctified thee, and I ordained thee a prophet unto the nations." Our God is supremely knowledgeable, full of understanding and wisdom. There is much spiritual depth to God's statement to Jeremiah. "God knew us before we were formed in the belly." If we existed in the mind of God, we had life. We have to remember from where we originated. How can we destroy what God knew prior to being born? We should follow the lessons of our Teacher.

In Isaiah 66:1, "Thus saith the Lord, the heaven is my throne, and the earth is my footstool: where is the house that ye build unto me? And where is the place of my rest." When this BIG GOD steps on the premises and speaks, we "Hear the word of the Lord, ye that tremble at his word...let the Lord be glorified" (Isaiah 66:5). King David states in Psalm 93:1, "The Lord reigneth, he is clothed with majesty; the Lord is clothed with strength, wherewith he hath girded himself: the world also is established, that it cannot be moved."

Psalm 97:9 says, "For the Lord art high above all the earth: thou art exalted for above all gods." Psalm 100:3 continues, "Know ye that the Lord he is God: it is he that hath made us, and not we ourselves; we are his people, and the sheep of his pasture.

David understood the majesty, beauty, and power of God. He was a humble servant of God and wrote songs of praise to the Almighty. This is the Lord God Almighty that confronts the upright and perfect servant, Job.

God immediately challenges Job to answer a number of questions. Job continuously fails each lesson. God reveals the beautiful wonders that only He has the power to perform. God questions, "Who is this that darkeneth counsel by words without knowledge?"(Job 38:2). God commands Job to, "Gird up now thy lions like a man; for I will demand of thee, and answer thou me" (Job

38:3). God is not in a playing games mood. He is serious about His mission.

God questions Job at great length throughout Chapters 38-40. God inquires about Job's whereabouts in Job 38:4-6, "Where wast thou when I laid the foundations of the earth? Declare, if thou has understanding? Or who hath laid the measures thereof if thou knowest? Or who hath stretched the line upon it? Whereupon are the foundations thereof fastened? Or who laid the cornerstone thereof."

We cannot match wits with God. We are totally incompetent in the presence of the Almighty. If Job could not correctly answer God's first question, would he have knowledge of anything else?

Job responds, "Behold, I am vile; what shall I answer thee? I will lay mine hand upon my mouth. Once have I spoken; but I will not answer: yea, twice; but I will proceed no further" (Job 40:4, 5). God continues a blistering interrogation of Job, chiseling away at his lack of knowledge. Job responds, "I know that thou canst do; every thing, and that no thought can be withholden from thee, who is he that hideth counsel without knowledge? Therefore, have I uttered that I understood not; things too wonderful for me, which I know not" (Job 42:2, 3).

Job is humbled before the Lord. He acknowledges his lack of understanding and knowledge. He recognizes that God has too many wonderful achievements that he has absolutely no comprehension of.

Job makes his most pivotal statement to God in Job 42:6, "Wherefore, I abhor myself, and repent in dust and ashes." At this stage, Job has completely submitted to the Lord. Now, he can be reconstructed by the Holy Architect into the being that God commands. God commands that we humble and submit to him in dust and ashes. This is seeking forgiveness at the lowest point of human dignity. God does not command us to kneel before man or any other idol. God commands that we bow in humble submission to Him.

The words in I Peter 5:6, "Humble yourselves therefore under the mighty hand of God, that he may exalt you in due time." Peter continues in verse 7, "Casting all your cares upon him; for he careth for you."

God rewards Job with "more than his beginning" (Job 42:12). God is a just God. When we are obedient to God, we will prosper in due season according to his will and grace. It is important that we only serve God. God gives us the grace and power to persevere.

Life is not always the way we imagine. Job trusted in God even at his lowest point. God awakens Job to a new horizon based on His judgment. We are secure in the fact that God is never wrong, never needs correction, and His tests are perfect. What is your testimony? Can you pass the test? If the test is unclear to you, will you trust in Him?

God instructs the elders to go to Job and offer up a burnt offering and "my servant Job shall pray for you: for him will I accept." Note these words from God "I deal with you after your folly, in that ye have not spoken of me the thing which is right, like my servant Job" (Job 42:8). The elders did as God commanded.

Throughout Job's ordeal "no one prayed for him." God commands that "Job will pray for you" (Job 42:8). This is the first time prayer is mentioned. We are reminded that we must pray for forgiveness, strength, mercy, and hope when pain, sorrow, and suffering arrives. Prayer changes things. Remember, the prayer of Job lifted the wrath from Eliphaz the Temanite, Bildad the Shuhite and Zophar the Naamathe.

"If any man speak, let him speak as the oracles of God; if any man minister, let him do it as if the ability which God giveth." We are all "partakers of Christ's sufferings; that, when his glory shall be revealed, ye may be glad also with exceeding joy" (I Peter 4:13).

God will bless us exceedingly when we maintain our commitment to Him. We are created by God, "For God is love" (I John 4:8).

In I John 5:21, "Little children, keep yourselves from idols. Amen."

May the grace and will of God be exceedingly great in your life. "Hereby know we that we dwell in him, and he in us, because he hath given us of his Spirit" (I John 4:13).

THE GREATNESS OF GOD

When boxing legend Muhammed Ali conquered the world of boxing and became heavyweight Champion of the World he shouted in front of a host of media, "I am the greatest!" As his resume of victories increased and after becoming a three-time champion, he proclaimed that he was the "Greatest of all Time!"

We have watched the brilliance of many mighty men who have done extraordinary things and overcome unbelievable obstacles to accomplish their lofty goals. We salute these mighty men of valor with awards, medals, gifts, titles, parades, and other symbols of triumph. In our generation we lift us celebrities, sports stars, singers, scientist, political figures, Olympians, Heads of State, authors, business executives, or military brass. The names would ring out like Einstein, Rosa Parks, Presidents John F. Kennedy, Eisenhower, Roosevelt, Lincoln, and Hoover, just to name a few; or Martin Luther King, Jr., Mother Teresa, Gandhi, Pope John Paul II, Michael Jordan, Joe Montana, John Wooden, just to name a few. O the record would be long if we listed every single person on a worldwide scale saluted for their notable accomplishments, their greatness.

If we had a local community survey, we could point out our school teachers, firemen, policemen, parents, brothers, sisters, clergy, or that unknown warmhearted person, who excelled in an unnoticed act, seemingly under extraordinary conditions and circumstances. Some of the achievements go beyond the depth and scope of understanding. Some triumphs shock us to a point to comment: "How in the world did they do that?" It's fascinating to read and watch people performing extraordinary acts under difficult and challenging situations. There is a certain joy and excitement that is demonstrated and appreciated when greatest is displayed for the betterment of mankind. Every person throughout history that has demonstrated greatest against the odds provides us inspiration to face obstacles and difficulties with a positive attitude and a means to take on the challenge with strength, confidence and power. It's an intriguing thing to witness a person climb higher than the imagination could ever conceive. Are you familiar with that hallow place deep in your heart that yearns/craves for greatness?

The bible states that the patriarch of Uz, Job, is "the greatest of all men of the east" (Job 1:3). His status in the Land of Uz was so great that princes covered their mouths when he spoke. He was a mighty man of God. But a strange and unique thing develops when the towering presence of God arrives on the premises to confront his perfect and upright servant.

God makes His presence known by appearing in a whirlwind over Job. God does not waste any time and immediately starts an interrogation of Job that is vigorous and right to the point. Job and the elders are crippled by the powerful voice of the Lord, and Job only speaks when God commands that he speak. The first question from the Lord of Host, "Who is this that darkeneth counsel by words without knowledge?" (Job 38:1)

We can imagine the fear in the heart of the men assembled when God speaks with a commanding tone. But God goes further and commands of Job, "Gird up now thy loins like a man: for I will demand of thee, and answer thou me" (Job 38:3).

Job is left in a state of bewilderment before the Lord. God gives Job a righteous interrogation and Job can only reach one conclusion: "Behold I am vile; what shall I answer thee? I will lay mine hand upon my mouth" (Job 40:4). Job becomes meek and humble before the Living God. He realizes that he is no comparison to the knowledge, understanding and wisdom of God.

God cites His awesomeness through questions beyond the scope of human intellect. The Almighty Divine Judge illustrates wisdom and creativity so far advanced above and beyond man's earthly knowledge that the question of man is: "Who can fathom the motivations of God?"

From generation to generation scholars and theologians have questioned and challenged the greatest of God. Job witnesses the greatest of God and says, "I have heard of thee by the hearing of the ear: but now mine eye seeth thee" (Job 42:5). Job acknowledges the sovereignty of God.

The great saints and prophets of scripture could not have achieved their objective without the power and will of God. Every notable accomplishment by men and women in the world starts with the exaltation of God. King David writes, "Great is the Lord, and of great power; his understanding is infinite" (Psalm 147:5). David elaborates in Psalm 147:6, "The Lord lifteth up the meek; he casteth the wicked down to the ground." Whether one is small or large, God dominates and controls all aspects of a person's rise to greatest. King David became a great king because of his willingness to submit to the power of God. And in his obedience to God, David was on the receiving end of many blessings from the Lord.

God possesses the impeccable credentials of righteousness, holiness, and power that place His greatness above all. God can lift up or tear down. He can bless or curse. He can destroy or deliver prosperity across the land. This is the mighty God of Abraham, Isaac, and Jacob. This is the God that delivered us out of Egypt. This is the God of our fathers. This is the Architect and Designer of heaven and earth. This is the God that delivered us out of the hands of the enemy. This is the great "I AM."

In all of our measurements and exaltation of self, we reflect upon the One that is responsible for every victory, triumph, and championship the God of Omniscience. And the great marvelous work that Jesus Christ did on the Cross bares the mark that "God is great." And through His greatness we receive grace, and this grace is justified only through Christ Jesus. Who measures up to the matchless character of Christ?

CHAPTER 9

THE RESURGENCE OF A MAN

"Humble yourselves in the sight
of the Lord, and he shall lift you up."
– James 4:10

What is a man without God? God rewards those that suffer in His Name. God is full of mercy and understanding. When a man humbles and submits himself to the Holy Father, then God will proceed to make that man better than he was. When a man thinks highly of himself, there is nothing God can do to lift him up. When God steps on the premises, we can bet it's serious business. Do we take God's presence lightly? Job realizes that God is extremely powerful. By way of God's holy power, man is capable of enduring much. God's power is overwhelming. When our worst nightmares and greatest fears surface to become reality, who will we call upon to fight the dark forces on the battlefield of life? Who will protect us from our drastic need for safety and security? Will God insulate us and keep us from falling?

Job had prepared many statements to confront God, upon his arrival. Notice that Job did not complete any of the confrontational phrases he had developed in his subconscious mind. The power of God is so high, gigantic, massive, vast and towering that it is beyond the finite limits of human evaluation. King David writes in Psalm 147:5,

> "Great is our Lord, and of great power: his understanding is infinite."

King David extols a God of greatness in every department. There is no comparison to our Lord and Savior; absolutely no other god can compete with Him.

GOD'S GOODNESS

David reveals a God of magnificent power from both sides of the aisle. In Psalm 149:1-6, David shows us that God is worthy of adoration for all his "goodness."

> "Praise ye the Lord. Sing unto the Lord a new song, and his praise in the congregation of saints. Let Israel rejoice in him that made him: let the children of Zion be joyful in their King. Let them praise his name in the dance: Let them sing praises unto him with the timbel and harp. For the LORD taketh pleasures in his people: he will beautify the meek with salvation. Let the saints be joyful in glory: let them sing aloud upon their beds. Let the high praises of God be in their mouth, and an two-edged sword in their hand."

King David advises us to praise God and be joyful with the power that God gives us through His mercy, compassion, patience, wisdom, and grace. We are required to submit ourselves to the Holy Father and glorify Him in every aspect of our lives.

GOD'S WRATH

There is another powerful quality of God. David reveals a God that will take vengeance against another, if provoked. In due time, God will strike those that violate his commandments and covenants. David writes in Psalm 149:7-9,

> "To execute vengeance upon the heathen, and punishments upon the people; To bind their kings with chains, and their nobles with fetters of iron; To execute upon them the judgment written: this honour have all his saints. Praise ye the LORD."

Our God possesses the power to bless or punish. Therefore, the words of wisdom from King Solomon tell us, "The fear of the Lord **is** the beginning of knowledge" (Proverbs 1:7).

JOB'S FIRST STEP BACK

Job revealed his fear of God when he totally humbled and submitted himself. Job proclaimed, "Behold, I am vile" (Job 40:4). In the presence of God, Job admits his weakness. He exposes his lack of knowledge on godly issues. Job was completely in awe of God's power and might. The Almighty's presence was "overpowering." Job felt the strength and force of our Heavenly Father in the whirlwind.

We closed the last chapter with reference to the powerful, thundering tone of God's commanding voice. God reveals a sampling of His awesome power and might to Job in chapter 40:

> "Gird up thy loins now like a man: I will demand of thee, and declare thou unto me. Wilt thou also disannul my judgment? Welt thou condemn me, that thou mayest be righteous? Hast thou an arm like God? Or canst

thou thunder with a voice like him? Seek thyself now with majesty and excellency; and array thyself with glory and beauty. Cast abroad the rage of thy wrath: and behold every one that is proud, and abase him. Look on every one that is proud, and bring him low; and tread down the wicked in their place. Hide them in the dust together; and bind their faces in secret. Then will I also confess unto thee that thine own right hand can save thee."

God challenges Job to answer questions to which only God has the answers. Remember, Job demanded an audience with God. Job gets his opportunity and he discovers that he cannot compare or compete with God. Job is speechless. The presentation God places before Job leaves him stunned and totally in awe. Job simply does not have the power, will, or wisdom to answer correctly the questions put before him. Job has no authority. Job's works are no comparison to God's mighty works. God is the judge of our works. Our works should serve God, not man.

The Rev. Dr. Martin Luther King Jr. said, "The ultimate measure of a man is not where he stands in moments of comfort, but where he stands at times of challenge and controversy."

GOD'S VOICE IN THE GARDEN

Another illustration of God's awesome power is exposed in the Garden of Eden. God was seated in heaven but He was able to perform the following act in Genesis 3:8,

> "and they heard the voice of the LORD God walking in the garden in the cool of the day:"

Imagine God's voice "walking in the garden." That is power. God's supply of power is unlimited and beyond human comprehension. God's voice continues through the Garden of Eden and He inquires:

"And the LORD called unto Adam, and said unto him, where art thou?" (Genesis 3:9).

Adam responds:

"And he said, I heard thy voice in the garden, and I was afraid, because I was naked; and I hid myself" (Genesis 3:10).

God responds to Adam:

"who told thee that thou wast naked? Hast thou eaten of the tree, whereof I commanded thee that thou shouldest not eat?" (Gen. 3:11).

We note that Adam was afraid when he heard the voice of the Living God pacing through the Garden of Eden. Adam was hiding because he feared the wrath of the Almighty. He had no idea how God would respond to his sin. Whether we sin or remain sin-free, it is wise to fear God.

Jesus Christ speaks of the ultimate power of God when He states that God, "is greater than all" (John 10:29).

JESUS' VOICE

Before Jesus' arraignment before Pilate, it was decided by the chief priests to send a band of men and their top officers. They carried with them weapons to bring Jesus before the court (John 18:3). The power of our Lord's *voice* is imposing when confronted by the soldiers, as John 18:4-6 reveals,

> "Jesus therefore, knowing all things that should come upon him, went forth, and said unto them, whom seek ye? They answered him, Jesus of Nazareth. Jesus said unto them, I am he. And Judas also, which betrayed him stood with them. As soon then as he had said unto them I am he, they went backward, and fell to the ground."

At the sound of Christ's voice the soldiers went backward and feel to the ground. What manner of man is this? This identical *voice* walked through the Garden of Eden. This is the *same voice* that spoke to Moses "in a flame of fire out of the midst of a bush" (Exodus 3:2). The same *voice* that commanded Abraham, "Take now thy son, thine only **son** Isaac, whom thou lovest, and get thee into the land of Moriah; and offer him there for a burnt offering" (Genesis 22:2). The *same voice* that commanded the Legions of demons, "Come out of the man, thou unclean spirit" (Mark 5:8). The same *voice* that told Satan in the wilderness, "It is said, Thou shalt not tempt the Lord thy God" (Luke 4:12). The *same voice* that set the framework for the universe by stating, "Let there be light: and there was light" (Genesis 1:3). The same *voice* that said, "Let us make man in our image, after our likeness" (Genesis 1:26). The same *voice* that said, "Now the parable is this: The seed is the word of God" (Luke. 8:11). This is the *same voice* that commanded Satan to restrict his level of destruction towards Job; the *same voice* that spoke in the whirlwind to Job. This is the *identical voice* that articulates to our hearts today, to instruct and guide us in His Word. The voice is real and persuasive. The Almighty's voice is filled with righteousness.

The word of Jesus Christ instructs us that God has given Him power to do wondrous things, as quoted in John 10:17-18,

> "Therefore doth my Father love me, because I lay down my life, that I might take it again. No man taketh it from me, but I lay it down of myself. I have power to lay it down, and I have power to take it again. This commandment have I received of my Father."

Blessed is the power of the Lord. His might voice is like "many waters." He directs and instructs us in the way to go. When we follow the voice of God, we will "see the glory of God" (John 11:40). Nothing or no one can compare or compete with God.

We do not invite difficulty, tragedy, or controversy into our lives. It happens at unexpected times. God permits these elements to enter our lives to prepare us for greatness. In addition, God's glory will be revealed if we endure. If we keep our attitude closely linked with Christ, we can rest with the blessed assurance that God will carry us through. In James 5:8 we are reminded,

> "Be ye also patient; stablish your hearts: for the coming of the Lord draweth nigh."

JOB'S REPENTANCE

Job has been patient. He has waited on the Lord. The Lord has commanded of him certain things. The Lord allows Job the opportunity to speak. Job responses to God in Job 42:1-6,

> "Then Job answered the LORD, and said, I know that thou canst do every thing, and that no thought can be withholden from thee. Who is he that liketh counsel without knowledge? Therefore have I uttered that I un-

derstood not; things too wonderful for me, which I knew not. Hear, I beseech thee, and declare thou unto me. I have heard of thee by the hearing of the ear: but now mine eye seeth thee. Wherefore I abhor myself, and repent in dusts and ashes."

Firstly, Job acknowledges that God can do everything. Secondly, he admits that he spoke with a lack of knowledge. He gives God total credit for understanding all things. In other words, Job *admits* to having "no knowledge" in the presence of God. Thirdly, Job *submits* himself to God for mercy, grace, and forgiveness. Job makes himself small before the Lord. He lowers himself to the level of "dust and ashes." He "rejects" self and "repents" before the Lord. Job goes into total submission before the majestic beauty, glory, and power of God. Now, he is preparing himself to receive the blessing from the Lord.

GOD'S FINAL RESPONSE

The Holy Father blesses Job. God accepts his sincere apology and repentance. God is pleased with his good and faithful servant. This is a prime example of how God restores us and makes us better than we were. God is in the restoration business, not the destruction business. He is a builder of men. He is a healer. The disciple James writes of Job in the New Testament in James 5:11,

> "Behold, we count them happy which endure. Ye have heard of the patience of Job, and have seen the end of the Lord; that the Lord is very pitiful, and of tender mercy."

Job has been redeemed. It is time for joyful praise unto the Lord. He has been made new by the forgiveness of his sins. When Job accepted his dismal state of affairs by turning it all over to God, he reached a realization that, if he emerged from his suffering, God would instill something new and amazing. That's the faith and trust we must place in the Lord. This is the mystery. We can trust God to make it better than we could ever imagine. We can imagine how Job felt upon receiving the blessing from the Lord.

Noted Christian author Max Lucado writes, "The big agenda item is God and His glory, not me and my comfort."

GOD'S UNFINISHED BUSINESS

God has spoken to Job, but he has other unfinished business with the elders. Can we overlook the behavior of the elders? God addresses the elders in Job 42:7,

> "And it was so, that after the LORD had spoken these words unto Job, the LORD said to Eliphaz the Temanite, my wrath is kindled against thee, and against thy two friends: for ye have not spoken of me the thing that is right, as my servant Job hath."

God is reserving his wrath against Eliphaz, the Temanite, and his two friends, for injecting messages to Job that were incorrect. The elders did not represent God in their meeting with Job. It's clear that God is upset with the elders. The elders offered up a plate of condemnation, judgment, and self-righteousness. They were simply inconsiderate of Job's difficulties. As "friends," they acted contrary to God's foundation of mercy, understanding, love, compassion, and prayer. James 4:10 gives us illumination on life's battlefield,

> "Humble yourselves in the sight of the Lord, and he shall lift you up."

This latter scripture is part of the foundation of God's holy word. We cannot permit a friend or enemy to deter us from the truth. Be not deceived by the "doctrines of devils." In the times of our trials and tribulations, the General Epistle of James 1:3 reveals to us how we should behave with God,

> "Knowing this, that the trying of your faith worketh patience."

Be patient and wait on the Lord; hope in His mercy and maintain total faith that He will arrive on time. We must continue to serve and glorify God, even in our afflictions. Judge not a friend in his days of suffering. But, extend a hand of comfort.

Job's friends failed to pray for him. In times of adversity, God wants us to PRAY. Pray changes things.

In Job 42:8, God instructs Eliphaz on what is required to save him and his friend for charging God wrongly:

> "therefore take unto you now seven bullocks and seven rams, and go to my servant Job, and offer up for yourselves a burnt offering; and my servant Job shall pray for you: for him will I accept: lest I deal with you after your folly, in that ye have not spoken of me the thing which is right, like my servant Job."

Job's integrity is restored. His prayer will make an impact with God but not the friends of Job. God makes His point with Eliphaz, that if he fails to follow His command, His wrath would be upon him. Do we need to consider how Eliphaz and his friends responded to God's command?

Job 42:9 reveals,

"So Eliphaz the Temanite and Bildad the Shuhite and Zophar the Naamathite went, and did according as the LORD commanded them: the LORD also accepted Job."

JOB'S TRIUMPH

The elders made the correct decision to follow God's command. Job's status is greater than before. Job 42:10 says,

"And the LORD turned the captivity of Job, when he prayed for his friends: also the LORD gave Job twice as much as he had before."

Job was once the wealthiest man of the east. God has given him twice as much as he had before. It is time to sing and rejoice at Job's prosperity. At this stage King David would shout, "Praise God! Praise God! Praise God!" There is no more sadness, only joy. In Job 42:11, Job is comforted by his brethren, sisters, and friends as they assemble to share the wonderment of the Lord:

"Then came there unto him all his brethren, and all his sisters and all they that had been of his acquaintance before, and did eat bread with him, and comforted him over all the evil that the LORD had brought upon him: every man also gave him a piece of money, and every one an earring of gold."

When God has lifted evil from the premises there is time for celebration and rejoicing. Even in modern times, we should reach out a hand of comfort, support, and encouragement. Our desire should be to lift up the person to a higher level and spread all the wonderful things the Lord has done. Sickness and difficulties are part of the mystery of life. When God signals us out to suffer in His name, we are receiving a gift. As troubling as it may appear, suffering glorifies the power and grace of God. And when He restores us to glory we can shout to the heavens how marvelous God performed His act of kindness. This is the blessed hope that keeps us anchored in the Word of God. Remember, God's grace is sufficient.

TO EVERY PURPOSE

King Solomon states in Ecclesiastes 8:6-7,

> "Because to every purpose there is time and judgment, therefore the misery of man is great upon him. For he knoweth not that which shall be; for who can tell him when it shall be?"

This sentiment is clearly stated to give us deeper understanding of the wisdom of God. God grants a time for every situation and circumstance. He remains in control of every point of reference in the universe.

Furthermore:

> "Every man also to whom God hath given riches and wealth, and hath given him power to eat thereof, and to take his portion, and to rejoice in his labours; this is the gift of God." (Eccles. 5:19).

JOB'S JOY

God has given Job joy. Job is better off today than he was yesterday. He suffered for a time but God reveals His grace and just reward to His good and faithful servant in Job 42:12; God's grace is his gift to us.

"So the Lord blessed the latter end of Job more than his beginning: for he had fourteen thousand sheep, and six thousand camels, and a thousand yoke of oxen, and a thousand she asses. He had also seven sons and three daughters."

Glory to God! Job kept the faith and submitted himself to God. God rewarded him with gifts beyond his imagination. King David wrote, "I will extol thee, O Lord" (Psalm. 30:1). God has delivered the goods. King David provides us with additional scripture to glorify God after the evil has gone, in Psalm 30:11- 12,

"Thou hast turned for me my mourning into dancing: thou hast put off my sackcloth, and girded me with gladness; To the end that my glory may sing praise to thee, and not be silent. O Lord my God, I will give thanks unto thee for ever."

Job's final blessings from God is exposed in Chapter 42:15-17,

"And in all the land were no women found so fair as the daughters of Job: and their father gave them inheritance among their brethren. After this lived Job an hundred and forty years, and saw his sons, and his sons' sons, even four generations. So Job died, being old and full of days."

OBEDIENCE TO GOD

Job lived a full life through the grace of the Almighty. Job kept the word of God throughout his life. He was the "upright and perfect man that feared God and escheweth evil." Christ states in John 8:51,

"Verily, verily, I say unto you. If a man keep my saying, he shall never see death."

For those doubters who fail to believe that Jesus Christ and God are one, the following scripture is provided from The Gospel According, John 1:1-2,

"In the beginning was the Word, and the Word was with God, and the Word was God. The same was in the beginning with God."

Also in John 1:27, the disciple, reveals his lack of significance before the Son of Man.

"whose shoe's latchet I am not worthy to unloose."

Glory to God! God may not always show us the complete picture while in the midst of our suffering, but one thing is certain: God rules Supreme over the ordeal. He's masterful in His planning. God designed a set of blueprints prior to the beginning of the world and He has never had to adjust His design. God is the Alpha and Omega. He offers us eternal life when we endure to the end.

Remember, Satan offers deceit and confusion. By the way, what happened to Satan? When God stepped on the premises, Satan made a swift exit. What does that reveal to us about this creature? It becomes clear that Satan fears God.

We are capable of living a sin-free life. We can do it. God desires that we live a healthy and prosperous life. God wants to bless us with a full life. He desires that every one of us will return to the heavenly kingdom. He does not want one of us to perish. When we keep God at the center of our lives, our chief adversary cannot penetrate the wall of protection that God has around us. Our Advocate in heaven defeated the adversary.

The enemy has a limited and restricted time to run free on earth. We have been released from the shackles of sin by the beautiful work that Jesus Christ performed on the Cross. Christ did not give up. He paid the ultimate price for our salvation. Remember, whatever we ask for in The Name of Jesus Christ, God will provide.

THE LIMITS OF EARTHLY POWER

How often we hear men boast about the power they possess? There is a classic scene in the New Testament when Jesus Christ is taken before Pilate for interrogation. As Christ stood before the court, Pilate elevates himself about the amount of power he possesses in John 19:10,

> "Then saith Pilate unto him, Speakest thou not unto me? Knowest thou not that I have power to crucify thee, and have power to release thee?"

Jesus Christ makes it abundantly clear to Pilate in verse 11:

> "Jesus answered, Thou couldest have no power at all against me, except it were given thee from above:"

The Apostle Paul reveals more to us about power in Romans 13:1,

> "Let every soul be subject unto the higher powers. For there is no power but of God: The powers that be are ordained of God."

All power in heaven and beneath heaven belongs to our Father. While facing the crucifixion, Christ elevated His Father in the presence of Pilate. He glorified God. Christ's example is one for us to follow. This action grants us the authority and power to resist the devil and his devices. By glorifying God, we will live more abundantly. We have the Victory!

O' Heavenly Father, we thank you for delivering us from evil. We praise and exalt your blessed holy name. There is no God greater than you. Although we suffered in your name for a while, you have restored us to glory. We are thankful for your patience, understanding and mercy. Most of all, we thank you for the increase you provide us each day. O' Father, we are only better because of you. You repair us when we are broken. Praise your blessed name. Forgive us for our sins. Father, keep us insulated from the perils of sin and teach us your way O' Heavenly Father. Your way is the right way. We submit ourselves to you in the name of Jesus Christ, our Savior. AMEN.

WHAT IS A HERO?

What is a Hero or Heroine? It is someone forged by the fire of their will, chiseled by the hand of their courage and tested by the Almighty for toughness of character through the most trying of times. In this uplifting, inspirational and motivating story of Job, we bring you the very, very best in a hero.

If you have been afraid, his courage will melt your fear. If you have been indecisive, his life will be a beacon in the darkness. If you have no dream, listen to the thoughts behind his deeds and get one.

The ancestors left a legacy testifying that you have been designed for accomplishment, engineered for success and, somewhere in-between, readied for a seed of Greatness by the Almighty Architect to let us know that the hero is within.

May the name of Jesus be glorified in your heart, mind and soul henceforth, now and forever more. AMEN.

CHAPTER 10

HOPE IN HIS MERCY

*"And in that day thou shalt say, O Lord, I will praise thee:
though thou wast angry with me, thine anger is turned
away, and thou comfortedst me."*
– Isaiah 12:12

We surface from the underneath and find God there. He is the power and force behind our resurrection from the depths of iniquity. We cannot surface from the ocean of affliction by ourselves. We need, depend on, and benefit from God's grace, mercy, compassion, and love.

The amazing thing about God is that when He is silent or quiet, His power is working for the betterment of mankind. His presence is there. Like Job you can feel and sense God's overwhelming power. Never doubt that God is around. God dominates every phase of social organization and every field of battle. God does not miss a beat. God is invisible, but His work is visible for us to view.

Those poor in spirit frequently inject all types of negative statements against God; statements such as, "God is not around, God is dead. Where is God when you need Him? God does not answer our prayers. Why does God let so many bad things happen? There is no God. Once this life is over, that is it. I treat everyone OK and I am a good person; I do not need a God. I can become a god by connecting with nature and the universe. There is so much evil in the world, why doesn't God do something?" The statements go on and on.

We must reach a level of understanding that God is the most exalted, holy and sacred Being in existence. We are part of God's ultimate plan. We were with God prior to arrival on earth. It's difficult to imagine in our physical form, but we were. That's why we should have total faith in God and resist Satan. Satan wants us to forget our origin. Satan had his opportunity to be with his Father in Heaven, but chose to disobey his Holy Father when iniquity was found in him. Satan is separated from God because of his disobedience. We are no longer separated from God, because of the sacrifice made by the Son of God, Jesus Christ. Glory to God! Satan is jealous of our relationship with God and is on a daily mission to destroy us. His goal is to fill up hell to an overflow. He has that much hatred for us. We have no other choice than to praise and give thanks to God for sending His Son to pay the ultimate price for us. God has made it clear that nothing will separate us from His love.

We must elevate our earthly thinking and learning to a more godly state of thinking. God is not our buddy, or the guy we play cards with every Friday night; nor is He the fellow we have a drink with nightly at the bar or club. God is a much higher authority and warrants our total submission. He cannot be measured by human standards of measurements. His holiness and purity is beyond human comprehension. We must place ourselves in a position to mimic the walk of Christ and not march against His teachings.

When suffering and affliction comes, we need God more than ever. We need His support, grace, power, and eternal mercy and compassion. We need God to assist us in our patience and faith. God wants us faithful until the very end. He does not want us to deviate from His holy word. To question, challenge, and condemn God when suffering comes is to lower our Father to a finite level, based on our limited intellect. We must not be like the well-learned Pharisees that challenged the Son of Man. Let us continue to elevate our understanding of the true purposes of God. Job lifted up his eyes to heaven while in the grips of Satan and said, "Although you slay me I will trust in thee." Job became humbled and meek before the throne of grace, placing all his trust and faith in the Lord. He sat an example for us to follow in modern times. God grants us mercy and compassion even when we don't deserve it. His mercy pours out like Niagara Falls. This is the eternal love that God has for us. The bible says, "His mercy endureth forever." We will be strengthened, not weakened or fearful when confronted with the shadows of death. "For God hath not given us the spirit of fear; but of power, and of love, and of a sound mind" (II Timothy 1:7). God is the Light of the World.

God is here to give us the ring and crown of glory. Be prepared and expect to receive your ring and crown because of your faith, obedience and hope in God's mercy. Do not be misled by false prophets and ministers preaching the "doctrine of devils." These disciples of iniquity exist today. These agents of the devil function in society to create confusion and destroy our ability to receive eternal life with God. We have to hold on to that blessed hope and endure these temptations as a "good soldier of Jesus Christ" (II Timothy 2:3).

When we reflect on all the deformities in man, we must acknowledge that if not for God we would exist in a wasteland of permanent displacement from the savior. It forces us to tremble at the thought that if Jesus Christ had not endured on the Cross our souls would be lost. Christ's work on the Cross is the ultimate illustration of God's mercy and compassion. It reveals the agape love of the Almighty. The Apostle Paul writes, "Let every soul be subject unto the higher powers. For there is no power but of God: the powers that be are ordained of God" (Romans 13:1). There is no modern day system that can measure up to the superiority of Christ.

Micah 7:18 says, "God delighteth in mercy." God has cheerfullness in showering us with love. His mercy is evidence of genuine love. Within His mercy and compassion resides grace. His grace sustains us. His grace is a beacon of light in the storm and flood waters of life. His grace keeps us from eternal damnation. He has not changed from the start of the world. The identical mercy that He showed Adam and Eve in the Garden of Eden, exist with us today.

There is a certain mystery to the goodness of God. The Apostle Paul spoke about this mystery. The mystery is beyond the scope of our understanding. We cannot comprehend why God appears to permit suffering and pain in one arena and not another. We cannot adequately explain in human terms why one catastrophe happens here and not there. Why one will die and another live. It's a divine mystery. The Apostle Paul writes, "For he saith to Moses, I will have mercy on whom I will have mercy, and I will have compassion on whom I will have compassion" (Romans 9:15). This is the essential reason that we must fear God and remain meek and humble throughout life, never elevating ourselves with pride before the Lord because it's only through the Almighty grace of God that we stand.

The patriarch Job found out in the midst of his suffering that perfection in judgment can only come from God. God's holiness and righteousness rule supreme over man's limited intellect. Therefore when we trust and depend on God for the source of our supply, we will obtain His tender mercies and compassion. Trust God that He knows what is best for us. When tragedy arrives, let us mimic Job and fall to our knees and thank God for all things in a total, humble, and submissive manner. Thank God for all things and ask God to bless us with the power and strength to carry on. Keep prayer at the forefront of all things. God commands us to communicate with Him. And the best method is through prayer.

When God rewards us with His healing power and our increase is better than before, rejoice and praise His holy name. Loudly praise God for delivering us from the depths of pain and suffering. Praise Him from the mountaintop. God is great.

Let us pray.

> O Heavenly Father we exalt and praise your holy name and give thanks to Thee for your pure and sacred nature. Father you found us weak, worn down and filled with iniquity; and you took this sin and forgave us. Father we are strengthened by Thee and look to Thee for all things. We have nothing, and submit ourselves to you to be remade into your likeness. Thank you, Father, for carrying the burdens and load of pain and suffering that we place upon ourselves by our refusal to obey your rules and policies. Have mercy on us, Father; make us better than we are. We submit ourselves to you, O Holy Father, to cleanse us of the filth in our hearts and souls. Only you can do this, Father. Teach us, Master, to have better understanding of your holy work. Moreover, protect us, shield us, insulate us from the evil that lurks in this world and have mercy on us. Hear our cry, O Lord, as you heard the cry of King David. Father, we need Thee and only Thee. All Thine wondrous ways, we find pleasing to us. Father, we hope in Thine mercy, grant us the power and will to carry on in your name. Father, we ask of you these things and others in the Name of Jesus Christ, who sits on the right hand of the Father. Amen.

Harriet Beecher Stowe writes, "When you get into a tight place and everything goes against you until it seems that you cannot hold on for a minute longer, never give up then, for that is just the place and time that the tide will turn." God responds in due time. He is a patient god. We have to follow the instructions of our Teacher in order to pass the test. We need our Teacher to assist us in passing the exam. Remember, whatever we indulge in life, God is the absolute power and authority over all things in heaven and beneath heaven. Never doubt our Lord and Savior.

For Apostle Paul writes in Romans 8:38, 39,

> "For I am persuaded, that neither death, nor life, nor angels, nor principalities, nor powers, nor things present, nor things to come, Nor height, nor depth, nor any other creature, shall be able to separate us from the love of God, which is in Christ Jesus our Lord."

What a soothing revelation to know that nothing in heaven or earth can separate us from the love of God. It's this blessed hope that saves us (Romans 8:24). We must constantly reflect on the eternal mercies of God. And in doing so we are commanded to extend similar mercies to one another. We cannot receive "divine restoration" if we refuse to show mercy and compassion to one another. When we extend a hand to a wounded soul, we are practicing the divine nature of Jesus Christ. We must sow the seed that will reap life everlasting (Galatians 6:8). Jesus Christ says, "Blessed are the merciful for they shall obtain mercy" (Matthew 5:7).

Helen Keller was blind and deaf from the age of two. She was the first deafblind person to earn a Bachelor of Arts degree. She became a noted lecturer, author and advocate for people with disabilities. But, it was Anne Sullivan, who was her teacher and took the time to break through the isolation, allowing Helen Keller to blossom. Helen Keller wrote, "I thank God for my handicaps, for, through them, I have found myself, my work, and my God." This is a small snapshot of a person who showed mercy and compassion, offering a hand of strength to lift a person up from their suffering. Anne Sullivan's tender mercies and patience are evident in the enormous success she was able to achieve. Anne not only strengthens the character and self-esteem of Helen, but her spirit as well. One of the great triumphs for the fullness of life is when we show graciousness to a person in need.

Jesus Christ became the author of our eternal salvation. We rest all of our blessed hope in Christ. Within this blessed hope we must be obedient to God in order to receive the Promise. It is the heart of meekness and humility that pleases God. We are encouraged to seek out the excellency of His power and grace and glorify His precious name. And through all of our earthly crying and tears we can lift up our eyes to the heavens and find comfort in His mercy.

AFTERWORD

"He is the Rock, his work is perfect:
for all his ways are judgment: a God of truth
and without iniquity, just and right is he"
– Deuteronomy 32: 4

God is mighty and just. His judgments are perfect in all departments. "For God is not unrighteous to forget your work and labor of love, which ye have shewed toward his name, in that ye have ministered to the saints, and do minister" (Heb. 6:10).

How will you govern your life? The deceiver will come without reservation to destroy those that are conforming to this physical world. His mission is to get us to conform to this world. Any holy alliance to sin for a season will only bring about destruction of the soul by the deceiver. God will not play games on the Day of Judgment. His decision will be swift, accurate, and final. Eternal damnation in hell is permanent placement for those who refuse to follow the commandments, covenants, and commands of God. God is merciful, patient and compassionate, but will not take a back step to anyone that decides to take His honor, praise, and glory. In other words, all glory, praise, and honor go to God. God is the anchor, cornerstone, rock, and fortress that protects and insulates us from the enemy. God is our ultimate security against the disciples of evil and wickedness. God will defend His turf in a supremely aggressive manner that will leave no doubt that He is the Master of vengeance.

"The Lord is not slack concerning his promise" (2 Pet. 3:9). In John 3:2, 3, "Beloved now are we the sons of God, and it doth not yet appear what we shall be: but we know that, when He shall appear, we shall be like Him; for we shall see Him as He is. And every man that hath this hope in Him purifieth himself, even as He is pure."

We are sons of the Most High. We resemble Him. Our faith, hope, "and truly our fellowship is with the Father, and with his Son, Jesus Christ" (I John 1:3). It is commanded of us to conduct ourselves like God. We should reflect the likeness of Jesus Christ in every mission we undertake. We cannot become confused and classify right as wrong, or wrong as righteous. This is the *"doctrine of devils"* to confuse us and lose faith in the truth. Satan is a liar and masterful deceiver, dead set on destroying man and every image of Jesus Christ. He is not in a position to take anything from us, but his persuasive skills are potent. He has been stripped of all authority and the limited power that remains with him is restricted by the Almighty hand of God. All of our time, moment by moment, should be focused and committed to God. If we are truly about our Father's business we do not have the time or desire to participate in sinful pleasure for a season.

Job reveals to us that a man can remain committed to God and maintain the highest degree of integrity and character. Job illustrates in words and deeds, the ingredients necessary for God to acknowledge "that there is none like him in the earth, a perfect and an upright man, one that feareth God, and escheweth evil." Did you imagine while reading Job, what it would have been like to meet, converse, and listen to a holy man of his stature? God states that "there is none like him in the earth." This is a powerful statement from God regarding a holy man. Our hope in God allows us to measure up to this description. Remember, God sent us One that was greater than Job, and His name was Jesus Christ, the Son of the Most High.

In II Corinthians 5:14, 15, "For the Love of Christ constraineth us; became we thus judge, that if one died for all, then were all dead: And that he died for all, that they which live should not henceforth live unto themselves, but unto Him which died for them, and rose again."

We can rest with the confidence "that God was in Christ" (II Corinthians 5:19). Do not be deceived by those that state that Jesus Christ did not exist; or Jesus Christ was merely a prophet; or Jesus Christ died on the cross and his remains lie in an unmarked burial plot; or Jesus Christ never came to earth in the flesh or Jesus Christ is not God because God would never place Himself in a position to be crucified by mortal man. We have heard the stories promoted by the deceptive practices of "agents of hell." The Bible firmly cements "that God was in Christ." Where is the challenge to God's Absolute Authority? Do you have an arm to box like God? Are you in a position to call God a liar? Can you label yourself vile like Job? Will you admit to a lack of understanding and knowledge like Job?

There has been a sudden attack on the tradition of the family. Society is confronted with the urge and desire to accept same-sex unions, extramarital affairs, pre-marital sexual adventures, and other alternate lifestyles as acceptable in the Kingdom of God. Divorce rates have skyrocketed to nearly 50%. Marriage and family have gone about a tremendous assault. Adultery is promoted on the Internet as a playful game for couples seeking self-satisfaction. Job classified adultery as a "heinous crime; yea it is an iniquity to be punished by the judges. For it is a fire that consumeth to destruction, and would root out all mine increase" (Job 31:11-12). We have to be careful and understand the commandments and "voice of God." There are false representatives of God that claim that adultery and fornication are acceptable practices in the kingdom of God, because "He loves all His children." We cannot fall prey to this "ultimate deception." God is not in favor of filth and uncleanliness. God is holy. God defends His turf against the slightest order of sin. A cancer cannot exist in the presence of God. We cannot destroy the foundation of the family by promoting sin. Sin separates us from God. God created man to head the family and be responsible to his wife and children. God designed the woman to be a *"helpmate to the man."*

For those who continue to operate in sin, God will show mercy and compassion when we act like Job and "wherefore I abhor myself, and repent in dust and ashes" (Job 42:6). Then we proceed to the final act like Job, "I know that thou canst do every thing, and that no thought can be withholden from thee" (Job 42:2). We can not occupy a seat of righteousness in heaven while enjoying the physical pleasures and urges of this world. The Son of God will not allow any form of iniquity to enter the gates of heaven. Do not be deceived by those arriving in sheep clothing speaking a doctrine contrary to the scriptures. Remember, listen and adhere to the "voice of God." God will not accept our excuses when He steps on the premises to confront us of our sins. His doctrine is clear; reject the policies and procedures of this world and live with the faith and hope through the "grace of God." We have a chance at salvation through Christ Jesus. "For whosoever shall call upon the name of the Lord, shall be saved" (Romans 10:13).

The Apostle Paul states, "Flee fornication. Every sin that man doeth is without the body; but he that committeth fornication sinneth against his own body" (I Corinthians 6:18). Paul goes further in a pointed statement regarding God's holiness in I Corinthians 6:9, "Know ye not that the unrighteous shall not inherit the kingdom of God? Be not deceived; neither fornicators, nor idolaters, nor effeminate, nor abusers of themselves with mankind." Paul's words are written with the full authority and permission of God. Our bodies are temples to glorify God.

PLEASURE AND "ALTERNATE LIFESTYLES"

Giving in to our physical urges, lusts, and desires does not fall under the mandates of God. God has warned us against earthly pleasure that attack His temple of holiness. Our bodies do not belong to us. Our bodies must serve God. A heavy sacrifice was made at Calvary to present us as worthy candidates to meet the Father of Jesus Christ. Giving into such urges is all part of Satan's plan; a plan carefully crafted to bring a person down to a subterranean level.

Listen to God, He loves us, repent of this behavior, reject this unsacred behavior. Humble and submit yourself to God to "change your life" and "strengthen your integrity." Remember God loves good integrity. Satan cannot take your integrity without God's approval. Don't wait to change, accept God now without delay. Submit yourself to God "right now" without delay, without any degree of trepidation. Step forward and accept Christ. In addition, Christ will enter your life and change you into a better person. Christ can change you into an "upright and perfect man and one that fears God, and escheweth evil." God does not desire us to be dirty and unclean. Be totally honest with yourself: "Am I acting correctly in the present of God? Am I glorifying God by my actions or glorifying myself? Will my actions profit God or myself? Are you planting good seed or bad seed?" Apostle Paul writes in Galatians 6:7,

"Whatsoever a man soweth, that shall he also reap."

Be true to yourself. Do not intellectualize. Throw away
self-centeredness. Complete your inventory of self. Be
honest with yourself. Do not play silly games. God is
watching. God is the only answer we have. Glory is to
God who sits most high, Glory to His holiness and precious name. Amen.

Jesus put his immutable word on the record in Mark
13:31, "Heaven and Earth will pass away: but my words
shall not pass away."

MARRIAGE AND TRUTH

God is not like man. God is completely about truth. Man prefers to
play games between truth and the shadows of darkness that cover
his lies. Man fails to realize that God knows the acting out of our
habits whether in darkness or in the light. Therefore, how can a
Minister carry on a ceremony to marry two homosexuals or lesbians
when such a ceremony is not within the commandments or covenants of God? The Minister is not performing or acting on God's
behalf; he is performing on behalf of Satan. Man cannot marry man.
Woman cannot marry woman. Animals of the lower species behave
according to the rules of their kingdom. God placed man in governorship over the animal kingdom, yet our behavior sometimes sinks
to the level of that of a dog or cat. God has clearly established the
rules of conduct. Marriage is for a Man and a Woman. God's word has
not changed. Therefore, any Minister performing such acts in the
Name of God has violated the sacred covenant God ordained prior to
the beginning of the world. Instead of using common sense on this
issue, we have to use a divine perspective and ask the question: does

the act glorify God? If the pastoral community feels God is too rigid in this area, then one will have to consider: do we follow the voice and desires of man or God? Is modern day society truly convinced that God would endorse such acts?

God does not like His doctrine, commandments, and covenants violated. He prefers that His word remain as documented at the start of Creation. Any change would have to come from the Father himself. God's word is Masterful. God will not change because of *"group sensitivities"* towards individuals seeking nourishment for their physical pleasures of the flesh. All sin is punishable by death. We cannot tempt God and expect Him to be accommodating to sin. God is a holy and righteous God. He hates sin and all its components. God commands us to be like Him, not like man. God instructs us to mimic the attributes of His One and only Son, Jesus. God is a jealous God. Fear Him. You do not want to experience the wrath of God. Hear me clear today; you do not want to anger God. As an illustration, notice what God did to two entire cities that had given in to wanton behavior; consult the legend of Sodom and Gomorra (Genesis 18-19).

NEW TESTAMENT

In the First Epistle of John, John advises us to reject the earthly pleasure of the flesh. He encourages us not to fall prey to the desires of the flesh but receive strengthening in the Holy Spirit.

> "Love not the world, neither the things that are in the world. If any man love the world, the love of the Father is not in him. For all that is in the world, the lust of the flesh, and the lust of the eyes, and the pride of life, is not of the Father, but is of the world" (John. 2:15-16).

The New Testament scripture from John warns us that the desires of this world are not the desires of God. We cannot serve God and Satan. God is not wrong. God is not in error. We are wrong. We are in error. We are the sinners. Remember, John writes, "Lust of flesh, and the lust of the eyes, and the pride of life is not of the Father, but is of the world." You cannot have pride in that which is contrary to the Word of God. A prideful person serves the "doctrine of devils." Jesus Christ told Satan in a face-to-face encounter: "for it is written, thou shalt worship the Lord thy God, and him only shalt thou serve" (Matthew 4:10). Glory to God!

> Teach us, Father, to abide by your rules. Bless us with the power and will to resist sinful earthly pleasures for a season. Have mercy on us, Father. Father, we are weak and we need thee to make us strong. Forgive us of our sins, O' Heavenly Father. Praise to thee for your mercy, compassion, grace, understanding and love for us. Protect us from the evil of this world. Praise your Holy Name. Praise your teachings for the betterment of our lives. We thank you, Father, for all things. In the name of Jesus Christ, we pray, AMEN.

Today, we live in a world that's ever changing. It's easy for people to shout, "I'm doing my own thing." We observe other people doing their own thing and we immediately conclude that it's okay to engage in similar behavior because it seems right, or the person appears happy. But, would we consider for a moment and ask the question: Does God approve of me doing this thing? Proverbs 1:7 says,

> "fools despise wisdom and instruction."

We cannot be free when we remain shackled by desires and urges that are contrary to the Kingdom of God. Everyday we have to replenish ourselves with the "goodness of God." We have to reflect on all the great things God has done in our lives; the good and the not so good. Job illustrates to us that it requires us maintaining our integrity and character. We have to demonstrate courage. Eleanor Roosevelt says, "I gain strength, courage and confidence by every experience in which I must stop and look fear in the face. I say to myself, I've lived through this and can take the next thing that comes along." The former First Lady of the United States reveals to us her determined effort and commitment to courage and integrity. She looked the task directly in the face and refused to blink. She had stored up her confidence and reflected on her past to gain renewed strength in the present to tackle the task at hand. Anais Nin says, "Life shrinks or expands in proportion to one's courage." If Christ did not have courage He would not have gone to the Cross willingly. If Christ did not have confidence in His Father, He would not have commanded His spirit into the hands of God when He died. If Christ did not have supreme confidence in His Father, He would not have risen on the third day. Jesus Christ illustrates to us that we must "believe" in order for change to happen. Randy Alcorn says, "No matter how tough life gets, if you see the shore [of heaven] and draw your strength from Christ, you'll make it." Satan's mission is to destroy our confidence. He wants to strip us of our integrity and character so we can curse God to His face. But, when we look to the hills, like King David, for the source of all power and authority, we gain the courage to walk upright. Our faith and trust in the Lord is strengthened and the darts of the devil will not penetrate our mind or heart. When we are obedient to God, He blesses us beyond human reasoning. When we obey the voice of the Lord, no corruption will attach to our body. When we humble ourselves and repent of our sins, God will restore us to a higher plane. Proverbs 26:11 says,

> "As a dog returneth to his vomit, so a fool returneth to his folly."

Isaiah 5:20 says,

> "Woe unto them that call evil good, and good evil; that put darkness for light, and light for darkness; that put bitter for sweet, and sweet for bitter!"

God gives us the eternal warning of His anger against iniquity in Isaiah 13:11, 13, 19,

> "And I will punish the world for their evil, and the wicked for their iniquity; and I will cause the arrogancy of the proud to cease, and will lay low the haughtiness of the terrible. Therefore I will shake the heavens, and the earth shall remove out of her place, in the wrath of the LORD of hosts, and in the day of his fierce anger. And Babylon, the glory of kingdoms, the beauty of the Chaldean's excellency, shall be as when God overthrew Sodom and Gomorrah."

Great Kingdoms have fallen as a direct result of God's "fierce anger." Let us not be fooled by Satan's deception. God states it clearly that he possesses the POWER to "shake the Heavens, and the earth." We desire no part of God's fierce anger. We are warned by God's total destruction of Sodom and Gomorrah that we cannot "play silly, foolish games" with our Lord and Savior. God described the men of Sodom in Genesis 13:13,

"But the men of Sodom were wicked and sinners before the LORD exceedingly."

God states the men were "exceedingly wicked and sinners." Can you imagine the type of things these men were engaging in for our LORD to describe their behavior as "exceedingly wicked and sinful?" Here is an example:

In Genesis 19, Lot is visited by two angels of God as he sat at the gate of Sodom. The angels were sent by God to deliver a message to Lot to remove his family from the city because He planned to destroy it. Lot entertains the angels in his home. The men of Sodom suddenly arrive at Lot's home and proceed to hammer on his door to get in "that we may know them (the angels)." In verses 7 and 8 Lot pleads with the men of Sodom:

> "And said, I pray you, brethren, do not so wickedly. Behold now, I have two daughters which have not known man; let me, I pray you, bring them unto you, and do ye to them as is good in your eyes: only unto these men do nothing; for therefore came they under the shadow of my roof."

Lot knew he had angelic beings in his home, direct from the presence of God, true holy men, and he did not want these wicked men to attempt to do the wrong thing. The gang wanted to fulfill the lust of their hearts. Lot offers his daughters (the virgins) to the men to please their insatiable appetite. The result of Lot's offer is found in the following scripture:

> "And they said, stand back. And they said again, this one fellow came in to sojourn, and he will need to be a judge: now will we deal worse with thee, than with

them. And they pressed sore upon the man, even Lot,
and came near to break the door" (Genesis 19:9).

The mob was determined to know the angels. The urges and self-pleasures of the men manifests themselves as an "abomination." The angels pull Lot back into the house, and performed the following acts:

"And they smote the men that were at the door of the
house with blindness, both small and great: so that they
wearied themselves to find the door" (Genesis 19:11).

We cannot be misguided by the deceptive nature of Satan. God wants us to take the high standard of morality, not the corrupt standard that Satan desires. God wants us to reflect on His likeness and walk in righteousness.

God loves us more than we love ourselves. God will not tolerate intentional, direct violations of His commandments without a just punishment. To violate the Lord's commandments is to lower the throne under which our Father in heaven sits. We cannot toss mud in the face of God and expect Him to sit idly by and accept it. There is a just reward to being holy, and there is wrath when iniquity is performed. Jesus Christ spoke of God's absolute authority when confronted with a request that was outside of His jurisdiction. He responded directly and compassionately about his Father's authority.

GOD'S AUTHORITY

In Matthew 20:20-23, Christ speaks to a woman who makes a special request for her two sons. Jesus abides by his Father's AUTHORITY. Jesus does not disrespect his Father, nor does he attempt to ignore this woman. But, He elevates His Father because the decision is not His to make. Matthew teaches us:

"Then came to him the mother of Zebedee's children with her sons, worshipping him, and desiring a certain thing of him. And he said unto her, What wilt thou? She saith unto him, Grant that these my two sons may sit, the one on thy right hand, and the other on the left, in thy kingdom. But Jesus answered and said, Ye know not what ye ask. Are ye able to drink of the cup that I shall drink of, and to be baptized with the baptism that I am baptized with? They say unto him, We are able. And he saith unto them, Ye shall drink indeed of my cup, and be baptized with the baptism that I am baptized with: but to sit on my right hand, and on my left, is not mine to give, but it shall be given to them for whom it is prepared of my Father."

We note that God is always glorified through the Son. Jesus Christ listened to his Father's teachings in heaven prior to his arrival on earth. Jesus is always elevating his Father, never accepting praise for himself. We can learn how to honor our earthly mothers and fathers by the eloquent example set by Christ. It also provides us with evidence that God is the Supreme ruler of all things in heaven and beneath heaven. Jesus Christ is our perfect role model.

God has sent famine, flies, snakes, earthquakes, floods, fire, turned water into blood, and made a king live in the woods like an animal for years as punishment against violating His commandments and covenants. Do we want God to punish us in a similar manner or worse? Are we willing to repent? Are we willing to seek forgiveness from God for our sins? Are we willing to accept Jesus Christ as our only Savior? Are we willing to give up our old ways and wear the renewed garb that God has provided? These are questions we must examine. If man's 'churchology' is contradictory to God's Law, it is commanded of us to destroy man's policy. Let us be reminded of

what Job said about the marriage covenant and what would happen
if it is violated in Job 31:12,

> "for it is a fire that consumeth to destruction, and would
> root out all mine increase."

THE LORD'S MERCY

When we elevate our thinking we gather a clearer picture of God's
purposes. Some may wonder why God has not rendered a final
judgment on violations of His commandments. Lamentations 3:22
says,

> "It is of the Lord's mercies that we are not consumed,
> because his compassion's fail not."

God is not speaking of one particular sin or violation. God is
speaking of all sin. Micah 7:18 says,

> "Who is a God like unto thee, that pardoneth iniquity,
> and passeth by the transgression of the remnant of his
> heritage? He retaineth not his anger for ever, because
> He delighteth in mercy."

Exodus 34:6 says,

> "And the Lord passed by before him and proclaimed, the
> Lord, the Lord God, merciful and gracious, longsuffering,
> and abundant in goodness and truth."

Exodus 34:7 says,

> "Keeping mercy for thousands, forgiving iniquity and
> transgression and sin, and that will by no means clear
> the guilty."

Psalm 78:28 says,

> "But he, being full of compassion, forgave their iniquity, and destroyed them not: yea, many a time turned he his anger away, and did not stir up all his wrath."

Nehemiah 9:31 says,

> "Nevertheless for thy great mercies' sake thou didst not utterly consume them, nor forsake them; for thou art a gracious and merciful God."

Psalm 107:1 says,

> "O give thanks unto the Lord, for he is good: for his mercy endureth forever."

Psalm 130:7 says,

> "Let Israel hope in the Lord: for with the Lord there is mercy, and with him is plenteous redemption."

Daniel 9:9 says,

> "To the Lord our God belong mercies and forgiveness, though we have rebelled against him;"

Nahum 1:3 says,

> "The Lord is slow to anger, and great in power, and will not at all acquit the wicked; the Lord hath his way in the whirlwind and in the storm, and the clouds are the dust of his feet."

Romans 2:4 says,

"Or despisest thou the riches of his goodness and forbearance and long suffering; not knowing that the goodness of God leadeth thee to repentance."

God's goodness and mercy keeps us from being consumed in fire for our sins. God is all-merciful. God is all-compassionate. We exalt our Heavenly Father for His patience. God is not quick to condemn. Compassion and forgiveness are at the forefront of God's thought processes. Keep in mind, we are not cleared of our guilt, but we must immediately remove ourselves from sin and seek repentance from God. We cannot serve "sinful pleasure for a season" and justify it before God. Also, we cannot "tempt the Lord our God." God is here for us. Trust in God. Man is quick to condemn and judge. God is not like man. Let us glorify God for His eternal mercy, compassion and forgiveness.

A PERSONAL INVENTORY

When was the last time you did a personal inventory of yourself? Have you performed a brutally honest introspection of self? Did you like what you saw?

Ask yourself the following questions:
- What can I Do without Jesus?
- What can I Say without Jesus?
- What can I Be without Jesus?
- What can I Think without Jesus?
- Where can I Go without Jesus?
- Where can I Stay without Jesus?

The Traditional Celtic Prayer: "God to enfold me, God to surround me, God in my speaking, God in my thinking, God in my sleeping, God in my waking, God in my watching, God in my hoping."

GOD'S WRATH

God can express His anger in a devastating manner. We know not the time, nor the hour. It is important to repent of our sins quickly. God is merciful, forgiving, compassionate, and slow to anger. God reminds us of His Almighty wrath in the New Testament. II Peter 2:6 says,

> "And turning the cities of Sodom and Gomorrah into ashes condemned them with an overthrow, making them an ensample unto thou that after should live ungodly."

There is not a moment in life that we should not consider God in our actions and reactions to life's conditions and circumstances. When we place God at the center of our lives, there is nothing the enemy can do to extract us from performing a righteous act. God is not to be served when it's convenient. But, we lift up His Holy name moment-by-moment. When we sin, God provides an outlet, forgiveness at the footstool of Jesus Christ. Christ welcomes us with open arms. The angels rejoice in heaven when a sinner accepts Christ as their savior. God's forgiveness is permanent. He does not remind us of our transgression. If we are to avoid God's wrath, we cannot be violators of His Laws. We must fear God.

ON GOODNESS AND SUBMISSION

Have you ever heard someone describe another person as being "a good person"? How is good measured? Is decency included in the evaluation? Is there anything good within man? Jesus Christ says in Matthew 10:18,

"And Jesus said unto him. Why callest thou me good?
There is none good but one, that is, God."

The Son of God was clearly without sin, yet He refused to proclaim himself as "good." Christ did not elevate himself. He remained totally humble. No iniquity was found in Jesus. God searched the heavens and earth for the perfect deliverer for mankind and only His Son could fulfill the mission. Jesus fulfilled everything his Father asked of him. Jesus was the mouthpiece of God. Jesus did not sin. He is with his Father in heaven. How do we classify ourselves as *good* in anything? Man cannot assemble the thoughts of *"goodness."* We are too corrupt and wicked in our present form. The Son of God exalted His Father.

When Christ's hour drew near, He fell upon His knees and prayed with earnest to His Father. Mark 15:36 says, "Abba, Father, all things are possible unto thee: take away this cup from me: nevertheless not what I will, but what thou wilt."

Jesus Christ denies himself in the most humble submission to his Father. Christ does not demand or command His Father to perform anything, "but what thou wilt." Christ acknowledges that "nothing is impossible with God." He recognizes that God possesses all the power and authority. Christ elevates His Father and places his life in His hands. When we are in a state of anguish, do we fall to our knees, facing heaven with open arms seeking the face of God? Are we so strong that we can't become weak before God? Do we possess sufficient power to handle our daily affairs without any intervention from God? Will we ask God to remove the cup that burdens us?

There is only one that can deliver us from the obstacles of this world. There is only one power that rules supreme in heaven and earth; the Lord God Almighty. If we recognize any other source of power beyond God, we provoke the anger of the All-Powerful.

EXALTING THE FATHER ABOVE SELF

Jesus performed the will of His Father. He magnified God in every situation He faced. Jesus denied himself in favor of his Father. He never exalted himself to be on his Father's level, never submitting a list of accomplishments or achievements to his Father of all the "good work" he performed on earth. Jesus never documented his many miracles performed in the name of his Father. Jesus was always the humble peaceful servant, the mouthpiece of God. Christ never rendered judgment against another, but glorified his Father as the final judge of all things. Remember, Job's mighty works are well documented. Job reflected on those works while suffering through his misery. Jesus Christ performed many miracles, but remained a humbled servant. Christ showed us how to live an exemplary life. No matter what the circumstance or condition may be, God grants us grace. We reside under grace. Remember, we must persevere if we are to receive the Promise. Mark 8:3, 4,

> "And when he had called the people unto him with his disciples also, he said unto them, Whosoever will come after me, let him deny himself, and take up his cross, and follow me."

If we elevate ourselves we lower ourselves. How can we boast about anything in the presence of God? Are we worthy of His mercy? Do we have the arms to box like God? Do we have the capability to know what tomorrow brings? How can people make themselves the center of anything when all power in heaven and earth has been assigned to Jesus Christ? Only God is worthy of praise.

HUBRIS

The early twenty-first century abounds with people that converse about "how good they are"; boast that "I go to church every Sunday"; "I pay my tithes;" or "it's so unfortunate about the homeless so I gave this much to help them, or I could never see myself in that situation." Humble thyself before God, never boasting about anything or anyone. How can we rationize about our works if our faith is lacking? All things under heaven belong to the Father. And only the Father is "good." Job talks about his "works" for the Lord in verses Job 13:13-17,

> "If I did despise the cause of my manservant or of my maid servant, when they contended with me; If I have withheld the poor from their desire, or have caused the eyes of the widow to fail: Or have eaten my morsel the fatherless and myself alone, hath not eaten thereby."

Job acknowledges in verse 19 how he provided clothing for poor families in cold weather. Job was a powerful voice for the poor and downtrodden. He did not render judgment or condemnation. He was a voice for the less fortunate. He was a keen advisor to princes of the kingdom. People throughout Uz respected and admired the integrity and character of Job. Job willingly gave to others, especially the poor.

> "If I have seen any perish for want of clothing, or any poor without covering..."

Job followed God's standards when it came to helping the poor. Proverbs 19:17 says,

> "He that hath pity upon the poor lendeth unto the Lord; and that which he hath given will he pay him again."

Job continues to represent his commitment to the poor by the following action:

> "If his loins have not blessed me, and if he were not warmed with the fleece of my sheep..."

Job, being a man of gigantic wealth and influence in the Land of Uz, reveals in Verse 21 that he never used his power, influence and wealth against the unfortunate:

> "If I have lifted up my hand against the fatherless, when I saw my help in the gate."

Job speaks on the record about his total commitment to the word of God and correctness in his works. I John 4:17, 18 says,

> "But whoso hath this world's good, and seeth his brother have need, and shutteth up his bowels of compassion from him, how dwelleth the love of God in him? My little children, let us not love in word, neither in tongue; but in deed and in truth."

John makes the proclamation that loving in deed and truth permits us to serve others with dignity. We honor God when we help a brother in need. It is not work that we boast about; it is part of the Christian way of life. Job illustrates his commitment to serving the fatherless. Job assisted the widows in the midst of their grief. He did not dishonor the widows by sitting eagerly by their door to commit adultery. He feared that God would take away his increase. His high standard of care for the poor and grief stricken should live in our life today.

We glorify God in helping people in need of love, grace and compassion. If we are to help a person in need, it must be done with love

257

and truth. We do not glorify or magnify the Lord with lip service. God is a keen observer. He's always on the lookout for believers that serve Him relentlessly. He's always soaring overhead like an eagle, looking down on earth to select those that will be "servants of righteousness." When we service the less fortunate, the credit goes to God. We cannot salute ourselves as if we are good. God will show the world the attributes of a good and faithful servant. We build treasures in heaven when we help the poor and downtrodden. Job always did the right thing in his charity work. Job feared God. Remember, Job was "upright and perfect." Job understood God's commandments. Proverbs 21:13 says,

> "Whoso stoppeth his ears at the cry of the poor, he also shall cry himself, but shall not be heard."

Job abided by God's written word. Job did not deviate from God's teachings. He was a man that glorified God in all of his works. Job is so adamant about his level of purity and uprightness that he states in chapter 31 verse 22:

> "Then let mine arm fall from my shoulder blade, and let mine arm be broken from the bone."

Job continues on by saying his fear of being separated from God caused him not to do unscrupulous acts in life. When we sin we are separated from God. God does not find pleasure in sin. Job avoided evil on all corners. He feared the wrath of God. He did not want to be permanently separated from God. Remember, the first lesson in life is to fear God. Job continues in verse 23:

> "For destruction from God was a terror to me, and by reason of his highness I could not endure."

JOB'S WEALTH

Job was the richest man in the east. He possessed extraordinary wealth. All of his business interests were successful and he had a great family. He was the Bill Gates, Rockefeller, Vanderbilt, Getty, Ford, or Trump of his day. However, Job was not like most men of extraordinary wealth. He was a true servant of the Lord. He did not deviate from God's principles in handling wealth. Mark 10:23-25 says,

> "And Jesus looked around about, and saith unto his disciples, How hardly shall they that have riches enter into the kingdom of God! And the disciples were astonished at his words. But Jesus answereth again, and saith unto them, Children how hard is it for them that trust in riches to enter into the kingdom of God. It is easier for a camel to go through the eye of a needle, than for a rich man to enter into the kingdom of God."

Jesus made this revelation when a man with great possessions inquired of him, "Good Master, what shall I do that I may inherit eternal life?" Christ advises him of the Lord's Commandments. The rich man responds in Mark 10:20, "Master, all these have I observed from my youth." Jesus immediately advises him on how to obtain eternal life in Mark 10:21,

> "One thing thou lackest: go thy way, sell whatsoever thou hast, and give it to the poor, and thou shalt have treasure in heaven: and come, take up the cross, and follow me."

The man walked away grieved, unable or unwilling to give up his earthly possessions to carry the Cross for God. We should never be ashamed to know Christ. Jesus carried the heavier burden in order for us to have salvation. Christ died for the Jew as well as the Gentile. He covers every sin for all mankind. When you examine yourself are you fully devoted to serving the Living God?

Jesus Christ explains in Mark 10:24, "Children, how hard is it for them that trust on riches to enter into the Kingdom of God!" God wants us to trust in him first and most of all. Job did not glorify himself in earthly possessions. He did not place his trust in gold and silver. Job placed his total trust in God. Job is one of the few men of wealth that will enter the Kingdom of heaven.

O LET US PRAY

O Heavenly Father, teach us to obey your commands against all earthly challenges. Father, you provide us with a mind, heart and spirit to reason, but we consistently fail because we limit ourselves to our own intellect and do not strive to think and decide like you, Father. Forgive us, Father. We need you to abide in us in order to manifest the greatest of Christ in us. We are incompetent, lacking in knowledge and understanding. We are weak but made strong through the resurrection of the Living God. Our thought processes are weak because we have become foolish in serving thee. We ask for your forgiveness O heavenly Father. We are unworthy of your many blessings and patience, but thank you and praise your Holy Name for the mercy you have shown us. Father, help us to focus our minds on your Holy Word and only your Word. Let us glorify your name in all things that we do, that you will bless us with the wisdom to understand and the power and will to carry through your word against all forms of temptation. O Father, you are our Master, our Deliverer, and our Redeemer. Bless us to be like you Father, your principles are the best principles. We have no principles without Thee. O Heavenly Father, have mercy on us, deliver us from evil and when we walk in the valley of the shadows of death we will only fear thee, because thy rod and staff will comfort me. O Heavenly Father, in the name of Jesus Christ, our Savior we ask Thee. AMEN.

Job's wealth did not conquer him. He did not worship money. He understood that God gave him everything. Job 31:24 says,

> "If I have made gold my hope, or have said to the fine gold, Thou art my confidence..."

How often do we hear rich folks boasting about their wealth? In modern day culture we hear stories of rich folks worshipping their wealth. Job 31:25 says,

> "If I rejoiced because my wealth was great, and because mine hand had gotten much..."

Job continues to document his loyalty to God's principles. Job reveals that he was not overwhelmed by God's creations. Job 31:26 says,

> "If I beheld the sun when it shined, or the moon walking in brightness..."

Job wants God to know that He did not place a higher value on the creation than the Creator. Nothing created in heaven and earth measures up to God. Nothing created by the hands of God should be worshipped. There is only one God. Job 31:28 says,

> "This also was an iniquity to be punished by the judge: for I should have denied the God that is above."

JOB'S TREATMENT OF OTHERS

How often do we look upon our neighbors troubling circumstance and point an accusing finger? Who among us has said, "I told you he was up to no good?" Did Christ point an accusing finger, or did He show mercy and compassion? When Peter fell in the water, did Christ say, "You should not have tried to be like me and walk the water, learn how to swim?" Christ offered a helping hand.

Whether in heaven or hell God is there. He does not abandon us in the midst of despair or heartache. Job illustrated the same temperament when he witnessed a neighbor experiencing problems. Job turned the other cheek when hate was directed at him. Job 31:29, 30 says,

> "If I rejoiced at the destruction of him that hated me, or lifted up myself when evil found him: Neither have I suffered my mouth to sin by wishing a curse to his soul."

In verses 29 and 30 Job illustrates an honorable virtue that few men show even today. How often do we hear the victim scream hate at the violator in a criminal case? This is not to say that the victim's emotions are not justified. In the flesh we are subject to lash out and curse the violator. But, if we catalogue Job's integrity and character, we elevate to a higher spiritual level that glorifies God. When we heighten our awareness and attach to God, we become in tune to the wonderful attributes that govern the heavens. There is no corruption in God. His garments are not moth-eaten. God is wrapped in the spirit of holiness. His raiment is that of the King of kings, Lord of lords and Champion of champions. His integrity and character is far above man's limited knowledge and understanding. It is essential that we dwell in the shelter of the Most High. When we dwell in the house of the Lord, we will offer a hand to help; we will pray for one another; we will command of ourselves to love one another in the likeness of Jesus Christ. Job 31:32 says,

> "The stranger did not lodge in the street: but I opened my doors to the traveler."

In modern terms, Job provided shelter for the homeless and those traveling with no place to rest or sleep in order to continue their journey. It would be safe to assume that Job provided a hot bath, clothing, food, and a wholesome atmosphere for a worried traveler to rest and relax. We can imagine that a holy man like Job was an excellent host, practicing perfect decorum throughout his home. We would have welcome and right at home in Job's residence.

COMPARING OUR SINS TO OTHERS

As a parent, I instruct each child never to compare their sins or transgressions to someone else. My parents taught me the identical lessons. For example, "what I did was not as bad as what 'so-so' did" or "I wasn't as bad as "what's his name." How often do children and adults may excuses for their troubles or mistakes. How often do we take full responsibility for our actions? As a society we are always in search for excuses or valid reasons for sin. Rather than take the high road and accept full responsibility, the flesh cries out to locate a substitute, a reason or excuse to smooth the situation over. Job points out in Job 31:33, "If I covered my transgressions as Adam, by hiding mine iniquity in my bosom." Is Job desperate at this stage? How many of us compare our sins to others, stating in our minds that our sins are not as bad as our neighbor? We must learn to stand on our own merit, not measuring ourselves against another's transgressions.

Christ paid the price on the Cross for our covering. The check has been cashed and we have full access to His Father, but only through Him. When God commanded Job to gird up his loins like a man, God wants a man to take responsibility, not hide in the Garden like Adam and avoid the situation. And when God confronts us about our sins, He wants the truth, nothing less. We have to comprehend that we cannot hide the truth from God. God is All-knowing.

Every man and woman must stand before God on his own merit. Job makes the point that he was not going to hide his transgressions in his bosom. How often do we perform our insidious acts in the dark and walk with our head up in the light? How often do we sneak around in sin and conclude "what you don't know won't hurt you"? Sin is sin, and is punishable with death. God is aware of every sin that has been committed by man from the beginning of time. He will not miss one transgression.

God is above pettiness. All sin is wrong in the eyesight of God. We cannot make God feel guilty about our sins, especially when He has instructed us on how to live a life of holiness. God hates sin and has placed the punishment of death on all that sin. It is only through repentance through the blood of Jesus Christ that our sins can be forgiven.

Job was speaking to his three friends, who came to comfort him, as he struggled with the trials and tribulations that Satan had placed upon him. However, Satan's actions were totally under God's control and power. Satan can do absolutely nothing without God's permission.

God has been clear that works alone will not get us into the Kingdom of heaven. Job's record of purity is well documented. God was pleased with his servant. God is the absolute authority over all things in the Universe. God advises us if we have done a good job. Man cannot tell God about his "goodness."

The Book of Job confronts our modern day issues such as euthanasia, mercy killing, assisted-suicide, Dr. Kervokian, C. L. Jung, wealth, and other antidotes for our everyday usage. We looked deeper into the "physicalness" of Job's suffering and offered a closer examination of God's masterful handiwork. We conclude that God is always in control and He never punishes us unjustly. We understand that Jesus Christ is the Just One.

We have valuable lessons in life to learn. Let us never flee from our problems. Let us confront our problems and govern our circumstances, rather than permitting our circumstances to dictate to us. Our frustrations limit us in coping with various challenges in life. Our frustrations cut us off from true decision-making, because tensions and stress in our lives restrict us from living life more abundantly. Let us make a daily commitment to God, handing over all frustrations and tensions to Him. And we will watch our daily lives improve discernibly, or, as Job would say; "watch my increase."

The Hollywood actor Andy Griffith understood the presence of God and the challenges we face in life. He says, "I believe that in every situation, no matter how difficult, God extends grace greater than the hardship, and strength and peace of mind that can lead us to a place higher than where we were before."

Job's struggle is not difficult to comprehend if we open our heart, mind and soul to God's mission. If we lean completely on God and His eternal mercy and compassion, we are taken to a new horizon far greater than the past. God's vision is far greater than the vision that we have for ourselves. God has a blueprint for our lives that's far beyond earthly architects.

Satan's mission is to tear down all of the building blocks of God. He is jealous of man and everyone in the image of Jesus Christ. His method is to destroy man through fleshly desires. He wants us to doubt God. He wants us to feel guilty about sin. He attacks our faith and trust in the Lord. He is masterful in this area. But, when the mighty sword of the Lord is on the premises he flees, just like he did when God arrived on the premises to interrogate Job. Satan's objective is to embarrass man before God. Satan enjoys pointing out our weaknesses. He was convinced if God removed the hedge from around Job that he would curse God and die. He lost so terribly that he embarrassed himself. We have the same opportunity to celebrate before God when we turn away from sin. The Bible states that angels leap for joy whenever a sinner is saved. Just imagine the celebration in heaven. The angels are pulling for us to make it through the struggle. God's angelic warriors fight for the throne of God. They represent everything good about Christ. James wrote, "we count them happy which endure" (James 5:11). The Apostle Paul says, "But now, after that ye have known God, or rather are known of God, how turn ye again to the weak and beggarly elements, whereunto ye desire again to be in bondage?" (Galatians 4:9)

We cannot handle Satan alone. Only God can handle Satan. Christ handled Satan in the wilderness. Their head to head meeting was of colossal proportions. It was the heavenly God versus the demonic god of hell. We cannot play games with Satan, i.e. engaging in such behaviors as witchcraft, occult, fornication, adultery, gossip, wrongful treatment of our neighbor, failure to follow the Ten Commandments, fearing Satan over God, lack of faith and trust in God, etc. Ultimately, Satan will only humble himself before God. God has Satan in check. No matter how destructive Satan may be, we should feel absolutely confident that our Lord and Savior is in control. James 2:19 says,

"Thou believest that there is one God; thou doest well: the devils also believe, and tremble."

The biblical scriptures are clear that "the devils also believe, and tremble." If Satan and his demons fear God, why don't we fear the God of heaven and earth? King David said that God is our fortress, our supreme protector. God is our Master and he has provided us with all things. As in Job's case, Satan may damage or destroy the flesh of man "that the spirit may be saved in the day of the Lord Jesus" (I Corinthians 5:5). We fear the Lord Almighty who governs the flesh and soul.

Earthly pleasures of the flesh only lead to corruption of the spirit. Our sinful nature takes us on the back roads to hell. God has a road well lit for us to travel on. He has a road paved that is straight and narrow. He has His heavenly angels along the way to provide proper direction. We will not get lost along the way. The Apostle Paul makes an urgent appeal in Romans 12:1, "Brethren, by the mercies of God, that ye present your bodies a living sacrifice, holy, acceptable unto God, which is your reasonable service." Paul's comment is pivotal for believers. The sacrifice Paul speaks of is not of bulls and goats or dead animals. This is not about the physical world. God wants us to sacrifice our body, mind, and soul. He wants us to sacrifice our hopes, dreams, ambitions, and will. Christ made us holy and acceptable. His work on the Cross paid the price for our salvation. We must bring our body into submission to the will of God. We have been justified by Christ Jesus. This is a daily mission for all believers. We must not conform to this world but transform by the renewing of our mind to receive the perfect will of God (Romans 12:2).

Thank you Jesus! All praise and glory to thee, my Father in heaven, Watcher over me. Thank You Jesus! Amen.

JOB'S SUFFERING

James 5:13 says, "If any among you is afflicted? Let him pray. Is any merry? Let him sing psalms" (James 5:13). When we willingly accept God's purposes for us, we gain valuable knowledge and receive a greater blessing as a result. God is filled with eternal mercy and compassion and will not leave us in ruins. Whatever the struggle God will lead us to the Promised Land. He will not leave us in the wilderness.

Today, we must keep on the lookout for Christ. Christ puts us through problems, struggles, and obstacles to make us the person God wants us to be. God's wisdom is beyond human comprehension. We must look upon Job's struggles with compassion, and mercy, rather than condemnation. It is mandatory that we consider the question "How does it profit God?" instead of "How does it profit ourselves?" When we suffer, we do not suffer onto ourselves because our bodies do not belong to us. We suffer to glorify God. We suffer to reflect the likeness of Him who designed us. We suffer to reign with Christ. What choice will we make when it comes to suffering in the name of God? Can we endure the pain? At what level will our suffering be? Will we choose suffering or pleasure? Hebrews 11:24, 25 says,

> "By faith Moses, when he was come to years, refused to be called the son of Pharaoh's daughter; Choosing rather to suffer affliction with the people of God, than to enjoy the pleasures of sin for a season."

Moses picked affliction over pleasure of sin. God gives us that choice. Moses was given a choice: to continue to live under pharaoh's rulership—enjoying the sinful pleasures of the pharaoh's palace—or live amongst the people of God. Moses walked hand and hand with God. He served God willingly and justly. He made the correct decision, to carry the cross for God. Moses listened and obeyed God and led the people out of bondage into the Promised Land. We are happier today because of Moses' decision. Moses was a great Ambassador of God. Like Moses, we have decisions to make. We have to make a clear choice. Do we choose pleasure for a season or affliction? Whether in pleasure of affliction we must choose God, the author and finisher of our faith. God gives us the ability to choose right from wrong. When we consider the decision that Moses made, it gives us strength and confidence to make the righteous decision. It is not about us and our desires and urges; it is about God and His Almighty purposes for us. If we abide in God and Christ lives in us, with God overhead, we will not be denied. We will make the right decision. And that decision will be based on the glorification and magnification of God. Self will not play a part in our decision. Exaltation of the Holy Father will be at the forefront of our decision.

Suffering makes us stronger and, hopefully, wiser. There are many lessons of life that God can teach us. We are so limited in our human form. However, with God in us, around us, beneath us, and high above us, we have every opportunity to understand and transcend our transgressions. Through the grace of God, we have salvation and renewed hope to endure and conquer every bombardment from Satan. Satan cannot harm us when God is in control. Keep in mind, Satan undertook his mission in order to be like God and overthrown His heavenly kingdom. Satan was sadly mistaken; he made a bad decision and it cost him His relationship with God. He resides permanently in hell as a result of his selfish decision. God's holy warriors kicked Satan and his angels out of heaven.

SATAN'S STRUGGLE

The following provides a brief description of what transpired when Satan and his angels attacked God. Revelation 12:7, 8, 10 says,

> "And there was war in Heaven: Michael and his angels fought against the dragon; and the dragon fought and his angels; and prevailed not; neither was their place found any more in Heaven. And I heard a loud voice saying in Heaven, Now is come salvation, and strength, and the Kingdom of our God, and the power of his Christ: for the accuser of our brethren is cast down, which accused them before our God day and night."

We have the victory because "our accuser has been cast down." Our accuser is totally defeated. God's undefeated record remains in tact. God showed Satan that He is unbeatable in battle. Moment by moment, Satan presents himself in council before our Lord, degrading us and making a mockery of our less-than-perfect lives, always expressing his confidence before God that he can surely make us "curse God to his face." The Bible says Satan accuses us before God "day and night" (Revelations 12:10). Satan believes every man is unstable and weak. He feels his corrupt nature can persuade man to sin before God. Revelations 12:9 says, "the Devil, and Satan, which deceiveth the whole world." If he has deceived the entire world how are we equipped to take him on in hand-to- hand combat? If we are not suited up in prayer, righteousness, faith, and the "blood of the Lamb," we have no defense against the arrows of the devil. It's the blood of Christ that protects us from the devil, and the devil hates that protection. He despises the holy protection of Jesus Christ. We are warned of Satan's intense hate in Revelations 12:12, "Woe to the inhabiters of the earth and of the sea! For the devil is come down unto you, having great wrath, because he knoweth that he hath but a short time." Consider for a moment how destructive this creature will be, knowing his time is short. Will you be without fault before the mighty throne of God? Will you serve sin for a season?

Satan has documented man throughout time and knows how man enjoys pleasure. When we take on Satan, we must be properly attired in salvation, righteousness, and faith. The hand of Almighty God must be upon us. Christ must manifest himself in us. Now, we are prepared to fight. But, we cannot enter the ring without being blanketed with the "blood of Christ." It is the blood that washes away our sins. It's the blood that cleanses us from head to toe. Remember, Job was covered with boils from the top of his head to the bottom of his feet. That's a snapshot of how the enemy deals with us. He desires to make our appearance as sickly as possible. But, the blood of Christ heals us from the top of our head to the bottom of our feet. In addition, He dwells in us. It's the blood that intimidates Satan and his cohorts. The blood injects fear into Satan. He knows the blood of Christ is pure, holy, and just. He knows that Christ is incorruptible. He cannot stand anything that resembles the likeness of Christ. John 2:1-3 says,

> "My little children, these things write I unto you, that ye sin not. And if any man sin, we have an advocate with the Father, Jesus Christ the righteous: And he is the propitiation for our sins: and not for our's only, but also for the sins of the whole world. And thereby we do not know that we know him, if we keep his commandments."

Remember, Satan deceived the whole world; Jesus Christ saved the entire world by His marvelous work on the Cross. Satan desires that we forget what Christ did on the Cross. He wants us to accept the modern day message from non-believers that proclaim that

Christ remains in the grave, that the Son of God has not been resurrected. This is a false doctrine. Satan has deceived the world to think that Christ has not risen. John 2:22, 23 says,

> "Who is a liar but he that denieth that Jesus is the Christ? He is antichrist, that denieth the Father and the Son. Whosoever denieth the Son, the same hath not the Father: {but} he that acknowledgeth the Son hath the Father also."

Glory to God! Let us not be deceived by the wicked one. The enemy realizes that he only has a short period of time to perform his destruction. Christ is with us. We are born of God through Jesus Christ for a life everlasting. We cannot conform to this world, because this world does not love God. We have to conform to the world of heaven. We must be governed by the spirit of God, not by man's earthly pleasures. When we reject fleshly things, we gain incite into the spiritual world that God has created for us. The flesh will return to its rightful place, the dust of the earth. The spirit will raise into the bosom of Abraham, the father of faith. Let us be obedient to God and our resurrection will bring merriment to the heavenly beings because we will be like Him.

RIGHTEOUSNESS

> John 2:29 says, "If ye know that he is righteous, ye know that every one that doeth righteousness is born of him."

> May the Lord grant us the wisdom to understand the reading of His word for the daily edification of our hearts. Holy and Glorified is our exalted Father in heaven. Most holy is His name. AMEN.

Satan is jealous of God and despises man. Knowing this, we must strive in earnest to be a reflection of Christ. When we improve our integrity and character, God becomes pleased with us. God loves uprightness and perfection. Remember, God said Job was perfect and feared God. God-like character is the best character to possess. Satan is a powerful creature and we must not fall prey to his persuasive skills and tactics. Satan is the ruler over all things evil, all things contrary to God's principles, commandments, and covenants. Jesus Christ noted the following regarding Satan:

> "Ye are of your father the devil, and the lusts of your father ye will do. He was a murderer from the beginning, and abode not in the truth, because there is no truth in him. When he speaketh a lie, he speaketh of his own: for he is a liar, and a father of it" (John 8:44).

Satan is out of his league when faced with the ultimate and absolute power of God. Remember, Satan trembles in the presence of God. Let us not be fooled. In the beginning we were made in the "image of God." If we act like our Maker, we exalt the Holiness of the Creator. We can become like Job, "Perfect and upright, fearing God and escheweth evil." God is too fully equipped to fail us. God cannot fail. His word is divine and holy. He is majesty and glory.

NEW TESTAMENT ILLUSTRATIONS OF FEAR

When we speak of fearing the Lord; we speak not only of man but Satan too. Jesus Christ shows us how the demons fear and tremble in His presence when an army of powerful demons possessed a man. Mark 5:15 describes the scene:

"Because that he had been often bound with fetters and chains, and the chains had been plucked asunder by him, and the fetters broken in pieces: neither could any man tame him."

The demon saw Jesus Christ from afar; the man ran and worshipped him (verse 6). In verse 7, the demons submit themselves to Jesus:

"And cried with a loud voice, and said, what have I to do with thee, Jesus, thou Son of the most high God? I adjure thee by God, that thou torment me not."

The demons do not appear so tough in the presence of Jesus Christ. They acknowledge that Jesus is the Son of God. Now, this is coming from an army of demons who have deceived the world. They plead on the name of God for mercy from torment from Christ. Does that sound like a demon? In the presence of our Lord and Savior the demons come off begging and pleading for mercy. It's clear that they fear Christ and tremble in His presence. Jesus Christ responds to their loud cry in a commanding voice in verse 8,

"Come out of the man, thou unclean spirit."

In verse 9, Jesus Christ demanded an answer to the following question: "What is thy name?" And he answered, saying, "My name is Legion: for we are many."

Rather than destroy them, Jesus directed the demons into the swine, and the swine drowned in the sea. We can rejoice convinced that the Son of God possesses Almighty power and authority in heaven and earth. Demons are no challenge for the Son of God. Why didn't Satan appear for backup? We can rest with confidence that Satan was as fearful of Christ as his demonic followers.

This is the same Christ, the Son of God that sits on the right hand of the Father in heaven. He is our Advocate and voice of reason to the Father. He is our Savior. Satan is without command of the Father. Satan is a loser. Satan cannot conquer God. Remember, King David called God, "my fortress, my rock, my deliverer, my God, my strength, in whom I will trust, my buckler, the horn of my salvation, and my high tower." God's foundation is as strong as a rock. God insulates us from all corners. Satan cannot reach us without God's permission.

> I am happy, overjoyed, confident, and in awe of our heavenly Father and his Son. God's power and will over all things in heaven and beneath heaven is such that we must rededicate ourselves to God. Our Father is so glorified and exalted that our imagination cannot perceive it. May the name of Jesus be firmly planted in our heart, mind, and soul. O Father, your word is so pleasing, so wonderful, so filled with grace, full of so much love and understanding, so much wisdom and it is so magnificent. Mankind needs to wake up and comprehend that we cannot continue with our incomplete worship and incomplete submission to your Holy Name. We are too stupid, Father, too weak to be in Thine presence; therefore, have Supreme mercy on us because we are fools. But, we are thankful for your Son Jesus and his Supreme VICTORY over all things. Praise Jesus! Praise Jesus! Praise Jesus! Thank You, God, for granting mankind this opportunity to be saved. Thank you Father. AMEN.

Yes, Job struggled and faced a tremendous challenge. He endured with patience, faith, understanding, forgiveness, and renewed hope. We need not be negative and seek to challenge God on

Job's condition. Let us look at Satan's evil intentions. Let us focus directly on Satan's motive, rather than God's high character and integrity. Job was a holy man and Satan was jealous of that. Satan is the tempter here, not God. Why did Satan want to destroy Job? Why does Satan want to destroy us? Satan is evil and in constant need to satisfy his thirst to destroy. James 1:13, 14 says,

> "Let no man say when he is tempted, I am tempted of God: for God cannot be tempted with evil, neither tempteth be any man: But every man is tempted, when he is drawn away of his own lust, and enticed."

DELIVER US FROM TEMPTATION

God gives us a choice between good and evil. When we serve Satan, we reject God. Our restoration back to God is only through Jesus Christ. When we are "drawn away by our own lust, and enticed" we separate ourselves from God. When we acknowledge our sins before God, humble and submit ourselves at the footstool of Christ, our sins are forgiven through the blood of the Lamb. Our Advocate is well established in heaven. Our Advocate will speak to the Father on our behalf and restoration is done.

In the name of Jesus Christ let His works lead us to a clearer understanding and wisdom of God's purposes when we are asked to "carry the cross."

With these verses firmly planted in our minds let us move forward in our lives to live with total and complete faith and trust that God will raise us up in due season.

JOB IN THE WORLD OF BUSINESS

Job has perfect business acumen. It is clear in God's description of Job that he maintained the highest degree of integrity, trust, and honesty in all his business transactions. Job's word was his bond. Let us visualize for a moment how Job conducted his business. Job was upfront and upright in every sector of his business. Job did not engage in under-handed tactics. He did not "bad-mouth" the competition. Job strongly rejected any businessman that approached him who was unprincipled in his dealings. Job was the ideal business associate, always presenting himself with the highest degree of professionalism; he was a true entrepreneur, with morals and ethics.

The lesson here is as long as you have God totally and completely in your life, the temptations brought by wealth are not temptations at all. Keep in mind, Job was the wealthiest man in the East, principled in every aspect of his life. Christ said, "Give unto Caesar what is Caesar's." God commands us to live our lives more abundantly. No matter how minute the situation may be, we need God. We are totally, completely, and absolutely dependent on God. There is no substitute.

Faced with the reality that we are merely a speck of dust from the earth from which we were created and to which we must return, man's humanness is revealed for the world to view. Life is based on new and renewed challenges and consequences. Challenges on the surface appear to overwhelm us, but the hope and renewed faith in our Lord and savior Jesus Christ is a power vested in all of us. Job's demeanor reveals man's significance with his own insignificance when confronted with the true will, power, strength, knowledge, and love of God the Almighty. The All Knowing, the

Creator, the Beginning and the End, Jehovah, King of kings, Lord of lords, the God of Abraham, Isaac, Jacob, Moses, King David, King Solomon, the maker of all things in the universe, Champion of champions, and our Father who Art in heaven, Holy Be Thy Name. This is the living God, the God in the Book of Genesis who, when his masterful art of the universe was completed, looked around and said, "it was very good" (Gen. 1:31). This is the God in heaven who sacrificed His only Son, Jesus Christ. "For God sent not his Son into the world to condemn the world; but that the world through him might be saved" (John 3:17).

There is a void in every person's life, as noted in the story of Job. That void can only be filled by God. His tender mercies and compassion sustains us. There is no substitute for the marvelous work that Jesus Christ performed on the Cross. Remember, we were filthy dreamers prior to the death, burial, resurrection and ascension of Christ. We are rooted in Christ. "Blotting out the handwriting of ordinances that was against us, which was contrary to us, and took it out of the way, nailing it to his cross" (Colossians 2:14). Christ is the firstborn from the dead that in all things he might have the preeminence (Colossians 118).

We can intellectualize about the reasons why God permitted Satan to take down a righteous man, but the point God illustrates is that His knowledge, understanding, and wisdom is supremely superior to man. His power is unmatched in the world. Job trusted God. He had faith in God. He knew that his Redeemer lives. Let us elevate our thinking processes, and conclude that God has a hand in everything that goes on in life. Isaiah had a vision of the wonderful majesty and glory of God in Isaiah 6:1-3,

"In the year that king Uzziah died I saw also the Lord sitting upon a throne, high and lifted up, and his train filled the temple. Above it stood the seraphim's: each one had six wings; with twain he covered his face, and with twain he covered his feet, and with twain he did fly. And one cried unto another, and said Holy, holy, holy, is the Lord of hosts: the whole earth is full of his glory."

Isaiah is humbled by his vision of the Holy Father in His glory and majesty. When Satan viewed his Maker in this position, Satan became jealous and wanted to be like the Father. Satan sought to destroy our heavenly Father, not love, worship and cherish him. For the iniquity that was found in Lucifer, God dealt with him accordingly. Satan did not care to be humble, but arrogant in his pursuit to over-throw and be like his Maker:

"And the great dragon was cast out, that old serpent called the Devil and Satan, which deceiveth the whole world: he was cast out into the earth, and his angels were cast out with him" (Revelations 12:9).

In other words, God cleaned house and disposed of all the garbage. There is no place in heaven for those in opposition to God's program. You cannot enter God's premises without complete submission to the heavenly Father. Job is merely a human being that was tested in order to receive God's salvation, mercy, grace, compassion, and glory.

Let it be known that God can detect the slightest sin in us. Your innermost thoughts cannot be hidden from God. He is the Maker and Creator of us and, with God, All things are Possible; without God, you have nothing. Are you willing to go into battle without God? Are you willing to leave home or go to sleep without God? Are you willing to eat a meal without God? We need God. God does not need us. God will surprise you. God is here. He is available to us. God is useful to us. Can you assemble any thought process without God? Consider for a moment.

OTHER INTERPRETATIONS OF JOB

Scholars of immense intellectual capacities, men with brains of gigantic proportions, have researched and analyzed Job's circumstances and psychological behavior. Some of these scholars have challenged God in writing as to "why would he send such a just and righteous man as Job to the depths of humiliation and despair without a reason?" Some say Job should have challenged God more forcefully, expressing anger at God's mistreatment of him. The question is simple: do you have arms to box with God? How can you challenge God? How can you confront the most powerful being in the universe? How can we be angry at the being that holds our very life force in the palm of his hand? How can you judge the Most High Judge? What jury panels can you put together, pure and holy enough to evaluate and condemn God? Firstly, there is no panel in heaven or beneath heaven that can judge God. Secondly, God is error-free. Thirdly, God is God. Consider the facts.

No man can face God one-on-one and win. It's impossible. God is spiritual and holy. Man is flesh designed from the dust of the earth. Is there any comparison to justify righteousness in the flesh? Under this comparison rule, man becomes insignificant in the presence of the Lord. Man lacks the ability to resurrect himself without the power, will, and grace of God. Remember, God's grace is a gift to us.

Job was an upright man. He found pleasure in serving God. The Lord showered Job with great favor. God was confident that Job would maintain his high ethical and moral standards to the end. But, Job could not have performed without God. God was in control throughout the episode.

Satan is an expert in exploiting our weaknesses for his benefit. He desires to fill every dark cell in hell to capacity with sinners. God wants everyone to be saved. The Lord knows why he designed hell. But, He does not want us to be an inhabitant of that cursed dungeon. It is quite clear, though, that Satan cannot solidly evaluate the outcome of his tactics while God can effectively evaluate the outcome of "all things." There is not a single doubt that God is the absolute authority in this situation.

JOB'S PHYSICAL STRUGGLE

Many scholars and readers of the Job saga marvel at the physicalness of Job's dilemma. Here is a man of true genuineness that is brought down to his knees. At one stage, Job denies his birth, wishes that he was never born:

> "Because it shut not up doors of my mother's womb, nor hid sorrow from mine eyes. Why died I not from the womb? Why did I not give up the ghost when I came out of the belly?" (Job 3:10-11)

Job appears to be stepping out of bounds, beyond his own reasoning powers due to the pain of his affliction. Job has no power over life or death. Job is not the Creator or Maker of Life. Job does not have the power to give up a ghost. Only God has that power. Man cannot determine the time of life or death. We have not been given the authority to know or make decisions about these things. Job later declares:

> "Let the day perish wherein I was born, and the night in which it was said, There is a man child conceived. Let darkness and the shadow of death stain it; let a cloud dwell upon it; let the blackness of the day terrify it" (Job 3:3-4).

A scholarly truism here is that Job is experiencing great pain and suffering. Job feels convinced that he is "upright" and his suffering is totally unwarranted. At this point in time, Job does not comprehend that God knows what is best for him. We must trust God. If we assault God on things we cannot comprehend, we insult the holiness of God. Remember, God said Job did not sin with his lips. He did not charge God foolishly. Proverbs 20:24 says,

> "Man's goings are of the Lord; how can a man then understand his own way?"

God is clearly telling us that we know nothing about our own goings. We are humbled by the latter scripture. The scripture reveals our lack of power and authority over anything, including our bodies. Our purposes in life is governed and supervised by God.

Job entered an abyss, but rose up a more improved servant of God. While in the smoldering ashes of despair he maintained his integrity and character. God loves sound integrity and character. When we are at low ebb, however, this is the point at which God can re-shape and remodel a man into the true being that he must become. He can become a man that walks in the footprints of the Living God. To become such a man, his moral and ethical codes have to go beyond man's meager laws and simplistic governmental policies. He must not embrace the systems of this world. He is commanded to live by the commandments and voice of God. Like Job, all pride and ego must be stripped away, permitting the Almighty glory of God to manifest itself. Worldly things are no longer significant and only the marvelous wonders of God have meaning. He must accept: that the power of God is infinite in every detail. He must understand that naked he came out of his mother's womb and naked he will return to the dust of the earth. He recognizes that the blessed hope rests with the Redeemer, Jesus Christ.

The good news is that, with God, there is renewed hope for the just and unjust; for the pure and unsure; for the weak and the strong; for the poor and the rich; for the Jew and Gentile. Christ died for all. Everyone has the opportunity to reign with Him. If we open our heart to receive Him, He will gladly come in. Let us join in and receive salvation from the Lord. God wants us to spend an eternity with Him. Isn't that a wonderful thought to consider?

THOU SHALT NOT TEMPT THE LORD

Let us not be divided about God's purpose. God's purpose for man is to worship only Him. God does not want us to worship idols. He wants our complete faith and trust. The ultimate control of all of life's circumstances lies with God and we must maintain a faith that whenever God sends a directive or allows a directive to be carried out, it is only for our betterment. If we endure until the end, God will give us the just reward. And it will be better than the original. Every single human being has a level of struggle he must face, some more potent than others. Often times, we feel our circumstances are worst than our neighbors, but if we knew the truth like God, you would conclude, "I'm not doing that bad after all." Jesus Christ demonstrates to Satan that we should not tempt the Lord thy God in Luke 4:2-12,

> "Being Forty days tempted of the devil. And in those days he did eat nothing: and when they were ended, he afterward hungered. And he (Satan) brought him (Jesus) to Jerusalem, and set him on a pinnacle of the temple, and said unto him, If thou be the Son of God, cast thyself down from hence: For it is written, he shall give his angels charge over thee, to keep thee: And in their hands they shall bear thee up, lest at any time thou dash thy foot against a stone. And Jesus answering said unto him, It is said, thou shalt not tempt the Lord thy God."

Some critics believe God was wrong for stripping Job of everything. These critics believe a just man was taken down without cause. If we conclude that God is unjust, then we are promoting that God is subject to error. If we conclude that God has made a mistake, then all of the fame accumulated on the Supreme nature of God is false. We would not have hope as a result of Christ's birth, death, and resurrection. The entire mystery surrounding God's preordained secret is null and void. We would have nothing to rest our hope on. Our death would be permanent and there would be no reason to seek this artificial God that encouraged us throughout scripture. The entire Bible would be a false doctrine. If we are to accept this limited conclusion that God erred in taking Job down to glorify His holy name, we would have no desire to preach the gospel to the poor and downtrodden. There would simply be no hope whatsoever because God was subject to error. The divine nature of God would be suspect. But, when we embrace the mystery with faith and believe that God sent the resurrected Christ to give us the blessed assurance that we will share in his glory, then, we are ready to go forth with confidence that God is perfect. We have the assurance that we will not perish but spend an eternity with Him. We can accept God's blueprint for our lives and advance forward aggressively towards the finish line. We can arise from a dead state and look towards the future with absolute faith and trust that Christ will be waiting for us.

Remember, all of us fall short of God's glory. It's the Almighty grace of God that sustains us. When we submit to God, we can "walk in the valley of the shadows of death and fear no evil." Job was in a valley, facing the shadows of death and only God could deliver him. We are weak without God. We have no power without God.

Jesus Christ, God incarnate, visited earth a couple thousand years ago to save man from himself. Jesus Christ is pure, sinless, and the Lamb of God. No form of iniquity was found in him. Yet man judged him and put him to death as an innocent man. The pain and anguish Jesus of Nazareth endured on the Cross for us was suffering of a divine nature. It was far and beyond the pain and suffering that Job faced. The Son of God did no wrong. He was beaten, stabbed, and crucified on a tree. Consider for a moment that all the sins of the world were placed upon Christ while on the Cross. I do not believe any human being could have taken the responsibility and endured like Christ. It took a God to accomplish this divine mission. When the job was complete Christ cried, "Father into thy hands I command my spirit" (Luke 23:46).

Christ fulfilled everything His Father sent Him to achieve. The Son of God repaired the damaged done in the Garden of Eden. Christ is our righteousness. Our citizenship in heaven has been restored. We can return to the greatness that was established with Adam as full-pledged members of God's family. The true Messiah has risen! Now, we can share in His glory.

LESSONS FOR THE PRESENT DAY

Today, Satan is in full operation. He and his demonic hierarchy have built their municipalities, principalities, commando units, priests, destroyers, and ministers of evil and sent them around the world on a global mission of evil and wickedness. His imps are actively engaging people weak in the faith. He has escalated his attack on the saints of God. He has organized an army of followers who have bowed to his power. He is on a reign of terror beyond the scope of human intellect. He is dead-set on exterminating the human race.

Jesus Christ was led by the spirit into the wilderness to be tempted by the devil (Luke 4:1). Christ had fasted forty days and nights and was hungry (Matthew 4:2). The enemy arrives to tempt the Lord. He takes Christ into an exceedingly high mountain and shows him all the kingdoms of the world (Matthew 4:8). Satan says, "All these things will I give thee, if thou wilt fall down and worship me" (Matthew 4:9). Christ responds in verse 10, "Get thee hence, Satan: for it is written, Thou shalt worship the Lord thy God, and him only shalt thou serve." This scene reveals that Satan has significant power in this world. When Adam failed in the Garden of Eden, God permitted Satan to take over the entire earth and set up his kingdoms around the globe. Satan is even called the "god" of this world (II Corinthians 4:5). God blessed Adam and Eve and said, "Be fruitful, and multiply, and replenish the earth, and subdue it; and have dominion over the fish of the sea, and over the fowl of the air, and over every living thing that moveth upon the earth" (Genesis 1:28). God gave Adam power over all the earth, but it was stripped from him when he sinned. God banished him from the Garden of Eden. God had His blueprint in hand on how He was going to restore man. Satan had no idea what the mystery was. No one in heaven or earth knew the exact plan of action, only God. And His plan was masterful. Satan never saw it coming.

Note that Jesus Christ did not object to Satan's claim of governorship over the five kingdoms of the world. Christ understood that his claim was only for a season because the New Adam had arrived on the earth and was prepared to sacrifice himself for the good of mankind. Satan could not seize the heart of Christ.

Can you imagine how Satan felt when God placed man on the landscape and created him in "our image, after our likeness" and granting man power over the entire earth. Satan's rage was ignited and he set out to take man down. In modern times, the deceivers plan is to tear down the entire infrastructure build on the cornerstone of Christ. His well-oiled machinery is active in our society creating confusion and cruel deception amongst the population. He is attacking on all fronts with a barrage of darts and arrows to tear down the saints of God. He is on full attack of the Church. He has select agents in the pulpit, choir, and deacon boards, etc. No part of society is off limits to him. He is on the street corners and school yards creating havoc. He has influenced administrators and court officials to take the name of God out of the school system and judicial courts. He is convincing leaders around the globe to go to war without consulting with God. He is influencing us to accept abortion, mercy killing, occult, and same-sex marriages as a right decision. The creature is performing every persuasive act he can conceive to tear down the family. He is destroying marriages and the children attached to them. If we listed every phase of social organization he has infiltrated, it would fill up a library. He will not slow down. He is relentless in his attack. If we fail to remain strong and vigilant in the Word of God, we will fall prey to his devices and tactics. God commands us to resist the devil and he will flee. We must reject temptation and become well seasoned in God's holy word. It is essential to our daily living and survival.

Satan's power is nothing for us to fear, because there is no eternal power but of God. Remember what Jesus Christ told Pontius Pilate, "Thou couldest have no power at all against me, except it were given thee from above" (John 19:11). Christ's latter statement is a divine testimony to the overwhelming power of God. We gain tremendous comfort in Christ's words to Pilate. His statement preserves us and amplifies the infinite goodness of God. There is no other power but GOD! Paul writes, "And all things are of God, who hath reconciled us to himself by Jesus Christ, and hath given to us the ministry of reconciliation" (II Corinthians 5:18).

Satan will run rampant for a season. Keep in mind, Satan is not omnipotent, omnipresent, nor omniscient. Only God possesses all three dimensions. God is in total control over all aspects of life in heaven and beneath heaven. The Apostle Paul writes, "As I live, saith the Lord, every knee shall bow to me, and every tongue shall confess to God" (Romans 14"11). That includes Satan and his agents.

Christ left us with the weapons of mass destruction to combat the spiritual battle with Satan. These weapons are prayer and faith! Paul writes, "having your loins girt about with truth, and having on the breastplate of righteousness, feet shod with the preparation of the gospel of peace, taking the shield of faith, wherewith ye shall be able to quench all the fiery darts of the wicked. And take the sword of the Spirit, which is the word of God. Praying always with all prayer and supplication in the Spirit" (Ephesians 6:14-18).

Move forward along life's solemn main road with the total confidence that God is the Absolute Authority over all things. Job's story is just one small outcry and testimony that God illustrates to us that His power is infinite and His restoration powers are unlimited. All of civilization is under the hand of God.

Job's story is deeper than the struggle of an upright man. It reveals the awesomeness of God's eternal "love, mercy, and compassion for us." It is a candid demonstration of His "Agape love," a love so deep that man cannot comprehend in human terms. He sent his only Son, Jesus Christ, that we will be "ambassadors of Christ" (II Corinthians 5:20).

Become saints and ambassadors for the Kingdom of God. Seek out the unsearchable riches of Jesus Christ. "And have no fellowship with the unfruitful works of darkness, but rather reprove them" (Ephesians 5:11). Christ will illuminate the landscape. The Almighty shadow of God will protect us and keep us safe. Remember, as servants of Christ, we are performing the will of God.

THE AUTHOR'S PRAYER

Today, as I write this testimony, I'm rejoicing and sending praises to heaven for God's perfect wisdom in sending Jesus Christ as the savior for mankind. I am enthusiastic that God saw fit to look down from heaven and find favor in me to rejoin His assembly in heaven...as sinful and disgusting that I am I magnify the Name of the Lord for His eternal mercy and compassion. I'm thankful today that I can view Job's suffering through my Fathers eyes and pray to Him for mercy, compassion and forgiveness; that I can genuinely depend on my Lord to deliver me from the gates of hell and into the bosom of Abraham. O Father, I accept you today as my only savior, as my only Deliverer, as my only Redeemer, as my only Healer. That you may take me and re-shape me into your own image, to do your work and not mine. I am satisfied that you know what is best for me, than what I know for myself. O Heavenly Father, let us pray.

O Heavenly Father, as I kneel before thine footstool, have mercy and compassion on me, because I am weak, without knowledge or wisdom and ashamed to know you before men. Father, I ask to submit myself to you to be remade into your workings, to become your humble servant, possessing the will and power of the Father. Father, I am nothing without Thee. I need Thee in every aspect of my life. Teach me, Father, your words of wisdom; strengthen me against earthly things that reign in Satan's domain. Make me stronger to carry the cross that Thine only Son, Jesus Christ, carried, and the resolve to carry that cross until you call me home. Grant me strength and power over the enemy. Grant me the power, faith, and will that when I walk in the valley of the shadows of death, I will fear no evil because Thy rod and staff is with me. O Heavenly Father, who sits most high in majestic beauty beyond my comprehension, lift me up, Father, that I will not be judgmental on others, but show compassion and mercy. Teach me to be a better son, a better husband, a better father, a better brother, a better man and a better follower of your word. Father, I need Thee more than ever. I am a sinner—incompetent in every capacity--that needs to be washed of his sins and reshaped in Thine image to perform Thine will. O' Heavenly Father, I accept your Son, Jesus Christ, as my savior, born of the Virgin Mary, preached the gospel among men and healed all that came before him, that Jesus came as your mouthpiece, not to condemn us, but to give us renewed strength and hope in knowing that the Father in heaven loves us without reservation. We are thankful for that, Father, that your Son died on the cross for us all that we might have a genuine relationship with the Father in heaven. O Father, this is the gift you give us -"salvation." Thank you, Father. I accept Jesus Christ as my savior, who descended into Hell, faced Satan, preached the gospel in Hell and was resurrected on the third day as He promised, witnessed by hundreds - and is accepted into heaven and sits on the right hand of the Father to administer justice. None of us can get to the Father but through the Son. O Heavenly Father, I am strengthened by Thine mercy, compassion, and love for me. Have mercy on me Father. Bless all that I do, protect me from evil and harm at all times. O Heavenly Father, remember me. I only inquire on these things in the name of your Son, Jesus Christ, our Lord and savior. AMEN.

Sensing and knowing his time was near, the Apostle Paul states:

"For I am now ready to be offered, and the time of my departure is at hand. I have fought a good fight. I have finished my course, I have kept the faith: Henceforth there is laid up for me a crown of righteousness, which the Lord, the righteous judge, shall give me at that day: and not to me only, but unto all them also that love his appearing" (II Timothy 4:6-8).

LIVE A FULL LIFE

Our behavior on the landscape of life has consequences. Life does not guarantee that we will not face difficulties. It's how we face those difficulties and challenges in measuring the depth and scope of living. The stage that we are performing on is temporary. It's a battlefield of good versus evil. There is a vast temptation system functioning in this world to make us fall under its grips. But, if we keep our focus on God, we will not experience grief under the peculiar odor of sin.

After all that Job endured, the Lord blessed him beyond his imagination. God doubled his wealth and gave him ten additional children. Job 42:17 says, "So Job died, being old and full of days." He lived a full life.

And we must keep our focus on living a full life in faith. It is not unreasonable but we must fuel our strength and power through Jesus Christ. Christ freed us from the sin. He conquered death. Jesus says, "I am come that they might have life, and that they might have it more abundantly" (John 10:10). II Peter 1:8 says, "ye shall never be barren nor unfruitful in the knowledge of our Lord Jesus Christ."

When we distinguish between what is good and what is evil and permit good to manifest itself in our lives, we can live a life of abundance. We will not be tortured by sin. We will not fall into the shackles of wickedness. We will become spiritually fit to take on the battle and enjoy life to the fullest. Christ showed us how to do it.

If we follow the marvelous example set by Jesus Christ, we will become obedient servants to God. We can no longer go backwards and become servants of sin. God solved that problem. Peter encouraged us to "abstain from fleshly lusts which war against the soul" (I Peter 2:11).

The Apostle Paul encourages us to remain obedient unto righteousness (Romans 6:16). And when we obey God, the temptations of this world are meaningless. When we seek the higher calling, when our face is lifted up to the heavens, when we search the hills for the source of our supply, we become meek and humble, knowing that the God of Abraham, Isaac, and Jacob will supply all our needs. And He will do it abundantly. Rejoice and live life to the fullest!

May you be deeply blessed and enriched with godly understanding, knowledge, and wisdom after reading this book. May God bless you with a "tremendous increase."